D0745427

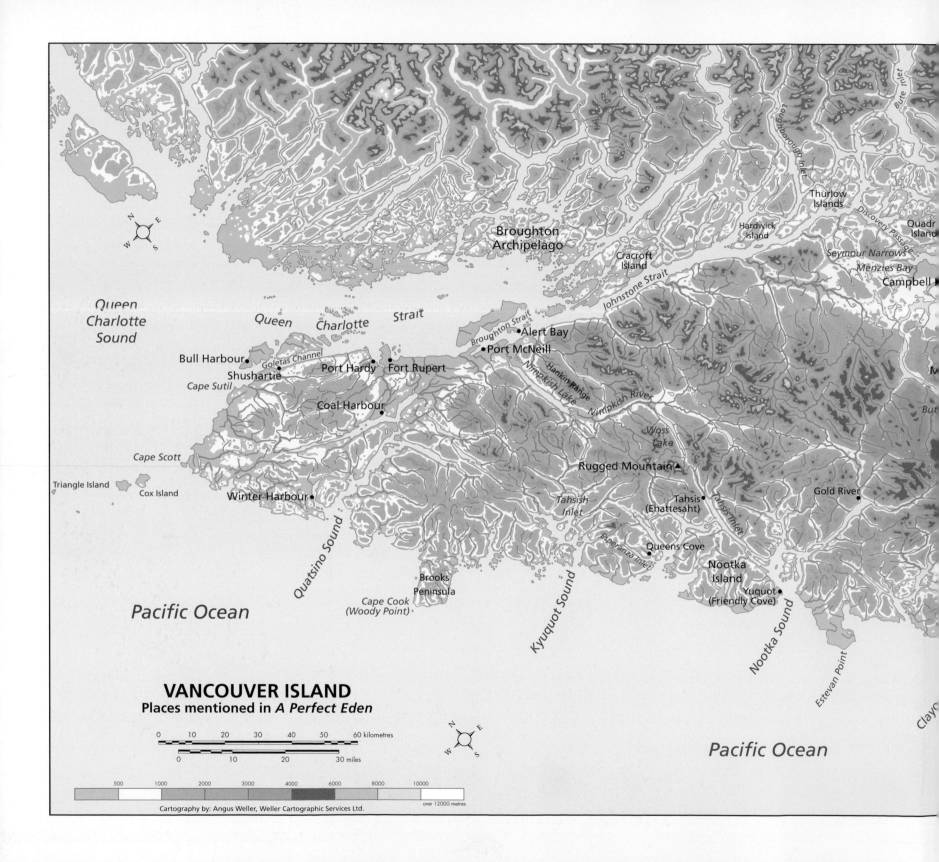

VANCOUVER ISLAND
Places mentioned in *A Perfect Eden*

Pacific Ocean

Queen Charlotte Sound

Queen Charlotte Strait

Broughton Archipelago

Thurlow Islands

Hardwick Island

Cracroft Island

Johnstone Strait

Seymour Narrows

Menzies Bay

Campbell

Quadra Island

Bute Inlet

Loughborough Inlet

Discovery Passage

Bull Harbour•

Goletas Channel

Shushartie•

Cape Sutil

Port Hardy•

Fort Rupert•

Broughton Strait

•Alert Bay

•Port McNeill

Hankin Range

Nimpkish Lake

Nimpkish River

Coal Harbour•

Woss Lake

Cape Scott

Triangle Island

Cox Island

Rugged Mountain▲

Winter Harbour•

Tahsish Inlet

Tahsis (Ehattesaht)•

Tahsis Inlet

Gold River•

Quatsino Sound

Esperanza Inlet

Queens Cove•

Brooks Peninsula

Cape Cook (Woody Point)

Nootka Island

Yuquot (Friendly Cove)•

Pacific Ocean

Kyuquot Sound

Nootka Sound

Estevan Point

Clayo

Pacific Ocean

0 10 20 30 40 50 60 kilometres

0 10 20 30 miles

500 1000 2000 3000 4000 6000 8000 10000

over 12000 metres

Cartography by: Angus Weller, Weller Cartographic Services Ltd.

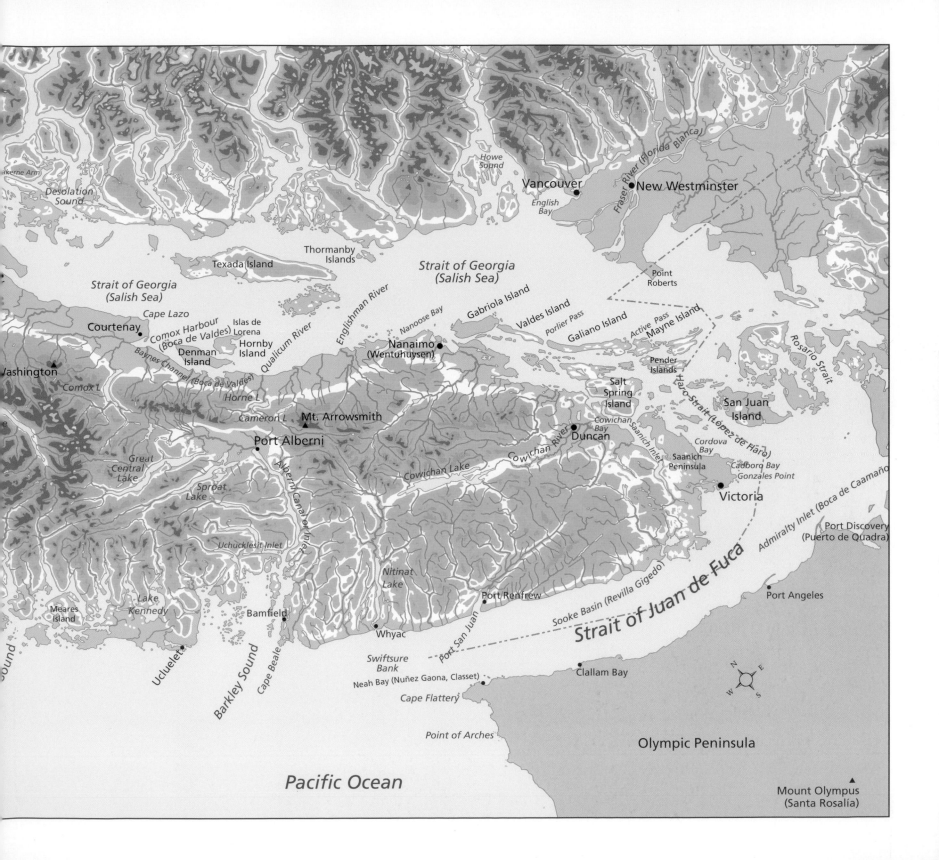

A PERFECT EDEN

ENCOUNTERS *by* EARLY EXPLORERS
of VANCOUVER ISLAND

MICHAEL LAYLAND

TouchWood
Editions

TouchWood Editions
touchwoodeditions.com

LIBRARY AND ARCHIVES CANADA CATALOGUING IN PUBLICATION
Layland, Michael, 1938–, author
A perfect Eden : encounters by early explorers of Vancouver Island / Michael Layland.

Includes bibliographical references.
Issued in print and electronic formats.
ISBN 978-1-77151-177-3

1. Vancouver Island (BC)—Discovery and exploration. 2. Vancouver Island (BC)—History.
3. Vancouver Island (BC)—Description and travel. I. Title.

FC3844.5.L395 2016   917.11'2042   C2016-904061-5

Edited by Marlyn Horsdal
Cover and interior design by Pete Kohut
Cover image: *Off Thormanby Island, June 25, 1792*, by Gordon Miller
Back cover image: A chart showing part of the coast of NW America (Historical Map Society of BC)
Proofreading by Claire Philipson

We acknowledge the financial support of the Government of Canada through
the Canada Book Fund and the Canada Council for the Arts, and of the
province of British Columbia through the Book Publishing Tax Credit.

This book was produced using FSC®-certified, acid-free paper,
processed chlorine free, and printed with soya-based inks.

PRINTED IN CHINA

20 19 18 17 16   1 2 3 4 5

❀ ❀ ❀

The place itself appears a perfect "Eden," in the midst of the dreary wilderness of the northwest coast, and so different is its general aspect, from the wooded, rugged regions around, that one might be pardoned for supposing it had dropped from the clouds into its present position.

James Douglas[1]

To Ferdie Chen
in gratitude

CONTENTS

✺ ✺ ✺

FOREWORD

Looking at george vancouver's great chart of the coast of northwest America, published in 1798, the untrained eye could be forgiven for initially overlooking the island that bears his name. It fits neatly into the southern end of a submerged coastal trough defined by the western continental edge and the high mountain range to the south, and encompassing numerous other islands, small and large, reaching north to Alaska. But there it is, the most distinctive coastal landform of the entire western littoral of North America. As an island, it presents itself as a unique entity separate from, but not unconnected to, its continental neighbour in ways both physical and developmental, but always maintaining a sense of its own space and place, and displaying an essential unity within its own diversity.

As did the first European explorers who approached the island by sea in the late 18th century, the first Indigenous peoples advancing down its coast would have considered it part of the continent. Others, coming through the mainland mountains, would have recognized its insularity as they crossed the water

to settle its eastern shores. The initial period of Spanish, British, and American exploration and trade between 1774 and 1792 served to define the island, and place it and the wider coast on the world map. But the island's history as a European settlement didn't begin until 1843, when the Hudson's Bay Company expanded its forts and continental activities onto the island with the founding of Fort Victoria. This followed the demise of the maritime fur trade and hbc's absorption in the 1820s of the overland fur trade pioneered by the North West Company.

The prime reason for the move to the island—which ushered in the beginning of non-aboriginal settlement, economic activity, and exploration of the island's interior—was not economic but political. It was driven by several factors: American settlers pouring into Oregon in the 1830s, coupled with the problems of navigation into and up the Columbia River to the hbc's Fort Vancouver; the company's successful 'hunting out' of the Snake River country; and the United States' clear determination that the 49th parallel would be the international border dividing the disputed Oregon Territory / Columbia Department. All these suggested to Governor George Simpson that an ultimate move of the HBC's regional headquarters away from the Columbia to the southern end of Vancouver Island would be in its best interests, both short- and long-term.

By the 1840s it had become clear that a trade-off between the twin prizes of Puget Sound and all of Vancouver Island, with a border along Juan de Fuca Strait, would be the most likely outcome of the boundary negotiations. As attention became focused on the strait and the island, Royal Navy hydrographers Henry Kellett and James Wood undertook important work to improve the charts of the immediate region. The existing charts, by then over 50 years old, were inherited from Vancouver, who himself had used the hastily done Spanish surveys of the island's southern coastline. From time to time, visiting naval vessels and the HBC's own surveyors contributed to improving the picture, until George Henry Richards—first on HMS *Plumper* and later on HMS *Hecate*, working over six summers from 1857 to 1862—provided the definitive charts that would serve mariners in the island's waters until well into the 20th century.

The establishment of Fort Victoria introduced the towering figure of HBC factor James Douglas to the island's story, although he didn't move to it permanently until 1849, when Vancouver Island formally became a Crown Colony. Within little more than a year, Douglas was combining his HBC duties with those of the colony's governor. As he oversaw the early development of Vancouver Island in the 1850s, Douglas was aided by a number of highly competent HBC colleagues including engineer/explorer/surveyor Joseph Pemberton and clerk, cum explorer and administrator, Joseph McKay.

Four key aspects of these early years were the evolving identification of, and relationships with, the island's native peoples; the development of agricultural land; the location of mineral deposits and the survey of accessible timber resources. Each involved exploration as the new arrivals sought to unlock the mysteries and potential of the island's geography.

The British government leased the island to the HBC with the understanding that land sales would establish settlement, and the company began implementing that condition of the 10-year lease. Douglas purchased native lands around Fort Victoria with a series of treaties, but by the mid 1850s there were still fewer than a thousand non-native settlers. Relationships with the aboriginal population were basically cordial as both original inhabitants and newcomers sought to benefit from each other's knowledge and skills. This was particularly true as the latter sought to explore the interior of the island and survey its resources, the most important of which proved to be agriculture in the Cowichan Valley and coal seams near Fort Nanaimo. The latter excited the colonial authorities, who saw in the extensive deposits a potential industry that could ultimately fuel steamships and railroads and facilitate trans-Pacific trade.

Coastal reconnaissance trips, such as Douglas and Pemberton's 1852 journey to inspect the coal field at Nanaimo, and probes into the valleys adjacent to the HBC forts at Victoria, Nanaimo, and Rupert (Port Hardy), were precursors to a series of longer-range forays across the island by Hamilton Moffat, along the well-established native grease trail from the northeast to Tahsis Inlet and Nootka Sound, by Adam Horne from Qualicum to the Alberni Inlet, and by Joseph Pemberton and Thomas Gooch from Cowichan to the Carmanah Valley, Nitinat Lake, and on to the coast. By the end of the decade, the vast and magnificent timber resources bordering the long, sheltered fjord of Alberni Inlet and Valley had been identified, and the area's first lumber mill was established in 1860. The following year, mounting pressure to find a more suitable way to the east coast than that offered by Horne's route led to exploration by

Richard Mayne and William Banfield to uncover the best track for a prospective road.

Thus did the nature of Vancouver Island begin to reveal itself—the detailed intricacies of her coasts left uncovered in the quick surveys of her earliest maritime explorers, the hugely difficult and often impenetrable terrain of her mountain spine, and the agricultural potential of the Cowichan and Comox valleys and the coal and timber resources that would form the backbone of her future industrial economy.

As Michael Layland notes in the afterword, however, knowledge of Vancouver Island remained far from complete. But the work of building on the early discoveries of the 1770s, '80s, and '90s had begun in earnest in the 1840s and '50s, and it set down the markers for the island's future destiny. The author's lively and informative narrative—generously illustrated with charts, maps, paintings, lithographs and photos, along with carefully selected quotations from contemporary journals, reports, and correspondence—reveals an exciting time of change, hope, and curiosity. Sadly, Vancouver Island's native peoples, who stride so colourfully through the pages of this particular book, would soon be largely swept aside. Pushed onto reserves and no longer valued as knowledge and trading partners, they would become subordinate players in a growing industrial labour force segregated by race, ethnicity, and gender. But that is another story, essentially absent from these early, happier years of encounter and exploration.

Robin Inglis
Former director of the Vancouver Maritime Museum and North Vancouver Museum and Archives; author of the *Historical Dictionary of the Discovery and Exploration of the Northwest Coast of America*, 2008.

PREFACE

IN *The Land of Heart's Delight* (2013), I traced the progress of cartographic knowledge about Vancouver Island. But I wanted to delve more deeply into the stories of those intrepid souls whose explorations helped shape the island's early maps and charts, those intriguing characters who faced physical hardship, technical challenges, and even mortal danger. Their motives were diverse, as were the circumstances and objectives that triggered their adventures.

A Perfect Eden recounts exploration stories from the earliest records—one-and-a-half millennia ago—through to 1864, the close of the era of Governor Sir James Douglas. Those encounters by new arrivals, mainly from Europe, were not just with the natural features on and around the island, but also with the many and varied people already resident here for untold generations. My intent is that each book will stand alone, while adding richer context to the other. Some overlap in the events and the people involved is inevitable, but I have tried to avoid repetition as much as possible, while preserving continuity for the reader.

INTRODUCTION

THE RECORDED HISTORY OF VANCOUVER Island is relatively short—Europeans first arrived on these shores just over two centuries ago. Nonetheless, their exploration generated a wealth of tales, puzzles, and fresh perspectives on wider issues that weave into the fabric of a much larger tapestry.

The northwest coast of this continent had long been a mystery to European cartographers. In the absence of reliable information, they attempted to reconcile myths and tall stories with wishful thinking. While they laboured to fill the gaps in their charts, Indigenous peoples continued to carry on their oral traditions of passing on intimate knowledge of their local homeland to their progeny.

In these pages I recount the impressions of newcomers from far-distant lands who found not an empty, uninhabited wilderness, but a place with a resident population that knew, nurtured, and had thrived in harmony with its environment. The explorers of Vancouver Island did not "discover" what they found. They merely recorded for their contemporaries the places and geographical facts known to peoples who had lived there for millennia. In most cases, local people accompanied the European visitors, or their knowledge provided guidance. The local people were mostly coastal dwellers—able seafarers, fishers, and hunters of whales. They undertook seasonal migrations and longer-distance voyages for trade and, frequently, for conflict with other tribes. They flourished on the wealth of the waters that surrounded them, and took full advantage of the products of the protective forests for shelter, sustenance, transport, and artistic expression.

Cartography does not seem to have formed part of the island's Indigenous graphic tradition. There are, however, many examples of how local elders immediately understood the purpose of the visitors' maps. The elders were able to contribute information about routes, place names, resources, and hazards the newcomers would face on their explorations.

Most of the early overland explorers took advantage of existing trading trails, guided by people who knew the route and could explain how and where to find sustenance during the journey. Interactions between the visitors and the residents were aspects inseparable from the exploration. The stories would be incomplete without those meetings.

In common with many earlier non-native writers about the island's history, I have grappled with the indigenous toponyms and ethnographic names. They appear in the accounts in an astonishing variety of forms, spellings, and usage. Such distortions from the original have been due, in large part, to the inadequacies of the European ear and alphabets to render them faithfully. They also reflect the very limited ability of the new arrivals to comprehend an enormously rich culture of language, kinship, social, and territorial relationships. For these books, I attempt to use the current, generally accepted versions, and respectfully request tolerance from those whom I might inadvertently offend by doing so.

One hears criticism of the early explorers, such as Vancouver and Galiano, that they did not adopt the native names for the places they visited and charted. To be reasonable, not only was there a host of distinct local languages and dialects, difficult to comprehend and transcribe into English or Spanish, but time did not permit the visitors to acquire a working knowledge of those languages—even if the meetings had been completely free of hostility. Some explorers and early traders did attempt to compile vocabularies, and acquired a smattering of conversation, enough for their limited objectives.

Renderings of some Aboriginal toponyms remain in use today—Songhees, Esquimalt, Saanich, Cowichan, Chemainus, Nanaimo, Comox, Nimpkish, Quatsino, Clayoquot, Tahsis, Wickaninnish, Ucluelet, Nitinat, Carmanah, Sooke, and Metchosin, for example. In some cases, names have returned to their origins—the Queen Charlotte Islands, for example, are once again Haida Gwaii.

The term I use in *A Perfect Eden* for the many descendants of unions between European men and North American First Nations women during the fur trade era is "mixed-race" rather than Métis. While the latter may sometimes refer to any person of mixed European and Indigenous ancestry, that definition is frequently challenged by Métis people who trace their own lineage to particular historic Métis communities.

Another area of difficulty has been in using Spanish surnames. I am fully aware of the formality in Spain and Latin America of including both the paternal and maternal surnames of an individual. However, English speakers have generally come to know these persons by just one—and frequently the incorrect one. For example, the naval officer Dionisio Alcalá Galiano has come down to us as just his maternal Galiano. It so happens that, on occasion, he signed his name as "Galiano." His contemporary, Juan Francisco de la Bodega y Quadra Mollinedo, was known to George Vancouver as "Señor Quadra." I have chosen to go with Galiano and Bodega y Quadra except at their first mention. *Les ruego su perdón.*

Michael Layland

FIG 1 Sir Francis Drake's galleon, the *Golden Hinde*, might have come to local waters in 1579 before he returned to England. This painting depicts an improbable theory that he even entered the Salish Sea, anchoring at Comox. [*Mysterious Voyage*, John Horton]

CHAPTER ONE

THREE PUZZLING VOYAGES: THE MYSTIC, THE RAIDER, AND THE OLD SALT

THE MYSTIC: HUI SHEN COMES TO THE LAND OF FOU SANG
Asiatic seafarers have probably visited the Pacific coast of the American continent for millennia. Scraps of evidence, individually inconclusive, have increasingly accumulated to support this theory. These include artifacts: stone anchors, ancient Chinese coins and ceramics, a rusting Japanese sword, chicken bones (domesticated, and of species not native to these shores) found deep within old middens, and implements of iron, a metal not found locally but in use by First Nations at the time of European contact.

Adding to the growing body of evidence are biological and cultural clues—introduced plants, human parasites, rainmaking rituals, belief in the magical powers of jade, linguistic root words, musical structures. A human flow out of China, Japan, Southeast Asia, and Polynesia—travelling deliberately or inadvertently—landed on shores from Alaska to Ecuador and perhaps as far south as Chile. Such arrivals must have been coming since well before the "discovery" of the Pacific with Vasco Núñez de Balboa's crossing of the Isthmus of Panama, or Ferdinand Magellan's voyage of circumnavigation.

The patterns of oceanic and atmospheric circulation, known generally as the North Pacific Drift or Gyre (see Fig. 2, page 6), strongly favour the clockwise passage of flotsam and continue to bring Asian materials—including glass floats from Japanese fishing nets, tsunami debris, and even disabled vessels—to these shores and thence southward toward Mexico. The return journey is much less likely. Nevertheless, the *Naos de China*, Spain's imperial trading galleons, sailed regularly between Acapulco and Manila for 250 years, starting in the 16th century. This demonstrated that the westbound passage was feasible. In the shipyards of Manila, Cantonese master shipwrights designed and constructed these enormous galleons—some with ten times the displacement of Columbus's *Santa María*—and Asiatic navigators and seamen provided their crews.

Chinese records appear to contain just a single example documenting the composition, purpose, and findings of an epic, round-trip, pre-European-contact voyage. This was the mission undertaken by a small group of Buddhist monks led

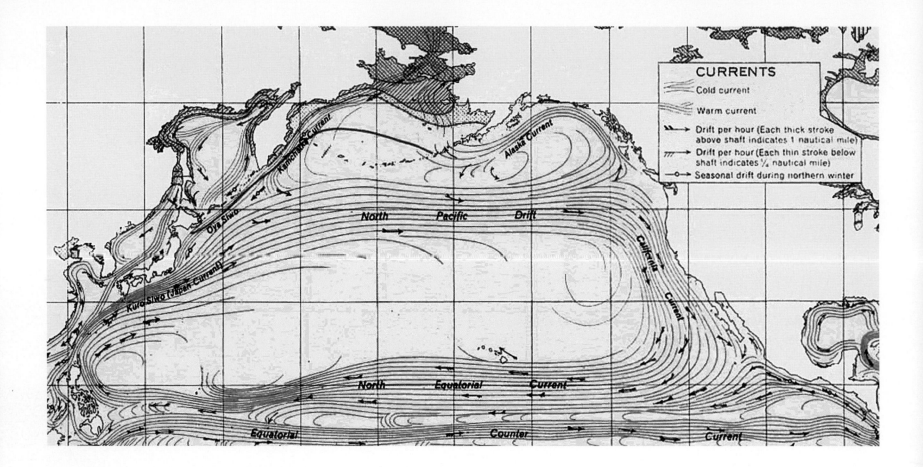

FIG 2 Year-round, the North Pacific Drift conveys ocean surface currents and associated weather systems from the East Indies past Japan and the Aleutians to Vancouver Island, then south as far as Baja, California, before returning east. [North Pacific Gyre, courtesy of Wikipedia Commons, US Army Manual]

by an Afghani mystic, Hui Shen, in the years between 458 and 499 CE (Common Era).

It was not until 1761 that European students of exploration history came to learn of Hui Shen and his mission to the kingdoms of Ta-Han and Fou Sang. The French sinologist Joseph de Guignes published a summary translation of the text in Volume 23 of the *Great Chinese Encyclopedia, 41st Book of Chuan,* covering the period 502–556 CE. After causing short-lived amusement at court, the translation lay forgotten for a few years until its rediscovery and incorporation into contemporary French and Italian maps. Cartographers Philippe Buache, Guillaume de L'Isle, and Antonio Zatta all positioned Fou Sang about latitude 50°—that of Vancouver Island—though with what justification is uncertain.

In 1885, Californian scholar Edmond Payson Vining, after comparing several translations and related texts, published his meticulous analysis *An Inglorious Columbus.* Generally endorsed by more recent scholars, Vining's theory was that Fou Sang was in Mexico. The following text is Vining's translation, from the account of Hui Shen's visit to Fou Sang some 1,260 years earlier.

> In the first year of the reign of the Tsi dynasty . . . (i.e., in the year 499 AD), a Shaman or Buddhist priest named Hwui Shän came to King-Cheu from that country, and narrated the following account regarding the country of Fou Sang. Fou Sang is situated twice ten thousand li (Chinese miles) or more to the east of the Great Han country [Kamchatka]. That land is also situated at the east of the Middle Kingdom (China). That region has many Fou Sang trees, and it is from these trees that the country derives its name. The leaves resemble [the Tung tree] and the first sprouts are like those of the bamboo. The people of the country eat them and the fruit, which is like a pear (in form), but of a reddish colour. They spin thread from their bark from which they make cloth, of which they make clothing. They also manufacture a finer fabric from it.
>
> In constructing their houses they use planks, such as are generally used when building adobe walls. They have no citadels or walled cities. They have literary characters, and make paper from the bark of the Fou Sang. They have no military weapons or armour, and they do not wage war in the kingdom . . .
>
> The title of the king of the country is "the chief of the multitudes." The noblemen of the first rank are called "Tui-lu"; those of the second rank, "Little Tui-lu"; and those of the third rank "Nah-to-sha." The king of the country, when he walks abroad, is preceded and followed with drums and horns . . .
>
> They have cattle-horns, of which the long ones are used to contain (some of their) possessions, the best of them reaching twice ten times as much as the capacity of a common horn. They have horse-carts, cattle-carts and deer-carts. The people of the country raise deer as cattle are raised in the Middle Kingdom (China). From milk they make koumiss [a fermented drink]. They have the red pears kept unspoiled throughout the year, and they also have tomatoes. The ground is destitute of iron, but they have copper. Gold and silver are not valued. In their markets there are no taxes or fixed prices . . .
>
> [I]n the year 458 AD, from the country of Ki-pin (i.e., Cophène, now Cabul) [Afghanistan] formerly, five men who were pi-k'iu (i.e., *bhikshus,* mendicant Buddhist monks) went by a voyage to that country, and made Buddha's rules and his religious books and images known among them. [1]

Interpretations and associated theories and arguments about the location of Fou Sang continue to surface and then subside. No one, however, has yet proposed a convincing answer to a key riddle linked to Hui Shen's mission: just how did his very detailed account of the places and peoples they saw get back and into the

Chinese record? The favourable oceanic forces that would have enabled his northeast-then-south voyage do not have an equivalent for the return journey, whether from Mexico or places to the north. His traditional wooden junk could well have been sturdy and seaworthy enough at the outset (see Fig. 3), but it would not have remained so for a second trans-Pacific crossing four decades later—even if the monks, by then probably more than 60 years old, had the necessary navigational skills and had retained the physical capability of handling the vessel over such an enormous distance. All in all, the story of Fou Sang remains an enduring mystery.

Recent research by cartographic historian Benjamin Olshin adds fresh colour to this mystery—a connection with the medieval Venetian merchant-explorer Marco Polo. Olshin has studied the controversial Rossi collection of 17th- or 18th-century copies of 13th-century parchments, from before the advent of classical cartography. They seem to substantiate the idea that Polo reached, not just the Silk Road and China, but Alaska and beyond. The most tantalizing of the collection is the so-called "Map with Ship" (see Fig. 4, page 9), now in the Library of Congress. It appears to show Borneo, Japan, Kamchatka, the Bering Strait, the Aleutian chain, the west and south coasts of Alaska, and a coastline trending north-south corresponding to that of British Columbia.

Two more are sketch maps, apparently by Polo's daughters, Fantina and Moreta, depicting a roughly similar coastal configuration and drawn, they said, from their father's letters. A third daughter, Bellela, writes of people on a peninsula "twice as far from China" who live on fish and make their houses "under the earth." Other references in the documents mention "Fusang," which means, in early Chinese, "land across the ocean." Olshin points out that this was written before the story of Hui Shen became known in Europe. Polo famously said, on his deathbed, "I did not tell half of what I saw."

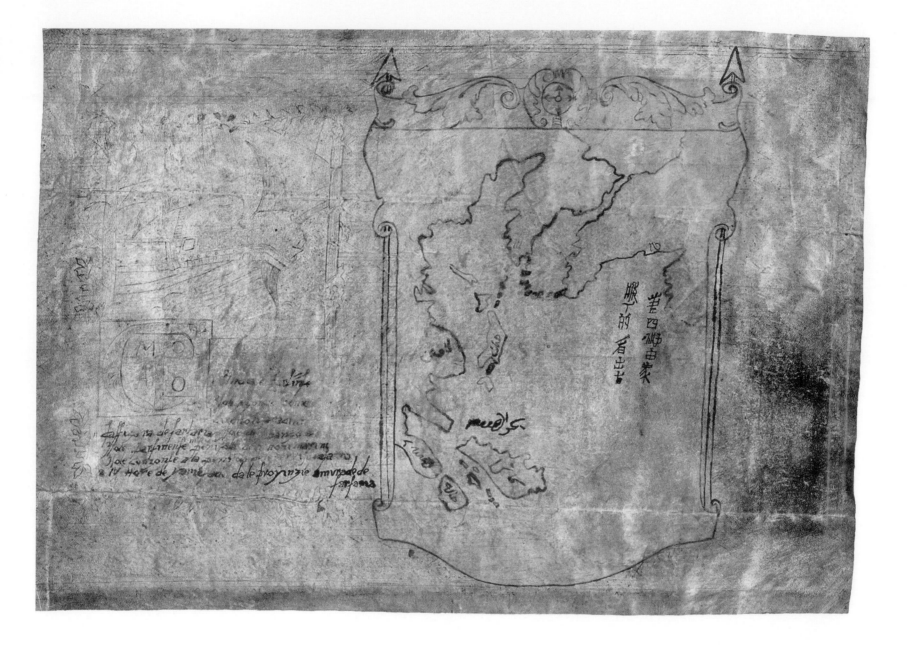

FIG 4 "Map with Ship," one of an intriguing group of documents seemingly connected with Marco Polo and hinting that the 13th-century Venetian explorer had learned about the geography of the northwest coast of the Americas from Chinese sources. [Courtesy of the Library of Congress, Washington, DC]

FIG 5 Francis Drake, the English freebooter, raided Spanish settlements and ships in the Caribbean and along the Pacific coast, acquiring a vast store of treasure. This portrait was based on a 1586 engraving by French artist Jean Rabel. On his shield, English galleons fire a broadside. [Courtesy of Christie's Catalogue]

THE RAIDER: "THICKE AND STINKING FOGGES"

The second controversial voyage though the waters off Vancouver Island—spawning even more theories and disputes than Hui Shen's journey—was that of the English adventurer Francis Drake (see Fig. 5). Did he, or did he not, approach the island, and if so, what did he do then?

To summarize the famous freebooting circumnavigation: Drake sailed from England in 1577 in command of five ships, including his own *Pelican*. His cover story was that he was to trade in Egypt, but his real purpose, revealed only when the ships were far into the Atlantic, was to cause mayhem in the so-called "Spanish Lake"—the Pacific. They were to transit the Strait of Magellan and breach Spain's Pope-endorsed monopoly, plundering as opportunity arose.

Having dropped two unfit ships—renaming his own the *Golden Hinde*—and regrouping after a ferocious southern storm, Drake led his men into the forbidden, and poorly defended, Pacific. They raided Spanish settlements at will—Santiago, Arica, and Lima—and took several prizes, including the gigantic treasure galleon *Cacafuego*. For half a year, the plunder proved rich and easy, requiring little violence. Aside from the silver and other spoils, Drake gained invaluable knowledge from captured charts, sailing directions, or "rutters," and directly from navigators experienced in these waters.

He had raided the small Spanish outpost of Guatulco, and, by then fully laden with booty—but needing a location for careening to clean and refurbish *Golden Hinde*'s hull—Drake decided to return home. He was aware of the fabled Strait of Anian or Northwest Passage—the navigable water route across the top of America believed to connect the Pacific and Atlantic oceans—and he seems to have decided to find it. Drake first headed due west from Guatulco at latitude 16° 10' north into the open Pacific, guided by information he had gleaned from captured Spanish rutters and pilots. This was known as the Spanish Route. The intention was to find a wind—expected some 1,500 miles (2,800 kilometres) offshore—capable of carrying them well to the north, and so it proved. When he felt well clear of Spanish presence, he turned back toward the shore (see Fig. 1, page 4).

An alternate theory has him taking that track in order to waylay another laden galleon returning from Manila.

For the careening, expected to take a few weeks, Drake needed to find a sheltered, shallow cove with a shelving beach protected from both the ocean and the enemy. He would need to unload and then beach the vessel at high water. He would then lay it on its side to remove the barnacles and other marine growth, replace any planks riddled by teredo worms, and recaulk all the seams. His first landfall proved most unsuitable:

> The 5. day of Iune, [1579] wee were forced by contrary windes, to run in with the shoare, which we then first descried; and to cast anchor in a bad bay, the best roade we could for the present meete with: where wee were not without some danger, by reason of the many extreme gusts, and flawes that beate vpon vs; which if they ceased and were still at any time, immediately vpon their intermission, there followed most vile, thicke and stinking fogges; against which the sea preuailed nothing, till the gusts of wind againe remoued them, which brought with them, such extremity and violence when they came, that there was no dealing or resisting against them.
>
> In this place was no abiding for vs; and to go further North, the extremity of the cold (which had now vtterly discouraged our men) would not permit vs: and the winds directly bent against vs, hauing once gotten vs vnder sayle againe, commanded vs to the Southward whether we would or no.

> From the height of 48. deg. In which we now were, to 38. we found the land by coasting alongst it to bee but low and reasonable plaine: euery hill (whereof we saw many, but none verie high) though it were Iune, and in the Sunne in his nearest approach vnto them being couered with snow.
>
> In 38 deg. we fell with a conuenient and fit harborough, and Iune 17. Came to anchor therein.[2]

Drake's nephew John Drake, who had sailed aboard *Golden Hinde*, compiled this account. It was published in London in 1628, from a manuscript by Francis Fletcher, the priest of the same voyage. While Fletcher's knowledge of navigation and technical matters was limited, to most experts the latitudes he gives seem likely to be correct within a degree or so, given the instruments then available and the poor visibility.

Surveyor, experienced sailor, and history aficionado Raymond Bishop studied Fletcher's description of their course changes as far as the "bad bay." He calculated, using wind and current data with later *Sailing Directions*, and allowing for various errors, that the landfall was located somewhere along the west coast of Vancouver Island. Although the weather reported would seem to modern readers unseasonably foul for June, it is not impossible, since that year was one of those known as the "Little Ice Age" in Europe—when the Thames froze so hard that large wagons could cross it.

After a week's running southward along the coast and reaching about latitude 30°, Drake found a suitable cove. He careened and made an act of possession, naming the land thereabouts as New Albion, claiming it in the name of Queen Elizabeth. He nailed a plate of brass to a large post to record the claim. He then headed once more westward into the Pacific, across to and through the Indonesian archipelago—the Spice Islands—and thence, via the Indian Ocean, around the Cape of Good Hope, into the Atlantic. After a three-year voyage in which he had circumnavigated the globe, Drake arrived home, where he received a royal welcome, a knighthood, and good share of the booty.

The politics of the day caused Elizabeth's advisers to seize all logs, charts, and other records of the voyage, and impose an order of silence on all participants. On pain of death, they were not to reveal where they had been or what they had seen. Secrecy was thus maintained for a while, but eventually some accounts did leak out, and even an official, probably adulterated, report was issued—to further confuse speculation with misinformation.

Several maps were published purporting to show Drake's track, but his own logs have never surfaced. Heightened by stories of the treasure brought back and the enduring fascination with the existence of a Northwest Passage, Drake's voyage generated a wealth of conjecture, imagination, and intrigue, which has continued to this day. Dozens of theories as to the location of the "bad bay," the careening bay, and New Albion have been proposed, shot down, debated, and investigated.

In reality, no one knows the true and whole story of this remarkable voyage of exploration and adventure. But for Vancouver Islanders, it is tempting to think that their home might have been part of it.

THE OLD SALT: "A BROAD INLET OF SEA"

Juan de Fuca is celebrated on Canada's west coast and on his island home of Kefalonia, in Greece, for having found and explored a navigable passage, now known as the Strait of Juan de Fuca, between Vancouver Island and the mainland. But the circumstances of that voyage remain cloaked in mystery and debate. Michael Lok, a 16th-century Englishman, provided a key piece of the puzzle.

A seasoned maritime merchant, Lok had traded for more than 30 years "through almost all the countries of Christianity," particularly in the eastern Mediterranean. As captain of his own ship, he had experienced first-hand the grip that his Turkish and Arab counterparts held over the western end of the Silk Road and the flow of Chinese goods along it: porcelains, pearls, gemstones, and, of course, silks. He resolved to devote effort and fortune to find a way to break the monopoly, and a trade route through the Arctic waterways to the Orient—a Northwest Passage—seemed to offer the best hope.

His earlier attempts had proved disastrous. In London, Lok invested heavily in the Company of Cathay's ill-fated Frobisher expedition of 1579 to seek that elusive alternate access to the East. The venture collapsed, with Lok losing everything. He struggled to recover, and eventually was contracted to represent the Levant Company, or "Merchants of Turkie," based in Aleppo. The company broke the contract and left Lok seeking recompense. In 1596, by now aged 62, Lok found himself in Venice still struggling to recover, when a seafaring acquaintance introduced him to an old salt with a fascinating tale to tell.

Lok records that the sailor was a Greek from the island of Kefalonia. He was named Apóstolos Valerianos (we now know that it was probably Ioánnis Apóstolos Phokás-Valerianos). However, he was known to his Spanish masters, and to posterity, as Juan de Fuca.

Lok transcribed the sailor's rambling tale, and eventually published it as part of a pamphlet on the probability of a Northwest Passage to the Orient. It seemed that for the previous 40 years, the Greek had been employed as a mariner and pilot in the service of Spain in the West Indies and other parts of the Spanish empire, including Mexico and the coast of the South Sea, as they called the Pacific Ocean. He claimed to have been aboard a returning Manila galleon when it was attacked and captured by the English buccaneer "Candish" (Thomas Cavendish). He lost his substantial investment in trade goods.

The Greek then began the chapter of his tale that held the greatest interest for Lok: how he had been sent to seek and explore the Strait of Anian.

> The Viceroy of Mexico, sent him out againe Anno 1592, with a small Caravela, and a Pinnace, armed with Mariners onely, to follow the said Voyage, for discovery of the Straits of Anian, and the passage thereof, into the Sea which they call the North Sea, which is our North-west Sea. And that, he followed his course in that Voyage West and North-west in the South Sea, all alongst the coast of Nova Spania, and California, and the Indies, now called North America (all which Voyage hee signified to me in a great Map, and a Sea-card of mine owne, which I laide before him) until hee came to the Latitude of fortie seven degrees, and that there finding that the Land trended North and North-east, with a broad Inlet of Sea, between 47. And 48. degrees of Latitude: hee entred thereinto, sayling therein more than twentie dayes, and found that Land trending still sometime North-west and North-east and North, and also East and South-eastward, and very much broader Sea than was at the said entrance, and that hee passed by divers Ilands in that sayling. And that at the entrance of this said Strait, there is on the North-west coast thereof, a great Hedland or Iland, with an exceeding high Pinacle, or spired Rocke, like a piller thereupon.

> Also he said, that he went on Land in divers places, and that he saw some people on Land, clad in Beasts skins: and that the Land is very fruitfull, and rich of gold, Silver, Pearle, and other things, like Nova Spania [Mexico].

> And also he said, that he being entred thus farre in the said Strait, and being come into the North Sea already, and finding the Sea wide enough every where, and to be about thirtie or fortie leagues [167 or 222 kilometres] wide in the mouth of the Straits, where he entred; hee thought he had now well discharged his office, and done the thing which he was sent to doe: and that hee not beng armed to resist the force of the Savage people that might happen, hee therefore set sayle and returned homewards againe towards Nova Spania, where hee arrived at Acapulco, Anno 1592. hoping to be rewarded greatly of the Viceroy, for this service done in this said Voyage.[3]

Lok went on to record Juan de Fuca's story about how he returned to Acapulco and reported his discovery to the viceroy in Mexico. The mariner was lauded for his efforts, but after two years, no tangible reward was forthcoming. He was told that the king himself knew of the achievement, and intended to reward him personally. For this, he needed to go to Spain. Once there, he again heard fine words of praise but still there was no prize. The mariner explained that, being old, tired, and fed up, he had quit Spain and was passing through Italy, headed for his island home and retirement. He suspected that Spain had not paid him because they thought their English rivals had given up looking for a Northwest Passage. He would now offer his services to Queen Elizabeth of England.

Lok recognized immediately that he had a vital piece of information in his hands, one that offered him a chance to restore his fortunes. He would persuade investors in London to finance an English expedition to capitalize on the discovery of the fabled passage. Lok returned to London to launch such a venture, supported by his pamphlet with the Greek's narrative, but was unsuccessful. The skeptical financiers required more proof of the story, demanding that Juan de Fuca present his findings to them in person. Lok's financial situation precluded him bringing the Greek to London, and eventually correspondence ceased when, in 1602, the old man failed to respond to Lok, and was presumed dead.

What is to be made of the yarn related by Fuca and transcribed by Lok? Quite apart from the known fact that no such journey would have been possible—since no such waterway exists or ever did—there are arguments to support the many who consider the whole thing to have been a hoax.

While Spanish records show that a Greek pilot known as Juan de Fuca did serve with them, to date no record has surfaced—either in Mexico or in the archives in Seville—to confirm the voyage or the claimed discovery. Spanish officialdom of the day took great pains to document any such activity, and many researchers have sought in vain for such confirmation.

Both Lok and Fuca were men in their twilight years. Both were in desperate financial straits and seeking, one last time, to recoup their losses. Both had personal agendas that would benefit from a windfall based on an attractive myth. Both would have wanted to make the discovery as enticing as possible.

Had the viceroy and his officials actually sent Fuca in search of the Strait of Anian and been presented with a report similar to that recounted to Lok, they would surely have mounted an immediate follow-up expedition to establish Spanish control of the waterway, and this, even more surely, would have generated extensive archival records. Also, whether or not they intended to reward the mariner, they would have appreciated the strategic significance of his discovery. It is inconceivable that they would have permitted him the freedom to sell his story to their rivals and enemies.

While there is a significant entrance—which now bears his name—with a prominent rock pillar, within about a degree of the latitude Juan de Fuca cites, some of his accompanying details are significantly wrong. He has the strait being 167–222 kilometres wide at the entrance; it is, in fact, only about 20 kilometres wide—out by a factor of ten. He has the coast trending about 90 degrees off the true direction. The pillar he describes seems to correspond with what is now called Fuca Pillar, close to and outside Cape Flattery. Adding to the confusion is another nearby islet, Duncan Rock, so named, erroneously, by George Vancouver to commemorate the visit in August 1788 by the fur trader Charles Duncan, who drew the first chart of the entrance.

Notwithstanding these inconsistencies and variances with known facts, there remain enough intriguing near-truths to provide fuel for ongoing debate and speculation. After all, he did report, apparently for the first time, a major inlet in the Pacific Coast at about the correct latitude, which led into a broadening body of water branching in several directions and containing "divers Ilandes"—features that equate well with Haro, Rosario, and Georgia straits, and Admiralty Inlet / Puget Sound. It would have been possible, just, for him to reconnoitre these within the 20-plus days he claims. There is even the remote possibility that he could have "pre-discovered" Vancouver's route from the Strait of Georgia, north past Cape Mudge, through Discovery Passage, Johnstone Strait, into Queen Charlotte Strait and Sound, thence back out into the Pacific.

There have been a few attempts to link or conflate the Juan de Fuca tale with the campaign of secrecy and leaks of misinformation surrounding the 1579 voyage of Francis Drake. Most of these, however, have been dismissed as too tenuous or too far-fetched. While most serious students of local history of that era retain prudent doubt about the reliability of Lok's transcript of Juan de Fuca's account, perhaps the last word on it has yet to be revealed.

Recently, Vancouver journalist Alan Twigg, curious about the man and his supposed discovery, visited the island of Kefalonia on vacation. He found his way to the remote village of Valeriano, and discovered that the locals were proud of their native son. On a plinth set in a small park is a bust commemorating "The Navigator Ioannis Apostolos Focas-Valerianos" (see Fig. 6). The accompanying plaque makes some rather extravagant claims, not reported by Lok—perhaps a product of understandable civic hubris.

FIG 6   A fanciful statue to a native son, nicknamed Juan de Fuca, graces the village of Valeriano on Kefalonia, Greece. [Courtesy of Alan Twigg]

FIG 7 In July 1774, the Spanish navigator Juan Pérez, in the frigate *Santiago*, encountered local people in spectacular canoes off the tip of Langara Island in Haida Gwaii. They greeted the visitors by sprinkling eagle down upon the sea. [*There Came to Us a Canoe*, Mark Myers]

CHAPTER TWO

FIRST CONFIRMED ENCOUNTERS: PÉREZ AND COOK CHANCE UPON NOOTKA

AN UNSHELTERED ROADSTEAD: JUAN PÉREZ SIGHTS SAN LORENZO
In the early 1770s the Spanish Viceroy of New Spain, Antonio María de Bucareli, became suspicious that Russian fur traders were encroaching along the northern coast of Alta California, which Spain considered part of its territory. He also feared that Spain's English rivals were intent on discovering a navigable Northwest Passage from the Atlantic through to the Pacific. Both of these developments threatened Spanish sovereignty over the region. In particular, Bucareli feared for the safety of the trading galleons, which often approached the north coast on their return to Acapulco from Manila (see Fig. 8, page 18).

To counter these threats, the viceroy decided to launch his own voyages of exploration, and to establish tangible confirmation of Spain's possession. The first ship—the frigate *Santiago*—set sail from San Blas on January 24, 1774. In command was the viceroy's most experienced mariner, the 32-year-old ensign Juan Pérez, supported by Esteban José Martinez as pilot and some 80 officers and men. They headed first for the outpost mission of Monterey, Mexico, taking supplies and colonists.

Pérez also carried secret and detailed orders from Bucareli that he was to continue northward along the coast, with the overall objective of enlarging the king's territories by landing and making an act of possession at latitude 60° north. Such acts involved a strict protocol to establish title that would be recognized by other European powers. Also, he was to bring to "the numerous Indian inhabitants . . . the light of the Gospel which will free them from the darkness of idolatry," [1] as well as search for any sign of foreign settlement.

By the time Pérez had delivered the colonists to Monterey and resupplied for his voyage into the unknown, it was mid-June, already well into the favourable season for these latitudes. The prevailing winds obliged him to head well offshore in order to make any progress northward. A month later, they had only reached latitude 52° and were running short of fresh water, so they headed northeast toward land. In dense fog and rain, they sighted a promontory they called Cabo de Santa Margarita, but were unable to find an anchorage, and did not land. Some canoes came out to trade with them (see Fig. 7, page 16).

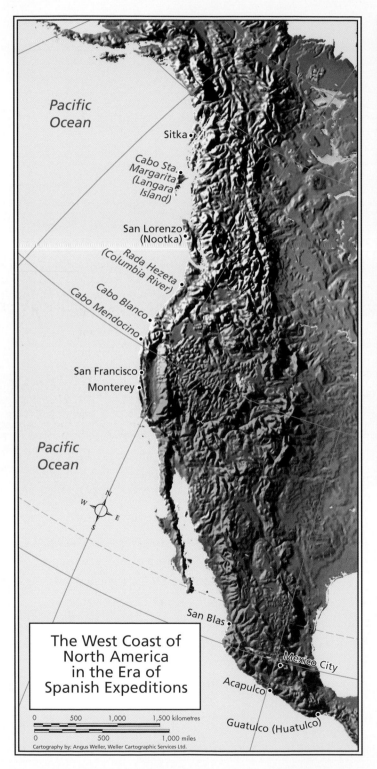

Pacific
Ocean

Sitka

Cabo Sta.
Margarita
(Langara
Island)

San Lorenzo
(Nootka)

Rada Hezeta
(Columbia River)

Cabo Blanco

Cabo Mendocino

San Francisco
Monterey

Pacific
Ocean

W — N — E
S

The West Coast of
North America
in the Era of
Spanish Expeditions

San Blas

Mexico City

Acapulco

Guatulco (Huatulco)

0   500   1,000   1,500 kilometres

0   500   1,000 miles

Cartography by: Angus Weller, Weller Cartographic Services Ltd.

FIG 8 (LEFT)   The west coast of the Americas showing places related to Spanish explorations of the 18th century. [Map by Angus Weller]

FIG 9 (ABOVE)   *Man of Nootka Sound.* John Webber, official artist with James Cook, used his time at Nootka to record faces, places, and natural history. [Courtesy of the State Library of NSW]

Pérez noted that the locals were "of good stature, well formed, a smiling face, beautiful eyes and good looking." [2] They had arrived at Langara Island, at the northwestern tip of today's Haida Gwaii.

Unable to make further progress north, Pérez recorded that he saw another point of land, across a wide entrance with a fierce cross current. This he called Santa Magdalena (now Cape Muzon) whose latitude, 54°40', would go on to be a significant factor in resolving imperial boundaries. The body of water separating the two capes was later called Dixon Entrance, after a British fur trader. It was here that Pérez abandoned both his search for fresh water and his mission to reach 60°.

Ordering the water ration to be reduced, he decided to return to Monterey. From Langara, wind and weather permitting, he would head south keeping within sight of the coast, seeking an anchorage where he might land to make an act of possession. Two weeks later, Pérez's report to the viceroy noted:

I was gaining [latitude] until 49 degrees 30 minutes north where I anchored on the 8th of the said month [August 1744] in a road-stead which appeared suitable to me for the purpose of taking possession, although it was unsheltered. [He was outside today's Nootka Sound.] But being becalmed and seeing that I was in 25 brazas [42 metres] of water, I anchored close to shore with a kedge anchor, spending the rest of the night in a calm sea.

The 9th dawned with the same conditions. Seeing that the weather was giving me some hope, I ordered the launch into the water, which was done very quickly because everyone shared in my desire to land. However, sir, when I was preparing to head for land a wind suddenly sprang up to the west so furious that in an instant it raised the sea, causing alarm, as that anchorage is uneven and extended about 4 or 5 leagues [22 or 28 kilometres] to sea. The condition of the sea and wind were becoming threatening. Seeing this unexpected contingency, and that the frigate was dragging the stream anchor and going rapidly toward the coast, I saw the need to order the stream cable cut; and I set sail to escape the danger of all perishing. Finally, with God's help and under a full press of sail, I managed to get away from this bad place, in which only the desire to land and comply with Your Excellency's orders had obliged me to drop anchor. It was not to be God's will, or, what is more certain, I was not deserving of it.

In this place many Indian canoes came out to us, which stood guard by us off the bow and stern all night. They came alongside the next day, and gave us sardines, and the men picked up some sea otter and seal furs in exchange for Monterey shells. They are very docile and not so lively as the ones earlier, but just as white and handsome as the others [see Fig. 9, page 18]. They are also poorer and, by their appearance, less talented.

As I have explained to Your Excellency, I set sail with the launch at the stern as soon as I retired from this bad harbour. I prepared to take it on board, which was accomplished with a great deal of trouble from the heavy sea running and because of the men's weakened condition—there were already many of them afflicted with the evils of scurvy.

We continued running with the foresail all day and night, descending to the south, always endeavoring to keep the land in sight if the weather permitted—although the fogs did not allow us this one pleasure. Believe me, Your Excellency, the days we were not plagued by fog were few, as were the days we took observations. [3]

In a diary, the pilot Martinez also wrote about those few days in the vicinity of Nootka Sound. His observations were incorporated into navigator Francisco Mourelle's précis of the "narrative" for the voyage. The portion relating to the time spent at Nootka reads:

[T]hey saw the land 15 leagues [83 kilometres] to the North, finding themselves in 48°50' of latitude. Although the winds varied in the 2nd [SE] and 3rd [SW] quadrants, they tried very hard to get in close with the purpose of anchoring, which they effectively succeeded in doing on the 7th at 3:00 in the afternoon. Sounding first in 25 brazas [46 metres] of water, which lessened to 15 then increased to the same 25 in black sand and mud, a league [six kilometres] from the closest land, they stopped with a stream anchor, hoping to look for a better shelter with [the ship's] launch.

That point of its anchorage, which they named San Lorenzo, was found to be in 48°30' of latitude North, and they considered it West of Monterey 3 degrees 51 minutes.

Six leagues [33 kilometres] to the Northwest of there was a point that was called Santa Clara. There was another, two leagues [11 kilometres] to the Southeast, which they named San Esteban, from where a point of rocks extended three-quarters of a league [4 kilometres] seaward, which took its direction to the Northwest and caused large breakers.

In that place they were approached by fifteen canoes of Indians who began trading with the ship's crew, from whom they received mother-of-pearl shells for pelts and sardines, which they handed over before receiving the agreed-upon price with neither suspicion or deceit.

Once again they saw small items of copper, which is an indication to them of mines of that metal. The natives asked for cutting instruments.

The people are said to be very robust and as white as the whitest Spaniard. It was the same with the only two women they saw, the dress of both sexes being pelts that without other arrangement cover their backs. [The sailors] having requested to know of them [the natives] if they had any knowledge of other civilized people, they apparently had never seen any.

The lands on those shores were modestly elevated, but in the interior they were very high and covered with forests.

The commander resolved to seek suitable shelter for their tasks. The launch was put in, and when it was ready the wind blew from the West exactly abeam, for which reason he sought to weigh anchor and set sail with the aim of avoiding the danger which threatened. But the wind freshened quickly, obliging him to cut the stream cable and make ready to sail immediately, in which case he followed a course South Southeast while the winds wheeled around to the 4th [NW] quadrant.

A remark found in the pilot's diary noted that a distance of five leagues [28 kilometres] from the anchorage at San Lorenzo there was a stepped sandbank at least 25 brazas [46 metres] deep and five or six leagues [28 or 33 kilometres] from North Northwest to South Southeast. Beyond that point, sounding continued with much unevenness and a bad anchoring ground.

Afterward they continued sailing in sight of the coast, hoping for improvement in the weather, searching for shelter in which to enter. The 11th, being in 47°47' of latitude, they saw a high mountain covered with snow, very perceptible, standing out alone, because the lowland stretching on all sides was heavily forested and populated with people as indicated by the number of smokes they saw. They named this mountain Santa Rosalía, considering it to be in 48°07' of latitude.

Mourelle's summary was critical, scathing even, of the results of the Pérez expedition.

The little fruit that resulted from this voyage is immediately apparent . . . In the days after they discovered the coast, they were doing no work . . . and the entire description they made of it is in approximate terms, which characterize the insufficiency of the commander and pilot . . . except for finding out that the coast continues to the northwest, we remained almost in the same ignorance after the voyage.[4]

As soon as Pérez had returned to his home port of San Blas, he sent a second report to the viceroy:

> Attached are verbatim copies of the diary which I have kept during my voyage . . . in which you will see noted, Your Excellency, everything concerning the voyage and the ship's course outbound and on its difficult return, not with that excellence we would have liked, but if everything contained in them is the pure truth there is no doubting that Your Excellency will excuse the defects found in them for they are not intentional.
>
> It has not been possible to construct a map of the coast discovered because the rolling aboard ship rendered it impossible, as well as the inconveniences suffered in these quarters of which Your Excellency is not unaware. It has been left to my care to send to Your Excellency a rough draft of everything, although it is not [done] with the excellence to which drafting instructors are accustomed.[5]

Despite Mourelle's harsh opinion of the fruits of the expedition, it did pave the way for several further sorties. As a preliminary reconnaissance, it acquired some valuable intelligence, such as the nature of the rugged, heavily wooded, coastline, populated with non-bellicose people keen to trade. It also demonstrated the extremely difficult sailing conditions during that season and the advisability of having a second vessel of shallower draft to accompany explorations along uncharted coasts.

What did the Mowachaht make of their visitors? The arrival of Pérez clearly made a major impression on them. Fifteen years later, they were able to point out to an American fur trader, Ingraham, exactly where the *Santiago* had anchored, and remember how the visitors had been dressed. The Indigenous people of the Pacific Northwest were steeped in a complex system of beliefs. To them, the spirit world was a constant and immediate presence. Denizens of that world frequently appeared in this one, taking on human and animal form, and transforming at will. The visit of the *Santiago* would probably have been viewed from this perspective.

Juan Pérez participated in the next voyage of exploration, departing from San Blas the following year aboard *Santiago*. Once again, he reached the latitude of Nootka but again, made no landing. He died from the effects of scurvy soon after returning from this second venture.

The Pérez voyage of 1774—particularly his contacts with the Haida at Langara Island and the Mowachaht at Nootka—constituted the first recorded encounters between Europeans and the peoples of the Pacific Northwest. For this, it merits an important place in the history of the exploration of Vancouver Island.

PROVIDENCE SEEMED TO ATTEND US: JAMES COOK ENTERS KING GEORGE'S SOUND

The authorities in London were well aware of the strategic significance implicit in Michael Lok's promotion of Juan de Fuca's claims. To be the first to discover, investigate, and lay claim to a navigable Northwest Passage would bring enormous advantage to any European trading nation. It was imperative that England should be that nation, but they had to act with circumspection. They did not want to provoke Spain by encroaching on its dominion along the Pacific coast of North America, but there was some doubt as to the northern limit of such "possession." As far as London was aware, this was Cabo Blanco at latitude 42°, reached by Sebastián Vizcaíno in 1603. They also had intelligence that a later expedition had got as far

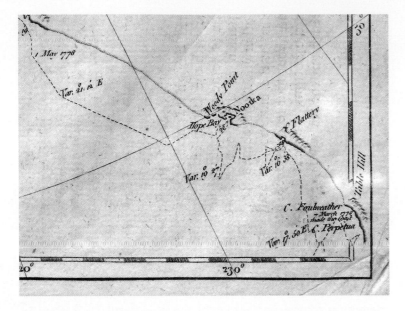

FIG 10 The portion of Cook's chart that records his track and landfalls at Cape Flattery and Nootka. His "Woody Point" was later renamed Cape Cook on the Brooks Peninsula. [Author's collection]

as 58°, but did not know the details. This, of course, would have referred to the Pérez voyage of 1774.

As a consequence, Captain James Cook, RN, in 1778, during his third great voyage of discovery in the Pacific, was ordered to investigate the coast north of 65° to seek the western portal of any passage through to the eastern seaboard. His secret orders were to make landfall only north of 45° and "to be very careful not to give any umbrage or offence to any of the inhabitants or subjects of his Catholic Majesty." [6]

As an added incentive, he and his expedition would be eligible, if successful, to claim the reward, recently announced by the admiralty, of ₤20,000 (worth about ₤2,000,000 today) to the officers and crew of any vessel discovering a passage to the Atlantic north of 52°.

Cook was also aware of the supposed entrance at about 47° reported in Lok's transcript of Juan de Fuca's story, and of another rumoured opening, the River Reyes, at about 53°, supposedly explored by a certain Admiral de Fonte in 1640 and reported in London in 1708. He considered both these possibilities rather dubious, but perhaps worth a look while he was in the vicinity.

The two ships of Cook's expedition—*Resolution*, under his command, and *Discovery*, captained by Charles Clerke—fresh from discovering the Sandwich Isles (now Hawaii,) made landfall on the Pacific coast of America at latitude 44°33'. Contrary winds and stormy conditions prevented Cook from advancing northward along the coast for a week before he decided to head offshore, seeking a favourable wind to carry them north.

He made a second landfall on March 22, a little north of 47°, but only briefly. It was foggy and getting dark, far too hazardous to linger near a rocky shore to investigate further. So again, he headed back out to sea. He named a point of land Cape Flattery in acknowledgment of the supposed entrance, recording:

It is in this very latitude where we now were that geographers have placed the pretended Strait of Juan de Fuca. But we saw nothing like it; nor is there the least probability that ever such thing existed.[7]

Had he arrived only a few hours earlier and coasted a short distance northward, he would have discovered a major entrance, which he would surely have been tempted to examine.

As it was, after gaining latitude offshore for two weeks, he found that the coast had veered to the northwest, so that he made yet a third landfall, this time, at 49°29'. He named the place Hope Bay, bounded to the north by Woody Point and to the south by Point Breakers. James Cook had arrived at Vancouver Island (see Fig. 10, page 22).

A flotilla of expertly handled canoes greeted the ships, and gestured that they should come around into the shelter of what would become known as Friendly Cove. Cook mistook one of the calls giving directions, "Nootka!" as being the name of the place. In fact, the locals' name for their summer village was Yuquot (see Fig. 11a, page 24). While initially Cook gave the name King George's Sound to the inlet, it would eventually be known as Nootka Sound.

As Cook looked around his fortuitous haven, he could see a variety of magnificent conifers, both standing and horizontal, as seasoned driftwood. Several streams poured into the sound from the surrounding hills. Here was the ideal place not only to refill his water casks, but also to replace some masts and spars before facing the rigours they could expect further north. Both ships had sailed from the Thames behind schedule and were poorly refitted. The Deptford dockyard had been overworked and rife with corruption; materials and workmanship suffered. The two vessels had originally been sturdy, stable Whitby collier-cats, shallow-draft sailing transports for the coal trade.

Chosen by Cook, who had served his maritime apprenticeship aboard these workhorses, they had been subjected to extensive modification and rerigging by order of the admiralty.

The quality of the officers, crew, and attached scientists had thus far largely compensated for the shoddy condition of the ships' fixed and running gear. Cook commanded the loyalty of a first-rate roster of both experienced and junior men. All aboard knew of the admiralty's prize for finding the Northwest Passage and hoped to share in it.

Among the names that would linger in the history of Vancouver Island was that of *Resolution*'s young sailing master, William Bligh. An excellent navigator and cartographer, Bligh nursed a short temper and a prickly nature. He, like Cook, had come up through the ranks. His name was given to the island in the middle of Nootka Sound where the two vessels anchored for their sojourn in Ship Cove. Another name to remain on today's maps is that of a midshipman aboard *Discovery* who, 14 years later, would command his own expedition to these waters and leave his name on a large island and two cities—George Vancouver. Three more, Nathaniel Portlock, master's mate to Bligh, George Dixon, a petty officer armourer, and James Colnett, a junior officer, were all soon to return to Nootka.

The men were in good health. Cook was a stickler for a healthy diet—he had made his 37-month second circumnavigation without losing a single life through scurvy or other disease. He insisted on fresh fruit and vegetables at all opportunities, fresh fish and meat whenever possible. Cook ordered his officers to set an example for the men during long periods at sea, with mandatory sauerkraut (both unpopular and ineffectual) and another, better, dietary innovation: lime juice. Two years earlier, Dr. James Lind had published a paper reporting the benefits of citrus juice as an antiscorbutic, and Cook had immediately adopted Lind's ideas into his provisioning.

FIG 11A *A Great Many Canoes Filled With Natives Were About the Ships All Day*—this painting by Harry Heine depicts the dramatic moment when Maquinna's Mowachaht people examined Cook's *Resolution* and *Discovery* outside what would be later called Nootka Sound. [Courtesy of Mark Heine]

FIG 11B Captain Cook and his men engaged in barter with Mowachaht people at Ship Cove, Nootka Sound, while repairs were being made to the masts of *Resolution* in Harry Heine's *Captain James Cook*. [Courtesy of Mark Heine]

Cook called upon yet another medicinal stratagem at Ship Cove. The fresh, green shoots of the local spruce trees were collected, boiled with molasses, and fermented into spruce beer. This was an excellent source of the yet-undiscovered vitamin C. The Royal Society awarded Cook their Gold Medal for intellectual achievement on his presentation describing his regimes.

At Ship Cove there was an isolated, flat-topped islet. While the vessels were laid up for refitting, the expedition's astronomer, William Bayly, set up two tents: one a portable observatory, the other for the marine guard. The observatory tent afforded room for both a large, precision quadrant with its observer and a wooden-cased, pendulum, regulator clock. Panels in the canvas roof could be selectively removed for observing the heavens. This was an excellent opportunity to accurately determine the latitude and longitude of a point on America's west coast.

Bayly, Cook, and Lieutenant James King, another specialist astronomer, together made more than 600 observations, using the "lunar distances" method decreed by the astronomer royal. This involved comparing the angle made between the moon and the sun or a fixed star, and referring to the official *Nautical Almanac* and other tables.

The astronomers could also verify the reliability of another technological innovation employed by Cook—the chronometer watch K1, invented by John Harrison and replicated by Larcum Kendall for testing by Cook (see Fig. 12). With this device, Cook had been able to know Greenwich Mean Time and thereby calculate his longitude—even while at sea—anywhere in the world.

The work of replacing both the foremast and the mizzen of *Resolution*, as well as recaulking and rerigging both ships, proceeded with all possible speed (see Fig. 11b, page 24).

FIG 12 John Harrison's marine watch-chronometer revolutionized the calculation of longitude. This version was made by John Arnold in London and sold to a Spanish expedition. [Museo Naval, Madrid]

CAPTAIN JAMES COOK.

OB. 1779

From the Original Picture by Dance in the Gallery of Greenwich Hospital.

JOHN TALLIS & COMPANY, LONDON & NEW YORK.

FIG 13 [Author's collection]

CAPTAIN JAMES COOK: BRITAIN'S FOREMOST NAVIGATOR AND HYDROGRAPHER

The epitaph on Sir Hugh Palliser's monument to James Cook declares Cook to be 'the ablest and most renowned navigator this or any other country hath produced.' Captain James Cook developed his skills as a hydrographic surveyor while preparing detailed charts of the St. Lawrence River for General Wolfe's assault and capture of Quebec. He then spent four years in command of a survey schooner charting the coast of Newfoundland and the cod fisheries of the Grand Banks. This experience, combined with exceptional leadership qualities, led the lords of the admiralty to select Cook, over several more senior officers, to lead the first of his three scientific voyages. Appointing a man who had joined as a lowly able seaman to such a position of prestige, in preference to high-born, socially prominent rivals, was a most unusual departure for the class-conscious Royal Navy of that era.

As it turned out, their gamble paid off magnificently. Not only did Cook far exceed the stated objectives of his expeditions, he established a splendid tradition of how such missions should be undertaken and the findings collated, described, and presented. Cook also trained a cohort of hydrographers to serve Britain's expanding global maritime interests (see Fig. 13).

FIG 14 An ink-and-watercolour sketch by Surgeon's Mate William Ellis shows Ship Cove in Nootka Sound with Resolution undergoing repair, and the tents on Astronomers' Rock where surveyors measured the local longitude. A marine stands guard. [Courtesy of the National Library of Australia]

whose business, as has already been observed, was to collect the vegetable and other curious productions of the countries through which we passed, were enabled to stock ourselves with a large proportion of culinary plants, which was of infinite service to us in our more northerly progress. And now having all things in readiness, we began to tow out of the cove into the sound, to which Capt. Cook gave the name of K. George's Sound, and with a light breeze and clear weather to proceed on our voyage: but we had scarce reached the sound, when a violent gust from E.S.E. threw us into the utmost confusion. All our boats were out, our decks full of lumber, and night coming on dark and foggy, our danger was equal to any we had hitherto met in the course of the voyage, though an especial Providence seemed to attend us, and to interpose in our favour, for by this storm a leak was discovered in the *Resolution*, which had it been calm weather, would probably have proved fatal to the crew. Having cleared the sound, we shaped our course to the westward, and so continued till day-light, when seeing nothing of the *Resolution*, we shortened sail; and before noon she came in sight, we pursued our course to the north-west-ward.[8]

Once more, the Pacific belied its name. A southeasterly hurricane forced them well offshore. Unable to regain sight of land until they were north of latitude 57°, they had passed both the Queen Charlotte and Alexander archipelagos, and were near Sitka. This was the area of the supposed entrance reported by Admiral de Fonte, and Cook was again dismissive: "For my own part, I give no credit to such vague and improbable stories, that carry their own confutation with them."[9]

England's greatest explorer now sailed out of the Vancouver Island saga, on to his investigation of the Alaskan coast, the Bering Strait, and into the Arctic Ocean. He decided to return to winter in the balmy Sandwich Isles, where he met his savage demise.

However, the expedition continued after Cook's death, going on to create, unexpectedly, the next stage of international interest in Vancouver Island. In Kamchatka the crew met Russian fur merchants from whom they learned that the sea otter skins and other pelts acquired in Nootka were valuable. A fur trader paid handsomely for two-thirds of their skins, about seven pounds apiece. All were well pleased with their profit—until the following year when they reached Macao. There, they discovered that on the Chinese market those same skins would fetch many times the price they had received from the wily Russian. One fine skin, obtained for a broken buckle, sold for £300. Here was a clear message: there was a fortune to be made by buying sea otter pelts in Nootka and Cook's Inlet and selling them to the Chinese. That message was not lost on crew members and others who read the published accounts of Cook's third and final voyage.

As their exotic visitors departed, Maquinna (also called Tsaxawasip) returned with his people to, so they thought, the normality of *nuh'chee*, their land. Over the next decade, the tranquil haven that had sheltered *Resolution* and *Discovery* for four weeks became the busiest seaport on the west coast of the Americas. In the process, Nootka Sound developed into a bone of contention, bringing rival European imperial powers Spain and Britain to the very brink of war.

IN COOK'S WAKE: THE FUR TRADERS

James Cook's superiors in London had urged him to exercise prudence in approaching the Pacific coast of New Spain. They were wise—it was a matter of extreme diplomatic delicacy. As early as Cook's departure from Plymouth in 1776, rumours had reached the ears of Minister José Gálvez in Spain about the voyage, and about British intentions to seek the supposed Straits of Anian. He instructed Viceroy Bucareli to dispatch a mission to thwart those plans.

It was not until 1779, however, that the reluctant Bucareli was even in a position to assemble a flotilla of two lightly armed vessels to attempt to intercept and apprehend Cook's far stronger force. By then, of course, it was much too late. Cook had already refitted at Nootka, ventured as far as the Bering Sea, and left the disputed waters.

Bucareli's vessels carried instructions to reach latitude 70°, if possible. Ignacio de Arteaga was given command, with Juan Francisco de la Bodega y Quadra as captain of the second ship. Quadra had, a few years earlier, ventured along the northern coast. Setting the now-customary course well out into the Pacific before heading north, the ships made landfall at about 55°, then explored northward up the broken coastline as far as Prince William Sound at 61°. There they made an act of possession, then coasted westward to Kodiak Island. By this time, the weakened crew, continuously hostile locals, and atrocious weather obliged them to struggle back to San Blas.

They reported having found neither traces of Cook nor signs of Russian encroachment, reinforcing Bucareli's conviction that this remote and difficult coast held scant interest or concern for Spain. Moreover, he felt that Spain had done enough to secure legitimate dominion over the entire coast. He died that same year and was not effectively replaced for another eight years, during which time British-Spanish rivalry flared into declared war, and the international situation cascaded into turmoil and revolution.

France was another rival to Britain's growing maritime dominance. In 1785, King Louis XVI ordered his own circumnavigating voyage of scientific exploration, led by Jean-François de Galaup, comte de La Pérouse. Provided with Cook's charts and instruments, and news of the potential for trade in sea otter pelts, La Pérouse was to make an act of possession on behalf of France north of 55°. He did so in 1786 at Port des Français in Lituya Bay, now Alaska, latitude 65°. By then he had lost 21 officers and men in a fierce tidal rip, and those remaining were exhausted. Low on men and provisions, he decided to abandon the search for the Northwest Passage.

He headed down the coast, adding a few details to Cook's chart as he went. Not long after passing Nootka, he noted a shallow zone of the ocean, and marked his chart "banc"—not realizing he was at the entrance to what was soon to be called the Strait of Juan de Fuca. He had missed the opportunity for a major discovery. In his report, he advised that further attempts by France to establish a presence along this coast would imperil the country's relationship with Spain.

The mysterious strait that Pérez, Cook, and La Pérouse had all failed to spot did not remain undiscovered—or, perhaps, rediscovered—for long. Cook's account of the commercial opportunity afforded by sea otter skins increased the number of ships heading off to exploit it. Even before the news had been made public, several of Cook's officers prepared to return to the northwest coast in search of more of the lucrative pelts. Some were sailing on their own account, others as members of established trading companies or syndicates based in London or Macao. A few, to evade trading restrictions of British and Chinese authorities, sailed under false colours. In Boston too, Yankee traders had learned of the new potential for business, and set out to investigate.

Their initial target had been Nootka Sound, but competition soon drove them to search for skins further afield, wherever the otters were plentiful. They did not hunt the animals themselves, but sought to trade with local experts in that art. Their purpose was primarily commercial, and not exploration to seek geographical knowledge. However, since many were trained naval officers, and keen to record details necessary to make profitable trading visits in the future, they made significant discoveries about the complex coastline.

In their pursuit of pelts, the traders ventured into previously unknown inlets on the west coast of what was to become known as Vancouver Island; they discovered and named the Queen Charlotte Islands (now Haida Gwaii) and the archipelagos further north, and produced some valuable additions to the chart. One of them, George Dixon, wondered, as had La Pérouse, whether this was the outer edge of a series of offshore islands, rather than the true coast of the continental mainland.

In July 1787, Charles Barkley made perhaps the most intriguing discovery in the fur-trading era, as far as Vancouver Island is concerned. The documentary evidence is scattered, confusing, and of questionable reliability, but the story has been investigated by such important historians as John T. Walbran, María Luisa Martín-Merás, Frederick W. Howay, W. Kaye Lamb, Willis Ireland, and is now generally accepted.

The 26-year-old Captain Barkley had commanded trading vessels for the Honourable East India Company, in whose service he had progressed since boyhood, when in 1786 he left the company to take up a new command. His vessel, *Loudoun*, was a former East Indiaman, weighing 400 tons, with 20 guns—a huge ship for her time. The new owners seem to have been a shadowy, renegade subset of directors and employees of the company (Barkley included), intent on skirting the monopoly trading rights enjoyed by the company: all most irregular.

Loudoun, newly fitted out in London, sailed for Ostend to provision for an extended voyage to the northwest coast. While it was there, two important things happened: Barkley met, courted, and married Frances Hornby, the 17-year-old daughter of an English clergyman, and the ship's name was changed to *Imperial Eagle*, with papers and the flag of the Austrian empire.

Barkley's log for the part of his voyage after he arrived on the west coast has been lost. It was first seized as security by customs authorities in China, then obtained by another fur trader, the nefarious John Meares (incidentally, a shareholder in the *Loudoun* caper, of whom more will be told), then returned to Barkley's family, who passed it on to the government as potential evidence at the Oregon boundary dispute. Thereafter, it disappeared.

Nonetheless, the momentous discovery was recorded in a related set of documents—the diaries and reminiscences of Frances Barkley. These were seen by Captain Walbran and summarized, but were lost in a fire before they could be completely transcribed. From a detailed study of all the remaining evidence, this appears to be what transpired: *Imperial Eagle* arrived in early June near Clayoquot Sound, then proceeded to nearby Friendly Cove in Nootka Sound, where Barkley was the first trader of the 1787 season. There he secured a good quantity of sea otter pelts—probably all that were available—and had an unusual visitor.

Shortly after the ship had moored in Friendly Cove, a canoe was paddled alongside and a man, in every respect like an Indian, and a very dirty one at that, clothed in a greasy sea-otter skin, came on board, and to the utter astonishment of Capt. and Mrs. Barkley, introduced himself as Dr. John Mackey, late surgeon of the trading brig *Captain Cook*. This visitor informed them that he had been living at Nootka amongst the Indians for the previous twelve months, during which he had completely conformed himself to their habits and customs, which Mrs. Barkley, in her diary, emphatically states were disgusting. Dr. Mackey had learned the language and had also made himself acquainted, more or less, with the surrounding country, thus making his services of great value to Capt. Barkley who, before the ship left this Sound, engaged Dr. Mackey as trader, a duty which he seems to have carried out to Capt. Barkley's complete satisfaction ... He had made frequent excursions into the interior parts of the country about King George's Sound, and did not think any part of it was the continent of America. But a chain of detached islands.

The previous year, another British fur trader, John Strange, had left one of his crew ashore with the Mowachaht to learn the local language and foster favourable trade with Strange when he returned the following season. It did not work out as well as had been hoped. Perhaps because Mackey transgressed a taboo, Maquinna and his people did not treat him kindly, taking all his clothes and other possessions. Notwithstanding his mistreatment, he did manage to acquire a passing command of the language and retain enough goodwill with the locals to help Barkley acquire most of the pelts available, not just in Nootka Sound, but also in the area.

After a month's trading with the Mowachaht, *Imperial Eagle* headed southeast to discover and enter yet another inlet, previously unknown to Europeans.

[W]e visited a large Sound in latitude 40.20 north, which Capt. Barkley named Wickaninnish's Sound, the name given being that of the Chief who seemed to be quite as powerful a potentate as Maquilla at King George's Sound. [This sound is now known as Clayoquot Sound.] Wickaninnish has great authority and this part of the coast proved a rich harvest of furs for us. Likewise close to the southward of this Sound, to which Captain Barkley gave his own name, calling it Barkley Sound. Several coves and bays and also islands in this Sound we named. There was Frances Island—after myself; Hornby Peak—also after myself—Cape Beale, after our purser, Williams Point and a variety of other names, all of which were familiar to us. We anchored in in a snug harbour in the Sound of which my husband made a plan as far as his knowledge of it would permit . . .

From Barkley Sound the *Imperial Eagle* again proceeded eastward, and to the great astonishment of Capt. Barkley and his officers, a large opening presented itself, extending miles to the eastward with no land in sight in that direction. The entrance appeared to be about four leagues [22 kilometres] in width as far as the eye could see. Capt. Barkley at once recognized it as the long lost Strait of Juan de Fuca, which Captain Cook had so emphatically stated did not exist . . . The *Imperial Eagle* did not go up the Strait, but kept along the ocean coast, which was now found to be compact and unbroken by bays or inlets.[10]

Soon after, Barkley lost a shore party of two officers (including purser Beale) and four men to, presumably, hostile locals. The next day, an armed search party discovered grisly remains confirming that their shipmates had been killed. Barkley, after naming the scene of the tragedy Destruction Island, departed for Macao to trade his furs.

The following season, 1788, saw two more fur traders venturing just inside the newly found strait. The first was John Meares, whose vessel, *Felice Adventurer*, lay at anchor in Effingham Bay, deep within Barkley Sound, where Meares planned to seek sea otters for trade. Benefiting from the maps and logs left by Barkley as deposit in Macao, he decided to send his longboat, under first officer Robert Duffin, "to explore and take possession of the strait and land adjoining in the name of the King and Crown of Britain."[11]

On this trip, Duffin and his crew came under attack by canoes of locals, fierce and armed with clubs and barbed arrows. It is not clear where this happened, but possibly in the vicinity of Port San Juan, since they could not have travelled much further in their week away from *Felice*. With several crew members and himself badly wounded, Duffin struggled back to rejoin *Felice* at Effingham. Included in Meares's book *Voyages*

Entrance of the Strait of John de Fuca.

FIG 16   John Meares used this fanciful depiction of Robert Duffin's 1788 foray into the Strait of Juan de Fuca to support his complaint against Spanish mistreatment at Nootka. [Courtesy of the Wayfarer's Bookshop, Bowen Island, BC]

is an attractive engraving of the longboat under full sail, six canoes filled with men paddling furiously in pursuit, approaching *Felice*, supposedly at the entrance of the strait off Claaset (see Fig. 16, page 34). As in many parts of the book, this picture seems exaggerated and deliberately misleading—far more so than artistic licence would permit.

Meares prudently decided to abandon further attempts at trading within the strait and head back to Nootka. There he met another trader, *Princess Royal*, under the command of Charles Duncan, a recently retired Royal Navy master—a specialized navigating officer. The two vessels were now part of an agreement for cooperation between two British syndicates operating on the northwest coast, and their captains exchanged information. Duncan decided to investigate the strait.

Duncan then headed south, picking up some pelts in Ahousaht on Flores Island before continuing directly to the strait identified by Barkley, and anchored off its southern promontory. He was greeted at Claaset by canoes of the local Makah people, with whom he traded for a few days, in the process acquiring some significant intelligence about the geography further down the strait. Duncan's logs were lost, but he did draw a clear sketch map of the entrance to the strait, which survived. As an annotation on that map he noted:

> The Indians of Claaset said that they knew not of any land to the Eastward and that it was A'as toopulfe—which signifies a Great Sea, they pointed out that the sea ran a great way up to the northward and down to the southward. On the East Side, they likewise said, that a good distance to the Southward, I should find men that had guns as well as I had.

This would seem to be a reference to what is now Seattle. Duncan continued his description:

> Pinnacle Rock appears to be about 34 fathoms [62 metres] high, its base in front about 10 fathoms. The top projects over the rest of it. The sides appear steep. It stands about half way between the Cape & Green Island. The distance between the Cape and Island is fi[ve] mile[s] not navigable in appearance. Green Island or to Tooches [Tatoosh] is about ¼ mile in length, covered over with green grass. On the east side is a small cove, very narrow and only navigable for boats. I saw some canoes go in and out and many Indians on the beach. On the east side is a large village and from the number of canoes that came to us from thence, I suppose it to be well inhabited.[12]

The rock he describes seems to match that mentioned by Juan de Fuca to Michael Lok and is now called Fuca Pillar.

Duncan then sailed for Canton, afterward returning to London. There he met and passed on his findings, including the sketch map, to Alexander Dalrymple. This man, formerly hydrographer to the East India Company, had been collecting all the information he could muster about the northwest coast (including the Barkley material) to support his campaign to have the East India and the Hudson's Bay companies join forces. They would create a powerful British commercial link with Asia, initially by the establishment of a "factory," or fur-trading base, on the northwest coast. Spain would have other ideas about that.

FIG 17 Painting showing Spanish naval officers of the mid-18th century engaged in hydrographic survey work. [Courtesy of España, Ministerio de Defensa, Archivo del Museo Naval]

CHAPTER THREE

SPANIARDS TAKE POSSESSION OF NUCA

IN THE LATE 1700S, A rumour circulated at the court in St. Petersburg that Russians and British had traded along the Pacific coast and even planned a base at Nootka. The rumour reached Spanish explorers when, southbound from Alaska, the French captain Jean-François de Galaup, comte de La Pérouse, landed in 1786 at Monterey, then a Spanish mission, where he chanced upon two vessels under the command of Estéban Martínez. This meeting eventually triggered a voyage north in 1788 by Martínez, with the very experienced pilot Gonzalo López de Haro in a second ship, to investigate the Russian intentions and any activity on the coast to the south of wherever he should meet any of them.

During the voyage, bad blood developed between Martínez and López de Haro—and most of the other officers aboard—largely as a result of Martínez's incompetence and drunken irascibility. After confirming that the Russians apparently intended to occupy Nootka, Martínez and López de Haro made separate returns to Monterey and San Blas, not stopping anywhere. The following year, 1789, the new Spanish viceroy

dispatched them to Nootka to pre-empt any attempt by foreign powers to establish a foothold on the coast. They were in for quite a surprise.

Martínez, again in command with López de Haro accompanying, carried orders to treat the local people well, convert them to the true faith, erect buildings and the fortifications needed to protect them, and make it look as though this were a permanent outpost. A few marines went with them. Foreign vessels were to be treated courteously and welcomed to the "Port of Nuca," but made to understand that they were in Spanish territory. Once this had been accomplished, they were to explore the coast between latitudes 50° and 55°.

In Madrid, the foreign threat was treated seriously and orders were sent to strengthen the naval force at San Blas. New vessels were to be constructed and deployed; the experienced officer Juan Francisco de la Bodega y Quadra (see Fig. 18, page 39) was promoted and placed in local command with six additional officers (see Fig. 17, page 36). A new viceroy, the count of Revillagigedo, was also due to arrive from Spain.

As Martínez arrived off Nootka, he met up with a vessel flying an American flag; he ordered it to stop, and the captain to report to him. There ensued a complicated affair of misinformation from both sides, exacerbated by the presence of other vessels in Friendly Cove, with several more due to arrive shortly. The situation had all the makings of a comic opera—if only the diplomatic stakes had not been so high. Over the coming months it became known as the Nootka Incident, leading to the brink of outright war between Britain and Spain. In the process, the hot-tempered Martínez seized some British ships, arrested their officers, crew, cargoes, and papers—including maps and logbooks—and conveyed them as prisoners under escort to San Blas, leaving the outpost unoccupied over the winter of 1789–90.

The American traders were known locally as "Boston Men" (in contrast to "King George's Men" from Britain). The senior of these was John Kendrick, who had ingratiated himself with both Chief Maquinna and Martínez, and even purchased a plot of land he called Fort Washington. Kendrick remained at Nootka as the Spaniards prepared to depart for the winter. Martínez, needing materials for paint—whale oil and ochre—sent a boat party to see if they were available from Maquinna in his winter village at the head of Tahsis Inlet. John Kendrick's son, Juan, who had joined the Spanish detachment, led the group. Returning, the party spotted a narrow side channel, which they investigated. They discovered that it led out to the Pacific, and deduced that Friendly Cove was on an island, to be called Mazarredo after a renowned Spanish naval official.

With international tension pervading Nootka Sound that season, little exploration of Vancouver Island had been possible. Another Boston trader, Robert Gray, in his ship *Lady Washington*, had ventured 17 leagues (95 kilometres) into the Strait of Juan de Fuca, but, finding no furs, retreated. The controversial John Meares, deeply embroiled in the Anglo-Hispanic dispute, published a map purporting to show that Gray had sailed through the strait, turned northwest, and returned to the Pacific north of the Queen Charlottes, which Meares deemed to prove the probability of a Northwest Passage.

The British and the Russians, anticipating trouble and even capture by Spanish warships, kept prudently well away from Nootka during 1790. The Spanish, from their newly expanded naval base at San Blas, however, were determined to re-establish Santa Cruz de Nuca as a defended outpost of empire. The new viceroy ordered that Martinez be given command of a squadron to re-occupy, fortify, and establish full control, then to continue the exploration of the surrounding coastline.

Bodega y Quadra had anticipated the order by preparing two expeditions with those same objectives. He did not, however, concur with Viceroy Revillagigedo that Martínez deserved any senior role in the mission. Instead, he gave overall command to the newly arrived veteran naval campaigner Francisco de Eliza, with Salvador Fidalgo and Manuel Quimper in command of accompanying vessels. Fidalgo was a seasoned hydrographer, and, while Quimper was new to command, he would have another experienced pilot, Gonzalo López de Haro, to provide able support. López de Haro had, the previous season, made a brief foray down the coast from Nootka as far as Port San Juan in a tiny schooner, *Santa Gertrudis la Magna*; this was a locally assembled vessel, *North West America*, seized from John Meares and renamed.

The Spaniards also conveyed a 70-strong company of militiamen, led by the highly capable Captain Pedro de Alberni of the Volunteers of Cataluña. Martínez—the subject of a damning enquiry conducted by Bodega y Quadra into the events at Nootka—was relegated to the ignominy of looking after trade in peltry.

FIG 18 In 1966 the Spanish Royal Navy presented this portrait of Capitán Juan Francisco de la Bodega y Quadra to the Canadian Coast Guard for the wardroom of the weather ship CCGS *Quadra*. [Courtesy of the Canadian Coast Guard]

FIG 19 Bronze bust of another Peruvian-born naval explorer, Manuel Quimper. Erected at Sooke Harbour to celebrate when, in 1790, he commanded the first European expedition to penetrate the Strait of Juan de Fuca to its eastern end. [Photo by author]

The initial flotilla was soon followed by a second, bringing more guns and supplies. Eliza's flagship was the cumbersome, 30-gun frigate, *Concepción*—the largest Spanish warship on the west coast. Fidalgo's command was the more manoeuvrable packet boat *San Carlos*, while Quimper and López de Haro were in the sloop captured from the British at Nootka and now renamed *Princesa Real*. For inshore work, they also carried another schooner, in kit form, to assemble on-site. This would be called *Santa Saturna*, or more familiarly, *Orcasitas*.

A month after his force re-occupied Nootka, Eliza complied with his orders to send a party north, to assess the current situation of incursions by foreigners. He dispatched Fidalgo in *San Carlos* to explore, chart, and investigate Russian activity. They found a few signs, including the presence of two warships, but made no direct contact. After making a token act of possession, Fidalgo headed back south. Unable to enter Nootka, he returned to Monterey, planning to proceed to San Blas.

At the end of May 1790, Eliza sent out a second exploring party, this time south from Nootka. It consisted of Quimper and López de Haro, with his capable apprentice pilot Juan Carrasco, aboard *Princesa Real*. They carried a quantity of sheets of copper to trade for sea otter pelts. This was a local initiative, a foray to see if they might share in the apparently lucrative business. They were to complete the journey within two months since the vessel was due to be returned to the previously arrested, but now freed, British fur trader James Colnett.

Quimper's first port of call was the large village of Chief Wickaninnish, inside Clayoquot Sound.

> Huiquinanichi lives in a great house adorned with columns of huge figures which held up three large pine timbers, as long as ninety feet [27 metres] and thick in proportion. The entrance is

a figure the mouth of which is a door. More than one hundred persons besides the king live in it.

There, to López de Haro's surprise, they also found Maquinna, nervous about a re-encounter with the disagreeable Martínez and reluctant to return to his own summer village of Yuquot at Friendly Cove. The Spaniards, keen to restore relations with both of these influential leaders, were generous with gifts of copper and scarlet cloth, and due ceremony. After assuring Maquinna that, although Martínez had returned, he no longer held any authority, Quimper provided the leader with a sail for his canoe to return home. The two leaders warned the Spaniard about entering the Strait of Juan de Fuca in such a small craft, since the locals there were *pizac*, equivalent in their language to very bad or treacherous. They were probably referring to the Makah at Claaset, who had murdered Barkley's shore party.

After spending a few more days charting some of the labyrinth of channels that form Clayoquot Sound, and not heeding the warnings, the Spaniards meticulously inspected several inlets along the northern shore of Juan de Fuca. At each place, they gathered information pertinent to the needs of a viable harbour—climate, access to fresh water and timber, protection from wind and seas, and the attitude of local peoples. They then made the time-consuming formal acts of possession, and gave the places Spanish names.

Inside the strait, *Princesa Real* ventured into Puerto de San Juan (or de Narváez, after a fellow pilot) where, to supplement the ship's longboat for inshore work, Quimper purchased two large canoes and 28 paddles from the locals. Continuing on, they noted Sombrio and Jordan rivers before arriving at what would later be known as Sooke Harbour; some local men in a canoe guided the longboat there. Quimper recorded:

On the 19th [I dropped anchor] in a port sheltered from all winds with a good bottom and fertile surroundings. I immediately caused a plan of it to be drawn up, and when this was finished I took possession of it on the 23rd, naming it Revilla Gigedo.

At sunset [López de Haro and Carrasco] returned and told me that the port was a closed one, and that they had entered the lagoon about half a mile, where they found the water almost fresh. About a mile inland he found the water entirely fresh but did not reach the source only noting that it came from the direction of a somewhat distant mountain. He said that everything close to the river was very flat land without trees, covered with much grass a yard and a half high and that the land in the distance, although covered with trees, was also flat . . . The tree where the bottle [with the document] of possession was buried stands in the angle which the tongue of flat land [now Whiffen Spit] with the entrance of the port makes [see Fig. 19, page 40].

Their next anchorage was Rada de Eliza (Pedder Bay) where they inspected, charted, and took possession, then sent out boat parties to Rada de Solano (Parry Bay) and Rada de Valdés y Bazan (Royal Roads). While they lay at anchor in Pedder Bay, some Strait Salish men approached. Quimper offered them gifts, and tried to find out more about the eastern end of the strait.

[They responded] with entirely understandable signs that there was a very large and wide [channel] which trended somewhat toward the northwest, and that at the end of the range of mountains on the south coast [the Olympics] there was another like it. They made a sign that this trended towards the southwest . . . I sent the armed longboat with the second pilot [Carrasco] to reconnoitre to the northeast to see if the information of the Indians that there was a channel there was true . . . On his return he reported that he had been in the channel and that it began at the point to the northeast, the one which has the two small islands close to it, and that it extended a long distance, as no land could be seen to the north except some mountains which could scarcely be made out. The west coast of the channel trended WNW [west northwest] he said, the land in sight to the northwest and that farthest northeast bearing E ¼ NE [east ¼ northeast] formed some large bays. Close to the islands and the shore were some rocks and small rocky islands, where he had found a strong current, and said the true channel was between the two islands and the coast to the east as it seemed to be clean and was much wider. He had gone ashore at the point at the first entrance and planted the Holy Cross which I had given him for that purpose, and said that it was flat with much green grass and other plants.

Rather than follow up Carrasco's reconnaissance of the entrance, Quimper crossed to the southern shore of the strait to investigate the other large inlet that sounded intriguing. Finding a wide, protected bay to which he gave his own name, Quimper anchored and sent Carrasco out in the longboat to explore further to the east. Carrasco discovered a second, much larger, entrance protected by an island; he named it Bahía de Bodega y Quadra (later also found by Vancouver, who called it Port Discovery). Just before deciding to return to his ship, Carrasco could make out what seemed to be yet a third shallow bay which he called Ensenada (cove) de Caamaño after yet another fellow pilot. This supposed cove must have been the entrance to the channel described by the Salish at Eliza: Admiralty Inlet leading to Puget Sound.

Although the sun had already set [Carrasco] had noted on the coast opposite, beyond the island, a kind of channel or port, and that in the first quarter there were two inlets in the coast, apparently small ones. In the middle of one he saw a front of high land and believed it ended there. This I named Fidalgo and the other . . . "Flon."[1]

Carrasco had evidently also glimpsed the entrances to Rosario Strait and Deception Pass.

Quimper suspected, erroneously, that the information he had been given by the people at Pedder Bay was questionable. In any case, time did not permit further exploration—he had scheduled orders for their return. Their vessel did not handle well to windward, so, to allow sufficient time, he chose to head back up the strait. The pilots concurred with his decision, but, as many subsequent sailors have found, this was far easier said than done. Capricious winds, combined with powerful and complex tidal streams, drove *Princesa Real* back across the strait to anchor in Royal Roads. They had passed by the entrance noted earlier by Carrasco that Quimper named Canal de López de Haro (now Haro Strait), and its western extremity, Punta de San Gonzalo (Gonzales Point). For at least the third time, they passed without noticing the entrance to what would be Victoria's outer harbour, but they did discover nearby a sheltered port that offered good anchoring, which they called Puerto de Córdova (Esquimalt Harbour). This they charted in detail, and traded with the friendly local people.

Crossing to the south shore once more, they struggled westward, eventually finding a cove just inside Cape Claaset, which Quimper named Núñez Gaona, after a senior officer. Fur traders had found this haven previously and had adopted its local name of Neah Bay. Quimper recognized that with its location, abundant supplies of fresh water, and fine timber, it would make a splendid and strategic harbour, so his people took a thorough set of soundings.

Tutuzí or Ta-toosh, leader of the local Makah people, soon made contact, offering plenty of sea otters and enormous salmon in exchange for copper and cloth. The Makah confirmed their reputation for trickery and ferocity by luring and then attacking a member of a shore party. Despite this, as a gesture of friendship, Quimper gave Ta-toosh the two canoes he had acquired earlier.

After a week or so, Quimper set sail for Nootka, only to find that dense, prolonged fogs and adverse winds prevented him from entering. Now perilously low on food and water, he too, elected to head south again to Monterey, where he found Fidalgo in *San Carlos*. Together, they returned to San Blas to report their discoveries to the base commander, Captain Bodega y Quadra, who was assembling a growing collection of cartographic data.

The charts, logs, and related records seized from the British ships at Nootka the previous year were by then in very capable and knowledgeable hands. Bodega y Quadra was compiling a new chart of the whole coast from all available information, and was able to identify the several gaps that still required investigation and detailed charting.

WINTER AT NOOTKA

Back in San Lorenzo de Nuca, Eliza's base at Friendly Cove, nothing was known of the findings or fate of the exploratory parties. While they were gone, Captain Pedro Alberni had employed his detachment of soldiers and the remaining seamen to good effect. Not only had they cleared and installed a fortified battery of 11 guns on an islet protecting the entrance, they had fundamentally altered Yuquot, the summer village of Maquinna and his people. They built barracks, officers' accommodations, an infirmary, a forge, a bakery, and pens and shelters for livestock; they dug wells and installed a system of aqueducts and sanitary facilities. Alberni had brought with him breeding stock

of sheep, pigs, goats, and poultry, as well as a wide selection of seeds and rootstock. He started to keep meteorological records, and planned to assess the optimum crops and timings for the soil and climate at Friendly Cove, so that the garrison might eventually become self-sustaining for produce.

Until this could happen, the Spaniards would depend largely on the goodwill and generosity of Maquinna, who kept them well supplied with fish, oil, and venison. There were unfortunate incidents, such as when an unsupervised party of soldiers commandeered at gun point a quantity of boards used for housing, but despite such occurrences, the relationship of Maquinna and his people with the Spanish arrivals remained amicable. Alberni worked at preparing a Nootkan-Spanish dictionary, and the fear and dislike Martínez had induced in Maquinna the previous year seemed to have been overcome. This improved rapport is even more noteworthy considering that the newcomers had expropriated the entire site of Yuquot, the Mowachahts' traditional summer home.

Despite Alberni's best efforts at establishing a working farm, the severe winter conditions of 1790–91, combined with devastating predation on the henhouses by weasels or mink, and on storehouses by rodents, left the food supply for the men and the livestock perilously low. Many of the Spaniards, including both the commander and Alberni, were stricken by scurvy and the "bloody flux"—probably cholera. After five sailors had died, Eliza decided to make *Princesa* a hospital ship, and sent her to San Blas with the 32 gravest cases, Alberni's deputy among them.

In early spring 1791, Bodega y Quadra sent two resupply vessels to Nootka: *San Carlos* under the command of Ramón Saavedra and the schooner *Santa Saturnina* under José María Narváez. A third ship, *Aranzazú*, followed them, bringing further instructions from the commander, including a summary of the newly signed Nootka Convention that permitted English fur traders to use the port of Nootka.

Earlier, Bodega y Quadra had sent explicit orders that this season, Eliza should take personal command of explorations, and he provided an excellent cadre of competent pilots. He also sent copies of Quimper's diary, López de Haro's chart, and his own compilation of all that was known of the entire coast, including a clarification of the place names. Bodega y Quadra's secret orders to Eliza highlighted the importance of good relations with the locals.

> Examine carefully the true latitude and longitude of the ports, the variation of the compass, the bearings of the capes and points and their latitudes, the force of the tides, the depth of the sea, the perspective of the coast, the nature and the character of the country, the quadrupeds, insects, birds, fish, metals, precious stones, plants, vegetables, and fruits, and the character and number of Indians and strangers . . . As one of the most essential points is to maintain harmony with the natives, you will treat them with benignity and kindness. Prudence requires this and the king orders it.[2]

Eliza complied with Bodega y Quadra's instructions up to a point, but the situation appeared to have changed. Some Mowachaht had brought news that a fleet of five ships had been sighted off Esperanza Inlet. Eliza sent Narváez in the schooner out around the back of Mazarredo Island to investigate. They learned that such a sighting had happened, but four months earlier, and more recently a schooner had been headed for Clayoquot. Eliza felt he needed to give greater priority to the defence of Nootka. Rather than use the robust and well-armed, but slower, *Concepción* for exploration as ordered, he switched commands with Saavedra. The latter was to remain in charge

of the base, while Eliza sailed aboard *San Carlos* accompanied by *Santa Saturnina* with Narváez in command, and the pilot Juan Carrasco (see Fig. 20, page 45).

Their departure was probably far too late in the season to reach the instructed latitude of 60°, but they did make a token effort to head north. After only a few days battling strong northwesterly winds, they realized that the schooner could not keep up with *San Carlos*. Eliza elected to turn about, go with the wind, and further explore the inlets to the south: Clayoquot, Carrasco (Barkley Sound), and the Strait of Juan de Fuca, including the intriguing channels at its far end, opening to the north.

Inside Clayoquot, Eliza focused on protocol and trade with Wickaninnish, sending Narváez and Pantoja to continue the exploration of its many side channels. Narváez found four previously unknown ones, but Pantoja in the longboat met hostility from the native people. Eliza learned that fur traders had been there earlier and had bought up the stock of otter pelts. When Narváez returned, Eliza dispatched him to explore Puerto de Carrasco and then to rendezvous at Córdova (Esquimalt).

No first-hand log or journal has surfaced documenting Narváez's forays while he was with the Eliza expedition of 1791. However, manuscripts were later seen in Mexico in the possession of Narváez's widow, who withheld them from the authorities pending resolution of her claims for a pension due to her husband. Thus, historians must rely on reports by Eliza and Pantoja at second hand, and on the often-ambiguous evidence from the various versions of the large map, with five inset maps, that resulted from their efforts and adventures.

Narváez spent about three weeks investigating what he called the Archipielago de Nitinat ó Carrasco, navigating the 36-foot [11-metre] schooner among the host of small islands now known as the Broken Group. To the northeast and

FIG 20 Packet boat *San Carlos* and schooner *Santa Saturnina* off Puerto de Cordova (now Esquimalt Harbour) on June 14, 1791, as a party sets off to explore Haro Strait. These vessels of the Spanish expedition were commanded by Francisco de Eliza. [*San Carlos and Santa Saturna off Royal Roads*, Gordon Miller]

northwest, he found two arms of the sea that seemed to lead northward, but contrary winds and days of continuous downpour prevented him from entering the second arm, which he evidently named Boca de Cañaveral (Toquot Bay.) Earlier, he had just managed to penetrate a third of the way up the Canal de Alberni. Eliza reported that Narváez:

> [H]ad seen five large settlements in the whole archipelago and believed that they contained more Indians than Nuca and Clayoquot, very warlike and daring and given to robbery . . . two hundred endeavoured to attack him on two occasions but he had held them in check by means of some cannon shot.[3]

Without realizing it, Narváez had sailed into an area at a time of clan warfare, when the locals were nervous. With food supplies almost exhausted, he left to rejoin Eliza and *San Carlos* at Puerto de Córdova. He named the headland at the southeastern corner of the sound (now Cape Beale) Punta de Alegría—Happiness Point. He does not seem to have noted the neighbouring, narrow passage that leads to Nitinat Lake.

Soon after Eliza had arrived at Córdova and anchored *San Carlos* just in the entrance, he sent the longboat—armed and with the young *pilotín* (apprentice pilot) Juan Verdía in charge— to enter, explore, and chart the Canal de López de Haro. This proved a very hazardous mission.

> [A]s soon as he had entered . . . six large canoes came out with from 16 to 20 Indians in each one. These were armed with long spears and each Indian had his bow and arrow. They began to menace our longboat, even over took it, so it had become necessary to open fire on them to get away from them. Continuing his defence he saw numerous Indians running along the land hastily launching many canoes. Embarking in these they directed

themselves towards the longboat with loud yells and shooting some arrows. The pilot, seeing that they paid little attention to the firearms and that at every moment more Indians were arriving, thought it advisable to retire in order not to endanger his men.[4]

Pantoja added that the longboat returned:

> in great haste . . . and having sent to the bottom a large canoe and killed some Natives among those who were striving the most to attack the longboat from all sides with some heavy spears having points of bone like harpoons.[5]

The reaction of the Straits Salishan Lekwungen men— probably from the Chilcowitch and Chekonein bands—is quite understandable. Although the Spaniards were unaware of it, the local villages had experienced many centuries of canoe-borne raiding parties of Cowichan, Nahwhitti, and even Haida warriors; they were well drilled in repelling intruders. A solitary longboat would not have intimidated them as the arrival of a three-masted frigate might have done, and by that time they would have been acquainted with trade muskets, and would not have been overawed by them.

If Verdía's account is to be believed, however, the nature of the defensive response—swift, fierce, and coordinated—seems anomalous when compared with the cautiously welcoming, rather than threatening, receptions experienced in most of the other Spanish forays. There is another possible discrepancy in the report. Either he penetrated the strait much deeper than his stated "as soon as he had entered"—perhaps getting as far as Cadboro Bay or even Gordon Head—or he overestimated the number of attackers. Noted archeologist Grant Keddie calculates that the indicated number of canoes and men would have required "a least three large villages" to muster such a force. The reaction was certainly robust enough for Eliza to await the arrival of his supporting schooner before attempting further sorties.

After *Santa Saturnina* had joined *San Carlos* at Córdova and the crew had had a few days' respite, Eliza again sent out the longboat, this time with the schooner in support. *San Carlos*'s pilot, Juan Pantoja, commanded from the longboat. He was a well-respected pilot and cartographer who had already sailed with Bodega y Quadra, Arteaga, and Maurelle on expeditions exploring this coast. Bearing in mind the reception evoked by Verdía's probe, Eliza decided that both vessels would be fully armed, and carry soldiers "able bodied and spirited," with provisions sufficient for a four-day mission. All this rendered both vessels crowded in the extreme.

Entering the Canal de López de Haro, they tried to sail in formation against what seemed to be "a very copious river." With the longboat falling behind, Pantoja changed approach. He furled the longboat's sails, and leaned to the oars again, but to no avail. The schooner hove to, allowing the longboat to come alongside and be taken under tow. In marked contrast to the situation reported by Verdía, during the whole day they spent in Lekwungen territory, they saw only one native and, on that occasion, without incident.

As dusk approached, they found themselves surrounded by a bewildering array of rocky islands, great and small, cloaked to the water's edge in a uniform blanket of first-growth forest, separated by deep channels of swirling tidal races, and extending into the misty distances. By nightfall, the schooner had anchored, apparently at the northwest end of today's Pender Island, and Pantoja joined Narváez to compare notes. It was clear that a full survey of all this would take far more than the few days allotted.

Next morning they headed south, then east down Swanson Channel, the longboat towing the schooner, both under oars. After passing a sheltered bay, which they named San Antonio (Bedwell Harbour), they managed to reach "a salient point," which they called Punta de Santa Saturnina (East Point, on Saturna Island). From there:

> [We] saw in the fourth quarter a grand and extensive canal. As the horizon was clear it was possible to see a long distance and in the middle of it could be made out, at the farthest point of vision, a small hill like a sugar loaf. It may be noted that the end of land or the parts of which form this canal are very high mountains covered with snow. This [Pantoja] named El Gran Canal de Nuestra Señora del Rosario la Marinera in honour of our patroness, as it was the most important place we had discovered up to the present.[6]

They had found the Strait of Georgia; those mountains were the Cascade Range, and the "sugar loaf" was, in all likelihood, Texada Island.

It was evening as they ventured into the new canal and they immediately felt a far more powerful current. A stiff northwesterly breeze brought them to their anchorage in the lee of a small island, thronged with seabirds, which they called *patos*, meaning ducks. They had also noted that the canal abounded in seals, tuna, and "whales of great size."

The following day they found themselves still in the confusion of islands, but they were unable to explore further because of a southeasterly rainstorm that lasted four days. By then, almost out of food and overdue to return to the anchorage at Córdova, they struggled back. Evidently, from the resulting chart, they rounded the northern shores of Orcas, Waldron, and Stuart islands to the western tip of San Juan Island, then into and back down Haro Strait to Gonzales Point and the Strait of Juan de Fuca. As soon as they could see *San Carlos*—probably as they came around Trial Island—they anchored, the crews totally exhausted by prolonged periods at the oars; the trip had taken over a week longer than planned.

A lookout spotted them, and Eliza sent out a second boat to bring Pantoja back to report. While they had been gone, Eliza had explored the land immediately around Córdova, finding it level in places and suitable for crops.

Pantoja's dramatic news of finding the Great Canal spurred Eliza to take advantage of the remaining summer conditions to extend their explorations—it was, by then, late June. The heavily manned schooner *Santa Saturnina* and the longboat had limited storage capacity, which restricted their operational range. Eliza proposed taking *San Carlos* into Haro Strait as far as feasible, to provide support for the smaller vessels. Pantoja respectfully pointed out that this plan held some serious risks—unpredictable winds; fierce currents, counter-eddies, and even vortexes—and the host of islands, narrow, winding channels, rocks, and reefs in otherwise deep water offered insecure anchorage.

As soon as the schooner joined them, Eliza called a council of his pilots, Pantoja, Narváez, and Carrasco. The new plan was that *San Carlos* would anchor in Puerto de Quadra (Port Discovery), while *Santa Saturnina* and the longboat continued exploring. Eliza gave Narváez command, and entrusted the longboat to Verdía, and both would be well armed. Pantoja would accompany Eliza, who was not well.

Soon after leaving their new base, Port Quadra, the pilots could identify the feature Carrasco had called Ensenada de Caamaño (Admiralty Inlet), but saw that it was much larger than had been thought. Planning to investigate it on his return, Narváez headed directly toward Bocas de Fidalgo (Deception

Pass) and entered, finding himself back in the archipelago they had visited earlier. After examining the shallow, double bay of Padilla and Bellingham, they re-entered the Gran Canal and sailed roughly northwesterly for eight days.

Following roughly the eastern coastline of the Strait of Georgia, Narváez noted Punta de San Rafael (the bluff near White Rock), Ysla de Zepeda (Point Roberts), Yslas de Lángara (Point Grey). Understandably, he had mistaken the low-lying lands of the Fraser delta for a continuation of Boundary Bay, and the two headlands for islands. He then passed Punta de la Bodega (probably either Point Atkinson or Ferguson Point) and Boca de Floridablanca (the Fraser River valley), noting the large quantity of fresh water that indicated the estuary of a major river. He travelled past Bocas del Carmelo (Howe Sound), and Lasqueti and Texada islands. Eventually, they reached the same latitude as Nootka, the northern end of Texada.

Realizing that they were running low on provisions, Narváez decided to return to Port Quadra, and crossed the strait. From the middle, he could see that the body of water continued northwesterly, and he noted a few features in the distance, including Punta de San Luis (possibly Sutil Point on Cortes Island or Hernando Island) and Ysla de Campo Alange (possibly Cape Mudge, Mitlenatch Island, or Kuhustan Point). On his map he also depicts Boca de Valdez (possibly Comox Harbour or Baynes Sound). There remains some debate about identifying most of these features. He anchored for the night just west of Qualicum Beach. The following day, at the mouth of today's Englishman River, he noted a large flock of wading birds, so he called it Rio de las Grullas—River of the Cranes—but these were more likely to have been great blue herons, still common in the estuary.

Narváez continued southeast along the shore of Vancouver Island, although he did not recognize it as such, and noted Boca de Rualcava (Nanoose Harbour). He then came upon an entrance, which he investigated, naming it Boca de Wenthuysen (Nanaimo Harbour). They anchored just east of Punta Casatilli (Orlebar Point, now known locally as Berry Point, on Gabriola Island). The next feature he recorded was a headland with a group of offshore islets, which he called Punta de Gavíola (now the Flat Top Islands off the eastern tip of Gabriola). Following what appeared to be the coastline, broken only by occasional gaps such as Boca de Porlier and the unnamed Active Pass, they reached the headland noted in the earlier sortie, Punta de Santa Saturnina.

Narváez drew the coastline as he had seen it, not realizing that he had been sailing along the outer edge of an almost continuous chain of islands between Nanaimo and East Point on Saturna Island. This error would remain on charts for the next 50 years. Narváez's last anchorage before returning to Port Quadra to rejoin *San Carlos* was off Guemes Island. They had been out for three weeks and time did not permit examination of Caamaño (Admiralty Inlet).

They reported that they had had little interaction with local people, and met no hostility, but there are some doubts about the truth of these claims. While the reports noted seeing no settlements on the islands or the adjacent coasts, the charts do show some. There were many, of course—it was a densely populated region. In Padilla Bay they had watched people digging for clams, and while they were at anchor off Lángara (Point Grey), a number of men in canoes (probably Musqueam) approached, bearing—to the Spaniards' relief—not weapons but salmon and other fish for trade. Through sign language the Spaniards learned some intriguing facts: the canal continued a great distance; people came from the east on horses to trade with them; and *Santa Saturnina* was not the first foreign vessel to venture into these waters. This earlier vessel might have been a fur trader; details of its story remain unknown.

As soon as Narváez had rejoined *San Carlos* at Port Quadra, Eliza ordered that *Santa Saturnina* be careened and reprovisioned, but he doubted that the schooner would be able to battle the seasonal northwesterlies anticipated for the return to Nootka. Needing Narváez's cartographic skills for preparing a composite chart to accompany his report to the viceroy, Eliza redeployed him to *San Carlos*, giving command of the schooner to Carrasco. They then needed two weeks to sail from Port Quadra out to Nuñez Gaona (Neah Bay), where they rested for two more weeks. While there, they noted the large island-village of Ta-toosh, from whose people they acquired some high-priced sea otter pelts.

Eliza had been correct in his doubts about *Santa Saturnina*'s ability to make headway against the wind to get back to Nootka. After a few days in the attempt, Carrasco lost contact with *San Carlos*, so he turned about and made for Monterey and from there, San Blas.

San Carlos continued to beat upwind, reaching the latitude of Nootka, but not for another two weeks did a shift in the wind permit them to sail into Friendly Cove. One day out, they had sighted two vessels leaving the harbour, but were unable to identify them. Eliza later learned that the ships had been the Spanish corvettes *Descubierta* and *Atrevida*, under the command of Alexandro Malaspina, on a worldwide voyage of exploration. They had been in the area for two weeks, making astronomical measurements and charting in detail the channels of Nootka Sound.

The pilots Narváez, Pantoja, and Verdía worked at compiling a chart of all that had been discovered up to that time, including the work of Malaspina's specialists. They had to reconcile their various notebooks and logs, which was not an easy task, as demonstrated by the ambiguities in the final result. They solved the conundrum of showing the maze of channels and

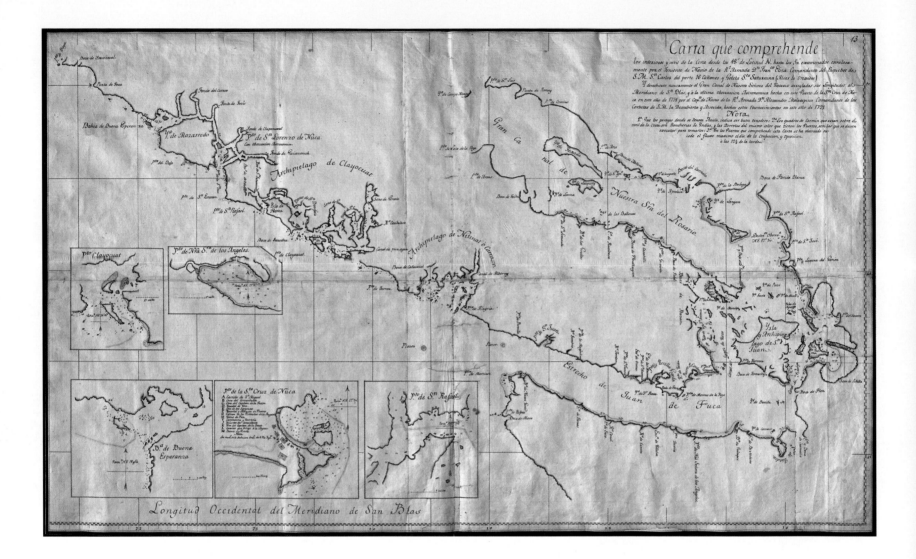

FIG 21 Commonly known as the *Carta que comprehende*, this 1791 chart records the significant discoveries made by José María Narváez when he explored the Gran Canal de Nuestra Sra. del Rosario (now Georgia Strait) that same year. [Courtesy of España, Ministerio de Defensa, Archivo del Museo Naval]

islands between Haro and Rosario straits by sketching a broken coastline of a large island they termed Ysla y Archipielago de Sn. Juan. They annotated their composite chart with good anchorages and Rancherías de Indios (settlements), and called it *Carta que comprehende los interiors y veríl de la Costa desde los 48° de Latitud Norte hasta los 50° . . . este año de 1791.* Since it accompanied his report to Bodega y Quadra in San Blas and bore his name, this document is often referred to as the Eliza Chart (see Fig. 21, page 50).

In mid-October, Eliza and Saavedra again exchanged responsibilities. The latter, now back in command of *San Carlos* with an exhausted Pantoja as pilot, was to personally deliver the report and chart. They could muster only a skeleton crew of 64, instead of the 80 aboard for the journey north. Of these, eight were "unable to render service, including the first boatswain." Rations were pitifully short, both on shore and for the journey. Most aboard had but one set of clothing, ragged and constantly wet. Their rat-infested ship was by then perilously short of anchors, sails, and rigging, heading into a season of storms, squalls, and dense coastal fogs. In three weeks they managed to struggle down to Monterey, where they rested for two weeks, replenishing and repairing before continuing to San Blas, which they reached at the end of December. In his report to the viceroy, Eliza referred to their discovery:

> I believe that if there is anything of particular importance or consideration to be explored on this coast it is this large canal, as according to my method of thinking, and that of my pilot, it promises much . . . I assure your Excellency that the passage to the Atlantic Ocean, which the foreign nations search for with such diligence on this coast, cannot in my opinion, if there be one, be found in any other part; it is either, I think, by this great canal, or it is continent.[7]

FIG 22   The fort and accommodations of San Lorenzo, the Spanish outpost at Friendly Cove, Nootka, in the early 1790s. A crowded war canoe approaches the frigate *Concepción*, at anchor with reduced masts and rigging. [*Vista de la Cala de Amigos en Nutka*, courtesy of Museo de América, Madrid]

CHAPTER FOUR

MALASPINA'S EXPEDITION ARRIVES AND EXPLORES: THE CORBETAS AND THE GOLETAS

Two brand new and identical *corbetas* (corvettes or sloops) of the Spanish navy—*Atrevida* and *Descubierta*—set sail from Cadiz in 1789 on a four-year voyage called the Royal Scientific Exploring Expedition. The ships had been specially built and equipped for this major mission, sheathed inside and out with copper for protection against teredos, wood-boring marine molluscs. In command was Captain Alexandro Malaspina, with Captain José Bustamante y Guerra as co-leader. The intention was to follow the examples set by Cook and La Pérouse, in the full spirit of the Age of Enlightenment, on a quest to acquire scientific knowledge, rather than for conquest or trade.

Malaspina was a follower of the French philosopher Jean-Jacques Rousseau, and had recently completed a circumnavigation in preparation for the major expedition. He gently advised Bustamante that such an extended voyage needed a different leadership style than the customary strict discipline. Rather, it would require leading through example, considering:

not what the orders are but rather what can be done and with what intent. On this commission, the scientific aspect rather than the military is what will contribute to public usefulness.[1]

This was a remarkably enlightened attitude for naval officers of any nation for that era. Malaspina was also concerned for the health of all aboard, paying close attention to cleanliness, ventilation, water supply, and diet. He had hand-picked all the officers for their outstanding merit.

They carried a team of renowned scientists with state-of-the-art chronometers and other survey instruments. In addition, Malaspina had a brief to report on the situation they found in any Spanish territory and outpost they visited. They had already crossed the Atlantic, run down the coast of Argentina, the Falklands, Patagonia, around Cape Horn, and up the western side of South and Central America before they arrived in Acapulco. Their original schedule had them next charting the Sandwich or Hawaiian archipelago, but new orders from Spain changed that plan.

Back in Seville and Madrid, various reports and maps had attracted official attention, describing and depicting the fabled Strait of Anian—what the British called the Northwest Passage—around latitude 59° or 60°. Malaspina's orders from Florida Blanca, Secretary for the Indies, were that he should now give priority to investigating this waterway. The expedition, briefed by Bodega y Quadra, took the recommended course of sailing due west until they found a steady wind to carry them north. They arrived in what is now Alaska and searched in vain for the Anian portal. Disappointed, they decided to return to Acapulco, stopping at Nootka and Monterey on the way.

At Nootka (see Fig. 22, page 52), after being welcomed by Saavedra and Alberni, Malaspina learned that Eliza was out on an expedition, but due back shortly, so he spent two weeks exploring locally. His astronomers set up an observatory, as Cook had done 13 years earlier, to get an accurate longitude for the site. Two young hydrographic officers, José de Espinosa and Ciriaco Cevallos, took a pair of armed launches to investigate and chart the island of Mazarredo and the five channels radiating from it, each with a settlement at the end. The senior hydrographer, Lieutenant Felipe Bauza, drew the resulting plan. Other scientists studied the fauna and flora, and the local population. Aboard were two artists, who made invaluable sketches of people, houses, artifacts, and ceremonies.

Malaspina noted that the Mowachaht were thin and apparently short of food, which he attributed to recent emphasis on hunting sea otters for trade instead of harvesting and preparing food supplies for the winter. He also detected tension between Maquinna and the garrison, and signs of inter-clan rivalry. Wishing to reinforce his connection with the moody Maquinna, and boost the leader's status, he was generous with respect, gifts, and praise.

Impressed with the organization and morale of the garrison and its farming activities, he gave due credit to Pedro Alberni. Before leaving, Malaspina was also generous toward the resident Spaniards, leaving with them a good supply of rations, wine, medicines, trade goods, and ships' chandlery. Unable to await Eliza any longer—and missing him by just two days—the expedition sailed south, intending to investigate the Entrada de Hezeta, thought to be the mouth of the great River of the West. Dense fog obscured the mouth of the Columbia River, so the ships abandoned the plan, and headed south to Monterey.

They had been there a few days, replenishing their depleted stores of food, when Carrasco in *Santa Saturnina* arrived, having come from Neah Bay at the end of Eliza's exploration of the Strait of Juan de Fuca. Details of their discussion have not survived, but it is safe to assume that Carrasco briefed Malaspina on what he had seen, without his notes, which would have been with Narváez aboard *San Carlos*. Thus would Malaspina have learned, before Bodega y Quadra and the viceroy, of the existence and apparent extent of the Gran Canal de Rosario.

In San Blas, Malaspina also learned that the viceroy had already had ordered Bodega y Quadra to prepare a follow-up expedition into the far end of Juan de Fuca, and that a newly built *goleta*—somewhat similar to a schooner—*Mexicana*, was the designated vessel under the command of Francisco Maurelle. He also noted that a second goleta was currently under construction.

Back in Acapulco, Malaspina successfully persuaded the viceroy that he was better suited than Maurelle to prepare the expedition—his new orders from Spain gave him specific responsibility for investigating possible passages to the Atlantic, and his officers were specialized hydrographers. He proposed that they should take command of both *Mexicana* and the second goleta, *Sutil*. After detaching the astronomer Lieutenant Dionisio Alcalá Galiano and Lieutenant Cayetano Valdés y Flores to the new mission (see Fig. 23a & b), Malaspina sailed with *Atrevida* and *Descubierta* for the Sandwich Islands. He was to have no further contact with the two officers.

THE VOYAGE OF THE GOLETAS

As they sailed from San Blas to Acapulco to prepare for their expedition, Galiano and Valdés grew increasingly horrified. Their two locally constructed goletas were seriously inferior to the specially prepared and well-equipped exploring vessels that the officers were accustomed to. The craft were small—46 tons (42 tonnes) compared with 300 tons (272 tonnes)—ill-equipped, and leaky, and they handled poorly. They were of shallow draft, good for exploring inshore, but not for sailing upwind, and their rigging plan was irregular and unworkable. The captains asked the viceroy for some radical alterations.

The rigging was rearranged to be more manageable, the decks lifted to provide more headroom and storage below, and the bulwarks heightened to retain sufficient freeboard to keep out more of the waves. Remediation was carried out by semi-skilled artisans with access to a limited range of tools; nevertheless, by early March 1792, *Sutil* and *Mexicana* were able to set sail for Nootka. True to Spanish custom of the time, the mission had an impossibly long list of objectives. For reasons unknown, Malaspina had declined to include Carrasco or any of the other San Blas-based pilots who had direct experience in the waters to be explored.

The expedition left Acapulco with a complement of about 40. In addition to the two captains, there were two pilots—Secundino Salamanca and Juan Vernacci, both well-trained hydrographers—and a draftsman, José Cardero. He had initially been an officers' servant aboard *Descubierta*, where his

In 1792 two young naval hydrographers were detached from a major Spanish expedition to explore into the Strait of Juan de Fuca.

FIG 23A (TOP) Expedition leader Dionisio Alcalá Galiano, in command of the goleta *Mexicana,* was skilled in astronomy. [Courtesy of España, Ministerio de Defensa, Archivo del Museo Naval]

FIG 23B (BOTTOM) Cayetano Valdés y Flores Bazán commanded the second goleta, *Sutil*. [Courtesy of España, Ministerio de Defensa, Archivo del Museo Naval]

innate drawing talent had come to the attention of Malaspina, who chose him to replace one of the team's professional artists. Cardero went on to create an outstanding visual record of the region at that time, and left a vividly written first-hand account of the expedition.

Galiano led the detachment in *Sutil*, with Valdés commanding *Mexicana*. Valdés, the two pilots, and Cardero had all been on Malaspina's voyage to Alaska and Nootka, but Galiano had missed it, remaining in Mexico to work on astronomical calculations.

Their voyage started badly; adverse winds forced the still-poor-sailing goletas southwest for three weeks before they could gain any progress north. They could manage barely half the daily progress of the corvettes, and had great difficulty maintaining a course. Whenever the wind permitted, they set as much sail as they could, with the result that a sudden gust snapped *Mexicana*'s mainmast. Uncertain of their true position, they struggled toward Nootka against storms, contrary winds, and currents. They finally arrived in mid-May, more than two months after their departure, only to run aground outside the entrance. Boats from the resident contingent had to tow both goletas into Friendly Cove.

Captain Bodega y Quadra had arrived before them, and awaited their arrival. He had been designated the new commandant of Nootka, and been given diplomatic responsibility for implementing the terms of the Nootka Convention with a British counterpart, also due to arrive. For a short period, no fewer than five Spanish vessels lay at anchor within the tiny harbour of Friendly Cove. Chief Maquinna remembered with pleasure the three officers who had visited a few months earlier. Salamanca recorded that the local leader was, once more, hospitable toward the garrison, bringing them fish regularly, without seeking payment.

A shortage of resources limited the assistance the garrison was able to offer the goletas. They could, however, help cut and rig two new masts for *Mexicana*, and replacement spars and yardarms for *Sutil*. They provided new ropes and a launch for *Mexicana* and repaired that of *Sutil*. A few soldiers, a gunner, and a carpenter joined the crews. The officers calibrated their chronometers to the reference time of the Nootka observatory, and Bodega y Quadra provided copies of Eliza's report and the latest available composite charts. López de Haro was back in Nootka, accompanying Bodega y Quadra, and he probably described to the goletas' pilots and officers his chart and his experiences in the Gran Canal the previous year.

In early June, they managed to sail out of Nootka and reach the new Spanish establishment of Núñez Gaona at Neah Bay. The viceroy planned for Bodega y Quadra to agree to leave Nootka to the British, and relocate their base to the more accessible south side of Juan de Fuca.

Salvador Fidalgo had sailed in the frigate *Princesa* directly from San Blas to Neah Bay, arriving at the end of May 1792 with a crew of 75 and a dozen soldiers. He carried orders to take formal possession, set up a battery of guns within a stockade, clear ground for buildings and cultivation, and construct the appropriate buildings for the new base. Again, the orders required him to treat the local people kindly and secure their cooperation.

By the time the goletas arrived, Fidalgo had been there just one week. Work had started on the stockade, and relations with the Makah seemed friendly, if still mutually wary. On the arrival of the Spaniards, the local leader, Taisoun, greeted them and came aboard with a gift of sardines. This honeymoon period lasted only a few weeks, but fortunately the situation was at its most amicable during the exploring expedition's two weeks at Núñez Gaona.

While the goletas lay at anchor in Neah Bay, the officers made a detailed chart of it, and fixed its coordinates. They also befriended a visiting leader, Tetacus, whose home, they understood, was at Machimutupusas, on the north coast of the strait. This was the village that previous Spanish expeditions had called Puerto de Córdova (Esquimalt Harbour) (see Fig. 24). Tetacus was clearly intelligent and inquisitive, displaying interest in all the workings of a European sailing vessel. He knew the names of several visiting captains: "Meas," Cook, and "Kimpair." He also revealed that two other ships, English, had recently entered the strait, with captains "Wancoobair" and "Bolton"—and that they were still there.

After a complicated charade for the benefit of the two anxious wives who accompanied him, Tetacus accepted an invitation to remain aboard *Mexicana* when the goletas started for the north shore. This left his wives to paddle home by canoe. Noting that the vessels required a breeze to make any headway, Tetacus went to the rail on the side of the ship from which the wind was needed, composed himself, then performed a ritual.

> He stretched out his arm and began to play with his fingers, doubling now one, now all of them, opening two, raising one and leaving it so for a while, and there was in all his actions something which indicated to us that he was praying mentally.

They soon found a favourable wind and steered to the far shore, then headed eastward, close to it. While at sea, Tetacus demonstrated his artist's eye, immediately grasping the concept of cartography.

> He recognized on the map the configuration of the strait and islands that had been discovered, and told us the names which he gave to them.[2]

FIG 24 Tetacus, a leader of the Esquimalt Salish people, sailed briefly with the Spanish explorers and provided many local place names for their chart. [Courtesy of España, Ministerio de Defensa, Archivo del Museo Naval]

FIG 25 The goletas *Mexicana* and *Sutil* under full sail along the northern shore of the Strait of Juan de Fuca, with Mount Baker in the distance. [Courtesy of España, Ministerio de Defensa, Archivo del Museo Naval]

The Salish toponyms he provided included: Quinicamet (Neah Bay), Chlayamet (Discovery Bay), Queuchinas (Admiralty Inlet), Machimusat (Sooke Harbour), and Sasamat (Fraser estuary and valley). As did many of the early explorers, the officers of the goletas collected and reported various words, with their meanings, in the local language. Some of the men added to the crew at Nootka had already acquired a smattering of the Nootkan dialect, and could tell if new groups they met were related to or distinct from the Mowachaht. Generally, however, communication between the Spaniards and local peoples was limited to sign language.

At Punta Moreno de la Vega (Bentinck Island and Race Rocks), Tetacus advised his hosts that they should take on water there as it was good and plentiful but would be scarce and ill-tasting beyond. He also piloted the goletas through the hair-raising Race Passage between the headland and the host of rocky islets. They arrived at Córdova that night and anchored outside, with Tetacus happy to remain on board. The ship entered the fine harbour next morning, and to Tetacus's evident relief and joy, his two wives followed not long afterward. That night the officers visited his longhouse, and were treated most hospitably.

With hindsight, the chance meeting of Galiano and Valdés with Tetacus makes for a striking omen: two young aristocrats of the Spanish navy strike up a brief friendship with the lord of the spacious, sheltered anchorage that would become, first, the home port of Britain's Pacific fleet, and then of Canada's western maritime command.

The Spanish record does not explain what Tetacus was doing at Neah Bay, in the heart of Makah territory, almost alone and with such confidence and apparent impunity. This man, seemingly a high-ranking Lekwungen Salish, was at ease among a warlike group from the arch-rival Wakash Nation. One possibility

is that he had formed an alliance by marriage with the Ta-toosh clan; another is that he had exceptional status.

> We afterwards learned that he was one of the most feared of all the chiefs who live on these shores, and that he had won the greatest respect and authority among them, on account of his bravery, ability and character.

An alternative theory holds that Tetacus was not Salish, but in fact was the same man—Ta-toosh or Tutuzi, leader of the Makah, the Neah Bay Wakash clan—reported by earlier European visitors, who could have had alliances with the Salish of the village of Machimutupusas.

The section of the viceroy's orders that applied to this phase of the mission directed that, once inside:

> Estrecho de Fuca, you will proceed with the examination of the inlets of that arm of the sea until you find out if they turn back to the western sea [the Pacific] or continue inland to Baffin Bay or Hudson's Bay, omitting no effort or time for that purpose.[3]

The officers interpreted this to mean that theirs was not a charting mission, but a reconnaissance to discover or refute the existence of the Northwest Passage. Their priority was to get to the eastern shore of the Gran Canal and investigate any waterways that seemed to lead eastward. This ruled out the Entrada de Carrasco (Admiralty Inlet) as it was reported—wrongly—to be navigable only by canoe, and anyway, it appeared to head south. The most promising prospect seemed to be the Boca de Floridablanca (Fraser River).

So, on leaving Córdova the next morning (see Fig. 25, page 58), they continued along the north shore of the strait, passing Punta San Gonzalo, the Canal López de Haro, and the

Archipielago de San Juan. They anchored at the southeastern tip of Lopez Island to take advantage of a clear night sky, their recently adjusted chronometers, and a scheduled event of one of Jupiter's moons. These factors helped them to make observations that improved the accuracy for the longitude of Nootka, and provided a reference for the coordinates of all other places they would visit during the expedition.

The next day they continued east and north, rounding Guemes and Lummi islands, when:

> [W]e saw two small vessels, one by her rig a small coasting vessel, and the other square-rigged. They were going along the coast northwards, and we had no doubt that they were the two English vessels which were in the strait according to the information which we had received from our friend Tetacus. We went on without changing our course, intending to navigate under light sail all night, and reach Point San Rafael [North Bluff] by dawn so as to be at the mouth of Floridablanca at the beginning of the morning. We proposed to enter it in order to make an immediate examination, since we had reason to think that it would be full of interest.[4]

As they passed Birch Bay they could see lights, which they took to be the British ships at anchor. Two hours later, off the estuary of the Nicomekl River, noting that the depth of water was decreasing, they decided to anchor until daylight would reveal the best approach. They awoke to find themselves in the middle of Boundary Bay and the realization that Narváez's chart was in error: Zepeda (Point Roberts) was the tip of a peninsula, not an island. Galiano corrected the chart, calling the bay Bahía del Engaño—Deception Bay.

As they were rounding Zepeda, they spied, approaching them, a square-rigged brigantine flying British colours. This was HMS *Chatham*, under the command of Lieutenant Robert Broughton, RN, who, following naval protocol, requested permission to come aboard *Sutil*, while all three vessels continued to sail along the coast. Galiano and Broughton exchanged formal courtesies, explaining their missions, which appeared remarkably similar, for the current season at least. They also exchanged what they had learned thus far. Galiano informed Broughton that Don Juan de la Bodega y Quadra was awaiting Captain Vancouver at Nootka for the diplomatic duties entrusted to them.

Broughton invited them to join the British at their anchorage, but the wind did not permit that, so he returned to *Chatham*, and headed back to Birch Bay. The goletas could barely manage to stay on course until they reached Lángara (Point Grey)—marked on the Narváez chart as "Ys" (*islas*, i.e., islands), but which they could see was in fact another headland. They anchored, planning to investigate the northern entrance to Floridablanca as shown on the chart (Burrard Inlet), next morning.

A favourable offshore breeze encouraged them to enter the apparent channel, but, while still two miles offshore, they discovered that the water had changed colour and become shallow, so they headed further out to sea. Suddenly, a powerful current caught and carried them across the strait, where they searched for an anchorage for the night. They found one toward the northern end of today's Galiano Island.

Just before dawn, Vernaci set out in a launch to seek a more sheltered place from which they might investigate the entrance noted by Narváez as Boca de Porliel [*sic*] (Porlier Pass), but they were prevented from doing so by a freshening contrary wind. Unable to return to the north side of the strait, the goletas made some progress toward Porlier, where they hoped to find shelter.

We reached it [Porlier Pass] at midday and easily entered it without waiting to send the launch forward to investigate it, since although the wind . . . left us . . . the waves carried us farther on, as they ran strongly in that direction.

When we made the entry, we found an archipelago of many low and small islands, and discovered that the channel divided into two chief mouths, one lying to the south-east and the other to the west. It was at once resolved to follow the former, in order to have always the help of the wind to get out if necessary. But when we had lost the shelter of the coast, the *Mexicana* experienced a sudden gust of wind from the direction of the channel, which was so strong that she was in danger of capsizing. We immediately realized the danger in which we should be among these islands, the channels between which we did not know and which we had no interest in exploring.

The wind, forced to pass through the narrow space which divided two mountains, blew with extreme violence; the currents were strong and were driven to take different directions owing to the numerous islands which barred their way, and as we saw no beach, it was clear that there would be no suitable anchorage. We could not pass far into this entry, since it was likely that much time would be spent on doing so to the prejudice of our main exploration of the mainland, and thus it seemed to be wise to put out sea without delay.

But the task of getting out of these channels was not so easy as we had hoped. The currents had gained such strength that we could not counteract them with our oars, the wind being light and soft. The result was that we had to spend two hours of great exertion and danger in order to get out of the channel . . .

On these channels there are several native settlements which have been abandoned, and there is one inhabited on the west coast of the entrance. From this five canoes came out with ten old men and nineteen young men, all very robust and of good

appearance. They reached the schooners and presented us with mulberries and shellfish, and received in exchange buttons and necklaces. When it was known that were in need of fresh water, they went to their settlement and presently brought us some casks full of it.[5]

The goletas were, indeed, fortunate to pass unscathed through the hazardous Porlier Pass in both directions. Apart from its ferocious tidal races, the narrow gap with rocky shores on both sides has several rocks, both visible and sub-surface, lurking mid-channel. Many craft, both sail and power, have subsequently come to grief attempting this transit in unfavourable conditions.

Aided by an easterly breeze and still hoping to find a safe anchorage, they continued northwest along the coasts of Valdés and Gabriola islands, now seeking Bocas de Wentuhuysen (Nanaimo Harbour). Passing between a small islet (now Entrance Island, with its lighthouse) and the point called Casatilli (Orlebar, but known locally as Berry Point), they found a sheltered haven and dropped anchor.

We called this roadstead "Cala del Descanso" [Cove of Rest], from our need of rest and our appreciation in finding it on this occasion.[6]

Evidently they were in Pilot Bay, not the present location of the ferry terminal called Descanso Bay. All were exhausted. As they were passing Casatilli, they had seen a few canoes of cautious locals, but were unable to entice them to trade. Ashore in Descanso, seeking sources of fresh water, they came across more men, locals, who made it clear that the sailors should not proceed.

They retreated to their anchorage to find that a flotilla of canoes, some 40 strong, had encircled the anchored goletas. The men in the canoes "were smiling and seemed to be docile," but still on edge. Many showed signs of disease, including blindness in one eye, probably due to cholera. They offered some smoked sardines and a few dog-hair blankets in trade for necklaces, abalone shells, and some rough pieces of iron. The Spaniards noted significant differences between the Snunéymuxw people at Wentuhuysen and those at Porlier, both in physical appearance and attitude.

The large assembly of canoes and the overall agitated behaviour have been attributed to the presence of many tribes from around the area gathered there before crossing the strait. They were headed to the Fraser Canyon for the seasonal run of salmon, bound for a traditional location known to be ideal for catching and wind-drying the annual harvest. Whatever the reason for their presence and mood, the Spaniards kept an alert watch that night, but no incidents disturbed their "*descanso.*"

The goletas remained at the Descanso anchorage for four days, during which the officers put into order their rough notes, sketches, and charts, and made a few astronomical observations, while the men replenished the water casks and repaired the ships and rigging. After two days of steady rain, they awoke to a lovely spring morning.

> Under a clear sky a pleasant country then presented itself to our view. The varied and brilliant green of some of the trees and meadows, and grand roar of the waters dashing upon the rocks in various corners charmed our senses and offered us a situation the so much [*sic*] more agreeable as we were the nearer to past dangers and fatigues.[7]

The following afternoon, a few men took the launch to explore deeper within Wentuhuysen Inlet, entering the present Descanso Bay, where José Cardero sketched some nearby sea caves now known as the Malaspina Galleries. They then found a much more significant tideway (Northumberland Channel) opening to the southeast. They correctly surmised that this would lead to the archipelago they had seen inside the Porlier entrance, but they did not venture too far into it.

Now revived, and restocked with wood and fresh water, they left Wentuhuysen and headed across the strait for Floridablanca, which took them a whole day and night. As darkness fell, one of the goletas struck a deadhead—a partially submerged tree trunk—which could have caused major damage, but luckily did not. They were still not out of danger, however. They were navigating blind among the treacherous shoals and sandbanks of the Fraser estuary, but managed to avoid grounding. At daybreak, they could see to carefully sound their way to Punta de Lángara.

A small group of canoes came out to meet them. Friendly locals of good appearance and obviously well off, if mostly naked, brought the visitors fresh salmon without showing interest in trading, then paddled off. After a few attempts to find an anchorage that was safe from changing tides and winds, they finally found such a place inside a creek, near what is now called Spanish Banks (off Point Grey near the campus of the University of British Columbia). Soon afterward, a second group of canoes approached, presumably Musqueam, this time led by "an old man of grave bearing who seemed to be a taïs" (leader), who came aboard with confidence. Disdainful of necklaces, he did agree to exchange a canoe for some small sheets of copper.

> [We] learned that the current in the part where we were anchored ran at four and a half miles an hour, and might therefore be supposed to be much stronger in the inner part of the channel. We were already in water which was almost fresh, and we saw

floating on it large logs, which indications confirmed us in the idea that the bay which we called Floridablanca was the estuary of a considerable river.[8]

The next morning, they spotted an approaching launch, which they immediately identified as coming from the English expedition, and Alcalá Galiano welcomed Captain George Vancouver, RN, aboard *Sutil* (see Fig. 26, page 64). He was returning from a two-day investigation of various channels in the area, and showed them the charts he had drawn. The Spaniards reciprocated by showing him their own charts, including that of Narváez. Galiano spoke some English, and a courteous relationship developed. Since their missions seemed similar—not to make complete charts of the area, but merely to check the continental coastline—Vancouver suggested that they join forces for their mutual benefit. They agreed to meet up as soon as the winds permitted.

While awaiting the arrival of the British ships, the Spaniards used launches to explore the nearby channels, some of which had been omitted on the charts they had copied. The scribe of the expedition—probably the artist Cardero—waxed lyrical about what he had seen.

> It would certainly be impossible to find a more delightful view than that which is here presented by the diversity of trees and shrubs, by the variety of animals and birds, when to this is added the pleasure of listening to the song of the birds, the observer is afforded many occasions for admiring the works of nature and for delighting his senses as he contemplates the majestic outlines of the mountains, covered with pines and capped with snow, when he sees the most precious cascades falling from them and reaching the grounds below with awe-inspiring rapidity, breaking the silence of these lonely districts, and by their

united waters forming powerful rivers which serve to give life to the plants on their banks, and in which a large number of salmon are bred.[9]

Sutil and *Mexicana* met with *Discovery* and *Chatham*, and they sailed together for a few days, anchoring each night. Eventually, they found a safe anchorage just inside Teakerne Arm, north of Desolation Sound. From this base, both teams sent exploration parties in launches into the many inlets. While the Spaniards felt their orders permitted them to accept the findings of their counterparts at face value, the reverse did not apply.

> Mr. Vancouver [explained] that while he had always the most complete confidence in our work, he did not feel himself free from the responsibility if he did not see everything for himself, since it was expressly laid down in his instructions that he was to explore all the channels along the coast from 45° to Cook River.[10]

They did work together taking astronomical observations to calibrate their chronometers and establish longitude, but were unable to agree on the result, mainly because of errors in the admiralty's *Nautical Almanac* and other official books of tables. They exchanged maps and information regarding the local geography, including opinions on whether or not the land to their west might be, in fact, a large island. This was soon proved so; during expeditions northward from the Teakerne base, Vancouver's officers noted that the flooding tide came from the north rather than the south, indicating that there must be a second opening to the ocean.

During their journey together, both parties had seen that the goletas could not keep pace with the British vessels, so they agreed to separate. Vancouver, like his Spanish fellow-mariners, was unimpressed with the goletas. He deemed them "the most

FIG 26 On the morning of June 21, 1792, while the goletas lay at anchor off Spanish Banks, a Royal Navy pinnace arrived, and Captain George Vancouver requested permission to come aboard. [*Encounter Off Spanish Banks*, Gordon Miller]

ill-calculated and unfit vessels that could possibly be imagined for such an expedition."

His officers convinced Vancouver that he should take his ships northward through the western passages. The Spaniards, against advice, elected to attempt a more easterly course through the complex archipelago they had found, using the new British charts as their guide. They left on extremely cordial terms with the British—"not only harmonious, but also of the closest friendship"—but soon came to rue their decision. The combination of variable winds and totally unpredictable tidal flows impeded progress for the first few days. Local people in canoes signalled friendly but clear warnings that the goletas should not proceed further. However, they persisted. At Arran Rapids, with a stiff following breeze, they attempted the passage against the tide.

> The *Sutil*, having steered to a point near an island, changed to the opposite course, and being caught by the force of a strong eddy, turned round three times with such violence that it made those who were in her giddy. Her crew freed her from this danger, rowing with all their might . . . The continual cross currents and eddies, sometimes in favour and sometimes against the [goletas], now driving them back and now driving them forward, making it always impossible to control them and leaving them at the mercy of the waters, alternately raised and mocked our hopes . . . the violent flow of the waters in the channel caused a horrible roaring and a notable echo, this producing an awe-inspiring situation, so that we had so far met with nothing so terrible.

Two weeks after separating from their English friends, the Spaniards emerged from the archipelago now called the Discovery Islands into Johnstone Strait at Hardwicke Island (see Fig. 27, page 67). After a brief skirmish with some locals at Cracroft Island, they met two men, apparently leaders of a neighbouring nation called the Nachimases (now 'Namgis), who were able to converse in Nootkan and knew Maquinna.

The senior of the leaders, Sisiaquis, invited the Spaniards to visit him at his village for ceremonial trading. He told them that English fur traders had been there and enjoyed his hospitality. He also indicated that two three-masted ships had also recently stopped there, presumably Vancouver's *Discovery* and *Chatham*. The Spanish scribe reported:

> We presently saw a large settlement, built in the shape of an amphitheatre on a small hill, surrounded by an attractive meadow and close to a stream; it was laid out in streets, and from the sea presented an agreeable appearance because the houses were painted in different colours and adorned with good paintings. It was the best settlement which we had met with since that of Tetacus.[11]

This was the Kwakwaka'wakw village at the mouth of the Nimpkish (the English rendition of 'Namgis) River, and the leader Sisiaquis was the man known to Vancouver as Cheslakees. The Spanish ships anchored there, but unlike the British, did not visit the village. They did visit another settlement, Majoa, just west of today's Port McNeill, which Cardero rendered in a fine drawing. They then crossed Queen Charlotte Sound to fix a position on the northern side.

By this time, it had become clear to the Spaniards that the mainland coast to the north continued in a pattern of islands and closed-ended fjords, similar to what they had already investigated. They had achieved their main objective: to prove that no navigable passage to the Atlantic could be accessed by way of the Strait of Juan de Fuca. The season of autumnal storms was coming, so, rather than expose their unseaworthy goletas to further punishment and danger, they decided to return to Nootka, by way of the northern shore of what they now knew to be a large island, then head south to explore the Boca (Entrada) de Hezeta (Columbia River).

En route, they anchored and rested for two weeks in Hardy Bay, enduring continual rain and southeasterly winds, but enjoying the abundance of fish. They took the opportunity to regulate their chronometers, while awaiting a more favourable northwesterly to enable their return to Nootka.

Meanwhile, Galiano took the launch to reconnoitre to the west, seeking a sheltered anchorage closer to the open Pacific and finding one at Shushartie Bay. He also made a celestial fix of the coordinates of Cape Sutil, the northernmost point of Vancouver Island and the western portal of Goletas Channel. During a brief lull, the ships struggled to make it to Shushartie, but a sudden change in the wind obliged them to anchor in the channel before making a run for Cape Scott. Forced back again by a wind now veering south, they turned about and made for the shelter of Bull Harbour on Hope Island, knowing full well that their craft could not weather a Pacific storm.

When the gale abated, they tried again. As they finally managed to round the cape, the wind shifted yet again and carried them south, under crowded sails, swiftly past Cabo Frondoso (Cook's Woody Point, now Cape Cook) and back to Nootka. They had been gone a few days short of three months, and had achieved the first circumnavigation of Vancouver Island.

Once more inside Friendly Cove, they found Bodega y Quadra there with a single Spanish ship, *Activa*. There were also three British vessels: Vancouver's *Discovery* and *Chatham*, which had arrived a few days previously, and the frigate *Daedalus*, resupplying Vancouver's mission. Bodega y Quadra and Vancouver were engrossed in protracted discussions on the diplomatic matters entrusted to them. Galiano furnished Vancouver with a copy of his charting activity and the coordinate fixes he had gathered since they had separated at Teakerne Arm.

Not wishing to delay their departure south, the officers of *Sutil* and *Mexicana* inspected their hulls and found them satisfactory for the rest of the journey. So, having quickly refitted and resupplied, they set sail the following day intending to investigate Hezeta and other stretches of the coast before continuing on to Monterey and the conclusion of the expedition at San Blas. They arrived there on October 23 with all aboard,

in perfect health and full of delight at the happy ending of an expedition which was very laborious and full of risk, taking into consideration the kind of vessel employed upon it . . . we handed them over . . . and prepared to return to Spain by way of Mexico and Vera Cruz.[12]

FIG 27 An awkward encounter between a Spanish longboat, as it ventured into the Canal de Salamanca (now Loughborough Inlet), and a menacing fleet of canoes. A few warning shots defused the situation without loss of life. [*El Remate del Canal de Salamanca*, courtesy of Museo de América, Madrid]

FIG 28　Untitled, but probably George Vancouver, by unknown artist. [Courtesy of © National Portrait Gallery, London, UK, 503 (edited)]

CHAPTER FIVE

THE ISLAND OF QUADRA AND VANCOUVER

GEORGE VANCOUVER'S FIRST SEASON

On August 29, 1792, when George Vancouver sailed into Nootka Sound, it was for the second time. Fourteen years earlier, as a midshipman aboard Captain James Cook's *Resolution*, he had first seen Friendly Cove. Now as captain of his own ship, *Discovery*, he was also the appointed representative of the British Crown (see Fig. 28, page 68). This time he was to formally receive certain real estate from his Spanish counterpart, Captain Juan Francisco de la Bodega y Quadra, in accordance with the Nootka Sound Convention of 1790 between their two governments.

His superiors had added this diplomatic duty to the requirements of his multi-season surveying mission to the northwest coast of the Americas. The first objective in his orders spelled out, in part:

The acquiring accurate information with respect to the nature and extent of any water-communication which may tend, in any considerable degree, to facilitate intercourse, for the purposes of commerce, between the north-west coast, and the country upon the opposite side of the continent, which are inhabited or occupied by His Majesty's subjects . . . [You are] required and directed not to pursue any inlet or river further than it shall appear to be navigable by vessels of such burthen as might safely navigate the Pacific Ocean . . . examination of the coast comprized [*sic*] between latitude 60° north and 30° north . . . and you are therefore hereby required and directed to pay particular attention to the supposed straits of Juan de Fuca . . . without too minute and particular an examination of the detail of the different parts of the coast . . .

He was also instructed on how to treat any Spanish surveying vessels he might meet.

You are to afford to the officer commanding such ships every possible degree of assistance and information, and to offer to him, that you, and he, should make each other, reciprocally, a free and unreserved communication of all plans and charts of discoveries made by you and him in your respective voyages.[1]

Six weeks after the ratification of the Nootka Convention, Prime Minister William Pitt ordered a two-ship expedition, with a third in support, to make ready. It would have two objectives: to establish or disprove the existence of a Northwest Passage, and to receive some properties—"land and buildings"—in Nootka Sound from the Spanish authorities.

George Vancouver was summoned to London, where he was offered and accepted command of the expedition. He was promoted to the rank of master and commander. The ships were to be *Discovery*, a merchantman of 330 tons, and the sturdy, 130-ton brig *Chatham* as armed tender. Both hulls would be sheathed in copper, and they would be armed appropriately. The support vessel *Daedalus* was to follow, report, and join them at the Sandwich Isles or at Nootka, bringing supplies and more detailed instructions regarding the arrangements with Spain.

Vancouver had known of secret earlier planning for a British penal colony at Nootka or in the vicinity, and he expected to learn more in due course. The voyage was expected to take up to three years, and his initial orders provided him with enough flexibility to accomplish the mission. It would end up taking a few weeks short of five years.

Vancouver was a rising star in the hydrographic ranks of the Royal Navy. He had been born of Dutch stock in Norfolk, the son of a customs official. After invaluable training during two of Cook's great voyages of exploration, he had completed a well-received charting of Kingston and other harbours in Jamaica. During that time, he had assembled an excellent group of subordinates.

For his new expedition, Vancouver could nominate some of the officers to serve with him aboard *Discovery*, and he called upon his team from the Jamaican harbour surveys: Lieutenants Peter Puget and Joseph Baker, and his trusted sailing master, Joseph Whidbey. As his first officer, Vancouver chose Zachary Mudge, who had been with them only briefly, but was well respected. Lieutenant William Broughton commanded *Chatham*, with James Johnstone as master. Vancouver, confident of his own and Whidbey's ability to take navigational observations, dispensed with a specialized astronomer. He was soon to change his mind.

One further person was assigned to *Discovery*: Archibald Menzies, a civilian botanist. The influential scientist Sir Joseph Banks, who had sailed—and clashed—with Cook, had nominated Menzies. Vancouver, aware of the earlier conflict, disliked the idea, but eventually warmed to Menzies. He grew to respect Menzies's calm, seasoned advice and his knowledge of medicine for mariners—particularly locally available, antiscorbutic plants. Menzies had previously circumnavigated the globe with James Colnett, even visiting Nootka.

The expedition's surveyors were able to count on the latest versions of new chronometers and related instruments, including high-precision sextants. The Hydrographer of the Navy, Alexander Dalrymple, had assembled a comprehensive collection of the best charts available, which included those of the various fur traders, but not those of López de Haro and Bodega y Quadra. He provided Vancouver with copies of these charts and of several accounts of voyages to the region.

Among the stores on board was a large and varied quantity of trade goods, mostly of metal and known to be of value to the people they would meet.

After waiting until early April 1791 for *Chatham* to complete a refit, the expedition got under way. By the time they had reached Madeira, Vancouver saw the advantage of having a specialist astronomer on the team; he sent a request that one be assigned and sent to join him.

Just over a year after they sailed from England, they reached the coast of California. Vancouver, remembering Drake's visit of 1579, referred to this as New Albion. Their voyage had taken them eastward around the Cape of Good Hope, along the southern coast of Australia—where they charted some 350 miles of coastline—and past New Zealand, Tahiti, and the Sandwich Islands. They made landfall in North America about latitude 40°23', a little north of Cape Mendocino.

After cruising northward along the coast of today's California and Oregon, making a running survey, they passed the entrance to the Columbia River, called on Spanish charts Entrada de Hezeta. However, rain squalls, heavy surf, and spray obscured it from view. They realized from the muddy colour of the water that they must be off the mouth of a major river, but Vancouver prudently opted for the safety of his expedition rather than risk venturing closer to the menacing shore.

A short while later they saw an American fur trader, *Columbia Rediviva*, captained by Robert Gray, and went aboard. Puget produced one of the maps drawn by Meares, indicating a supposed voyage by Gray through the Strait of Juan de Fuca and into an inland sea. Gray disclaimed any knowledge of such a discovery. He told them he had ventured just beyond the entrance, but had returned the same way.

Gray escorted the British ships around Cape Flattery, to a village called Classet (Claaset) in Neah Bay. Natives in a group of canoes came out to greet them and invited them to visit their village. Vancouver felt that the wind did not favour anchoring there, and sought a more sheltered place deeper in the inlet. It seems probable that Tetacus, who a few weeks later would befriend two visiting Spanish vessels, was in one of those canoes.

The British party continued along the southern shore of the strait, since that was the line of the continent they were to survey, and arrived at an ideal, sheltered harbour, which Vancouver named Port Discovery after his ship. They imagined

FIG 29 The Strait of Juan de Fuca and the mountains of the Olympic Peninsula are seen framed by an arbutus tree, first described scientifically by Archibald Menzies on Vancouver's expedition. [Chris Sheppard]

that they were the first Europeans to anchor there, unaware that the Spaniards Quimper and Eliza had preceded them into what they had called Puerto Quadra.

Once they had anchored, Menzies accompanied Vancouver on a brief reconnaissance of the shore. The naturalist noted, among many new plants, one he called an Oriental Strawberry Tree (see Fig. 29, page 71). Residents of southern Vancouver Island today know it well, and its scientific name, *Arbutus menziesii*, acknowledges his discovery.

Now the expedition's charting technique changed. Leaving the ships at anchor to undergo much-needed repair, Whidbey set up the portable observatory on land, while the surveyors took to the ship's boats to chart the coastline in more detail (see Fig. 30, page 73). Powered mainly by oarsmen, each boat was rigged with a mast for sailing as the wind would allow. The surveyors modified the running survey method by making landings at the prominent points. Here they would take compass bearings, forward and back, to all other such points that they could see, to produce, in effect, a compass traverse along the coast.

Immediately after the first boat expedition left Port Discovery, they found that the coastline turned southward to reveal a wide, navigable opening. They had discovered Admiralty Inlet. The boats traced the length of the dead-ended Hood Canal before returning to Port Discovery. From there, Vancouver spotted what seemed to be a group of islands to the north. He sent Broughton off in *Chatham* to investigate these—the San Juan Archipelago—while he repositioned *Discovery* to anchor close to today's Seattle. Vancouver and Puget explored, in boats, the complex of islands at the southern end of what is now Puget Sound. They discovered that this, too, had no outlet other than the one they had entered. *Chatham* joined them and Broughton reported that they had seen, to the northeast of the archipelago, an open horizon.

On June 4, the king's birthday, Vancouver ordered a royal salute of 21 guns from both ships and a double ration of grog for all hands to toast His Majesty's health. They had anchored off Tulalip Bay, north of the present-day city of Everett, in what is still called Possession Sound. With Broughton and other officers, Vancouver went ashore to conduct a formal ceremony.

[I] took possession of the coast, from that part of New Albion, in the latitude of 39°20' north . . . [to the] straits of Juan de Fuca; as likewise all the coast islands, &c. within the said straits, as well on the northern as on the southern shores; together with those situated in the interior sea we have discovered . . . I have honoured with the name of THE GULPH OF GEORGIA, and the continent binding the said gulph, and extending southward to the 45th degree of north latitude, with that of NEW GEORGIA, in honour of his present Majesty.[2]

This act seems to have been a piece of theatre by Vancouver, perhaps to build morale by stressing to the crew that their mission was of national and historic importance. So it was, but the act itself was contrary to Pitt's strategy of rejecting any Spanish claim made by right of such an act. It also ignored the fact of Spanish presence in Nootka, although Vancouver was still unaware of the earlier discoveries of the Gran Canal de Rosario, the open water that Broughton had seen.

The vessels made their way out of Admiralty Inlet across the eastern end of Juan de Fuca, and sailed north to anchor in Birch Bay. Boat parties surveyed the many channels between the islands of the archipelago and the mainland shore (see Fig. 31, page 74). Vancouver led a longer sortie probing northward, skirting around the shallow delta of the Fraser River and into the fjords of what is now called the Sunshine Coast. This party was the first Europeans to enter what would become Vancouver Harbour.

FIG 30 Vancouver's shore encampment at Port Discovery on the south shore of the Strait of Juan de Fuca seen at sunset, with a small, conical tent specially designed for astronomical observations for longitude, and ship's boats unloading supplies. [*The Encampment*, John Horton]

FIG 31 As dawn breaks over Boundary Bay, one of Vancouver's survey parties heads off toward Point Roberts. [*Dawn Departure*, John Horton]

As he was returning to *Discovery*, Vancouver saw two Spanish naval vessels at anchor in the mouth of a stream (now the North Arm of the Fraser), and requested permission to come aboard. Lieutenants Dionisio Alcalá Galiano and Cayetano Valdés y Flores greeted him, having already met Broughton. The meeting was courteous, but Vancouver acknowledged in his journal that he had come upon the Spanish ships with "no small degree of mortification." Nonetheless, he complied with his orders to be polite and cooperative with Spanish officers, and they soon formed a warm, respectful bond.

Discovery and *Chatham* met up with *Sutil* and *Mexicana* just off Point Grey and all four attempted to keep station. It became clear, however, that the copper sheathing on the hull and greater sail area of the English vessels made them much faster than those of the Spaniards (see Fig. 32, page 77). After a few days, the four ships found a sheltered anchorage just inside Teakerne Arm to the east of Cortes Island.

Two of the British boat parties explored to the north of the anchorage, and both made a key discovery. Johnstone took *Chatham*'s boat through the Arran Rapids to explore Bute and Loughborough inlets. As he left the latter, about opposite today's Kelsey Bay, he noted that the flooding tide now came from the northwest—not from the south, as before. This, he realized, confirmed that, in addition to Juan de Fuca, there must be a second opening to the Pacific, and that there might be a navigable passage around what must be a large island, or islands, to the west.

Soon after this revelation, the party heard a gunshot nearby. They came upon a large native village, and locals in several canoes, bearing muskets, came to greet them. Cheslakees, the leader of the village at the mouth of the Nimpkish River, enjoyed trade links with Maquinna and the Mowachaht of Nootka. From them he had obtained the guns and other trade goods.

Johnstone continued to explore westward along the strait that was given his name until, north of Hardy Bay, he reached Gordon Channel at the mouth of Queen Charlotte Strait. From here he could see the open Pacific. By now, the men were exhausted and nearly out of food, so, taking advantage of flooding tides, they returned to the Teakerne anchorage. They noted, but did not inspect, more inlets on the continental shore.

Meanwhile, Puget and Whidbey had been tracing the western shoreline of the "Gulph" and entered Discovery Passage. They too noted the tidal phenomenon, and drew the same inference. They had also seen a large native village, called Yuculta, at Cape Mudge. Opposite the village, they had found "a rivulet of excellent fresh water"—now called the Campbell River—before returning to the ships to report their finding about the change of tidal direction.

Once Johnstone had arrived with his report, Vancouver deduced that the two channels merged into one to give northern access to the ocean. Of the two routes to that strait, the western one seemed safer for *Discovery* and *Chatham*. Vancouver discussed the merits of the alternatives with his Spanish friends. They, despite knowing of the hazards, opted to keep as close to the continental shore as they could. Vancouver gave them a copy of Johnstone's preliminary chart, and they planned to follow his route. The two missions parted on excellent terms.

At first light on the morning of Friday, July 13, *Discovery* raised anchor, unfurled topsails, and sailed out of Teakerne across the northern end of the Strait of Georgia, to anchor temporarily off Cape Mudge. Vancouver sent Puget and Whidbey ahead to check for hazards up as far as a sheltered cove on the western shore. *Discovery* and *Chatham* joined them there. Vancouver named the cove Menzies Bay, to honour the expedition's botanist, by now his friend and confidant. This was the first topographical feature on Vancouver Island to be named by the expedition.

The advance party continued scouting northward and, taking advantage of an ebbing tide, they managed to transit the next hazard. Puget noted that "the Channel contracted to little better than half a Mile & between the Points the Stream could not run less than Six knots." Vancouver called it Euclutaw Narrows, after the village at Cape Mudge, but today it is known as Seymour Narrows. Puget had underestimated the velocity of the tidal race—it has been known to reach 15 knots. The tide carried them the length of Discovery Passage as far as Johnstone's Strait (the possessive "s" has now been dropped). With the next flooding tide, the boats returned to the ships anchored in Menzies Bay.

Vancouver, heeding the advice of Puget and Whidbey, waited for the next day's favourable ebb tide to run the gauntlet of the narrows.

> The tide, setting to the southward through the confined passage, rushes with such immense impetuosity as to produce the appearance of falls considerably high: although not the least obstruction of either rocks or sands, so far as we had the opportunity of examining it, appeared to exist.

He was mistaken in thinking the way clear. In the very heart of the channel the narrows concealed a twin-peak pinnacle that was later given the name of Ripple Rock. This menace—just beneath the surface at low water—would prove fatal to many vessels that followed Vancouver's route. The "falls" he described were the huge standing waves created by the force of the current swirling around the hidden hazard (see Fig. 95, page 201). He was extremely lucky: the boats came safely through.

Once they had rounded Chatham Point, where Discovery Passage becomes Johnstone Strait, it took them three days of difficult sailing to go just 85 miles along the narrow waterways. They found it impossible to make headway unless both the tide and wind cooperated fully. Menzies described the landscape:

> The South Side of this Channel rose in most places abruptly into high steep broken Mountains covered with a continued forest of Pines to their summits, which in some places was chequerd with patches of snow.[3]

He was viewing the rugged, northeastern coastline of Vancouver Island that provides a backdrop to Robson Bight. This is now an ecological reserve, the famous rubbing beach for orcas, or killer whales.

Discovery found safe anchorage off the large settlement near where Johnstone had heard the musket shot (see Fig. 33, page 78). The *tyee*, or headman, Cheslakees, coordinated a lively barter session for more than 200 sea otter pelts and fresh salmon. Vancouver described the village as:

> pleasantly situated on a sloping hill, above the banks of a fine freshwater rivulet, discharging itself into a small creek or cove [it was, in fact, the estuary of the Nimpkish River]. It was exposed to a southern aspect, whilst higher hills behind covered with lofty pines, sheltered it completely from the northern winds. The houses, in number thirty-four, were arranged in regular streets ... decorated with paintings and other ornaments ... too remote or hieroglyphical for our comprehension ... the whole, from the opposite bank of the creek, presented a very picturesque appearance.[4]

Trading with the Mowachaht had exposed Cheslakees's people—now called the 'Namgis, who live at Alert Bay—to the

FIG 32 For a few days in June 1792, Vancouver's two ships sailed with those of the Spanish expedition. As they passed Thormanby Island, near Texada, they encountered a pod of killer whales. [*Off Thormanby Island, June 25, 1792,* Gordon Miller]

FIG 33 John Sykes, a young master's mate aboard *Discovery* and a talented artist, drew this view of the "very picturesque" village at the mouth of the Nimpkish River, home of the 'Namgis leader Cheslakees. [*Cheslakee's (sic) Village in Johnstone's Strait,* author's collection, Vancouver's journal]

Nootkan language, and the visitors found that they could use the various Nootkan word lists collected by Cook and by the fur traders. Vancouver even entrusted two letters—one from Galiano, the other his own—to this cross-island trading route. He gave the letters, both addressed to Quadra, to one of the locals to deliver to Nootka. Neither arrived.

In an interesting example of cross-cultural differences, Cheslakees pilfered Vancouver's personal notebook. The leader was embarrassed when found out, but the captain was dismayed at what he viewed as innate dishonesty in the natives. He judged it to demonstrate "a natural inordinate propensity for thieving." He seemed unaware, however, that his own behaviour was just as reprehensible to Cheslakees. Vancouver assumed that he and his men were at liberty to take on fresh water, timber, firewood, plants, and berries without payment or even permission. The locals considered, quite reasonably, that such resources were their property.

Vancouver had moved *Discovery* near the entrance of Blackfish Sound, to rendezvous with *Chatham*. Broughton had earlier taken *Chatham* to explore and chart the inlets noted by Johnstone. The area to the north of the strait forms another archipelago, to which Vancouver gave the name of *Chatham's* skipper. It is another maze of narrow channels between islands large and small. After an anxious, five-day wait, *Discovery* sailed to reunite with *Chatham* on the south side of Queen Charlotte Strait. From there they resumed the examination, by boats, of Kingcome and other inlets of the continental shore. By now it was into August and the weather had deteriorated.

The entrance to the strait, where it becomes Queen Charlotte Sound, is far from clear sailing. Several chains of islands and hidden reefs constitute a perilous passage. Sailing westward, and about to leave the strait on a falling tide, *Discovery* struck a submerged rock, and remained perched there

until the next high tide. The ship then floated free, fortunately with her hull undamaged; the vessel was restored to sailing condition, and the crew rested after the exertion needed to escape from the rock.

Not long afterward, there came a second near-disaster, as *Chatham* also grounded on a hidden ledge. Night was falling, with a heavy ocean surge repeatedly banging the hull on the rock. Vancouver and his crew passed another anxious night. When the morning fog lifted, they saw, with relief, *Chatham* approaching under sail. In the various journals, there is a mysterious lack of accurate positions for the two grounding incidents, but it would seem that they occurred near the Deserters' Group of islands, north of Hardy Bay.

Immediately following the two groundings, fog obscured the narrow entrance to twin fjords penetrating the continental shore. Seymour and Belize inlets remained uncharted for another 73 years, until Daniel Pender discovered them in HMS *Beaver*. This was the only omission in Vancouver's thorough charting of the continental shore between capes Flattery and Caution. In any case, the rapids at the entrance would have precluded their use by ocean-going ships.

The expedition rounded Cape Caution, which guards the northern side of the entrance to Queen Charlotte Strait, to continue into Fitzhugh Sound. They anchored in a cove, which at first sight seemed to be Port Safety, found some four years earlier by fur trader Charles Duncan. Vancouver concluded that it was not the same place, and called his anchorage Safety Cove. To conclude their first season, the next nine days saw intense surveying activity with the ship's boats.

They had been based in the cove for about a week when *Venus*, a fur-trading brig flying English colours, entered to drop anchor close by. The captain, Henry Shepherd, had recently called in at Nootka, and had brought a letter from

Daedalus. The letter dealt a double blow to Vancouver. It reported the deaths of the original captain, Lieutenant Richard Hergest—Vancouver called him "my most intimate friend"—and William Gooch, the specialist astronomer requested by Vancouver. While they were ashore in the Sandwich Islands, natives had ambushed and killed them. Shepherd also informed Vancouver that Señor Quadra was impatiently awaiting his arrival at Nootka.

Vancouver decided that, rather than continue his survey of this stretch of coast for another few weeks, he would go to *Daedalus*, where he would collect and study his new orders and then meet with Bodega y Quadra. There was work that he and his crews could be doing afterward—the coastline of New Albion southward from their landfall as far as latitude 30° was still to be charted. On August 18, *Discovery* and *Chatham* raised their anchors, left Safety Cove, and sailed through Hakai Pass before heading south for Nootka. They arrived ten days later.

DIPLOMATIC NEGOTIATIONS

At anchor in Friendly Cove, Vancouver found *Daedalus* with his supplies and less-than-helpful new instructions. Bodega y Quadra greeted him, and the two began their discussions related to the second Nootka Convention, concerning the properties claimed by John Meares. A few days later, Galiano and Valdés arrived as well, and they shared and compared all survey notes most amicably.

Daedalus had brought supplies for the expedition and a suite of astronomical instruments, including a pendulum clock and three more chronometers. The Board of Longitude had supplied these for Gooch's use, but even without his specialist astronomer, Vancouver could bring them into service immediately, setting up an observatory on shore. He had been there when Cook had made his observations for longitude, and

knew how much effort had been devoted to the measurement. Vancouver wanted to ensure that his charting was firmly linked to his mentor's earlier work. He and Whidbey made well over a hundred sets of lunar distance observations, while diplomatic discussions with Bodega y Quadra proceeded.

In fact, Vancouver's final value for Nootka's longitude differed significantly from both Cook's and Galiano's. A local researcher, Nick Doe, has recalculated the longitudes using modern, more accurate tables. He shows that the three explorers were all first-rate observers and that the differences between their positions and the true one were due to systemic errors in the official *Nautical Almanac*. Vancouver was concerned by the apparent discrepancy, but was not able to discover the reason before he died.

Bodega y Quadra told Vancouver that Captain Gray had managed to cross the bar of the Entrada de Hezeta and had named it the Columbia River, after his ship. This was back in May, soon after he had met Vancouver off Cape Flattery. Quadra provided a copy of Gray's sketch map. This news added another survey task for Vancouver. Before entering Friendly Cove, he had considered charting the island's coastline south from Woody Point, but fog and unfavourable winds had prevented *Discovery* from getting close enough to shore for an accurate running survey. Besides, he now knew it was part of an island, not the continental shore. His orders meant that he was no longer required to chart it in detail.

The exchanges between Vancouver and his diplomatic counterpart could not reconcile their orders, so they agreed the matter would be referred back to their governments to resolve (see Fig. 34, page 81). Vancouver sent his first year's survey results and charts to London, together with his report on the issue and his request for further clarification and instruction.

They all partook of a feast provided by Bodega y Quadra and served on his personal silver plate and cutlery. Maquinna entertained his guests with ceremonial displays, dances, and a *potlatch*—presentation of gifts to the guests (see Fig. 35, page 82). Members of Vancouver's crew responded with reels and hornpipes to fife and drum. Maquinna expressed satisfaction over the event; it had greatly increased his status with his neighbour and rival, Wickaninnish.

As they were returning, a charming incident occurred, serving to highlight the mutual esteem of the two commissioners.

In our conversation whilst on this little excursion, Senr. Quadra had very earnestly requested that I would name some port or island after us both, to commemorate our meeting and the very friendly intercourse that had taken place and subsisted between us. Conceiving no spot so proper for this denomination as the place where we had first met, which was nearly in the centre of the tract of land that had first been circumnavigated by us . . . I named that country the island of QUADRA AND VANCOUVER; with which compliment he seemed highly pleased.[5] [See Fig. 36, page 83]

Two evenings later, Vancouver was able to return Maquinna's ceremonial hospitality by treating him to a display of "rockets, balloons and other fireworks," which they happened to have brought from England. While these developments continued on the diplomatic side, Vancouver still needed to fulfill some surveying responsibilities. He sailed down the coast to San Francisco and Monterey, where he was, again, treated generously by Bodega y Quadra, who had also left Nootka following the discussions.

After a few weeks of respite in the Sandwich Islands, *Chatham* and *Discovery* returned separately to the northwest coast. By now, it was 1793. *Chatham* arrived first, having headed directly for Vancouver Island. Puget attempted to approach

FIG 34 In 1957 the Spanish government donated this stained-glass window to the old church at Yuquot (Friendly Cove), Nootka Sound, to commemorate the meeting between Vancouver and Bodega y Quadra, August 28, 1792. [*Stained Glass Window in the Church at Friendly Cove*, Derek Hayes]

FIG 35 Mowachaht leader Maquinna publicly presenting his daughter at a coming-of-age ceremony at his winter village of Tahsis, in the presence of both English and Spanish naval officers, September 4, 1792. [*Fiesta en honor de la hija de Macuina*, courtesy of Museo de América, Madrid]

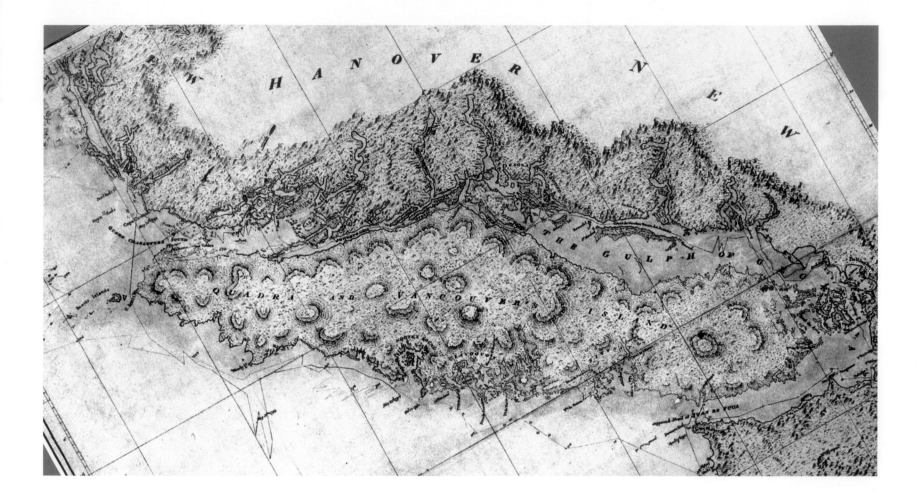

FIG 36 A section of George Vancouver's manuscript chart compiling his first season's work in these waters and commemorating the amicable working relationship with his Spanish counterpart, Juan Francisco de la Bodega y Quadra. [Courtesy of the Historical Map Society of BC]

FIG 3) The Victoria city street where the Christ Church Cathedral is located commemorates Bodega y Quadra. [Photo by author]

Nootka through Esperanza Channel, but in Nuchatlitz Inlet he ran into a dangerous situation of tidal races among shallow reefs that were not shown on the chart provided by Bodega y Quadra. He reached Nootka in mid-April. After waiting a month for *Discovery* to join them, Puget, following orders, sailed to recommence the survey of the continental shore from where they had left off the previous season.

The Spanish garrison at Santa Cruz de Nuca, under their new commander Salvador Fidalgo, had spent yet another miserable winter. Some had died; many others were starving and sick with scurvy or other maladies. Now several of *Chatham*'s crew also fell victim, but the relationship remained good. *Chatham* provided some much-needed food and antiscorbutics; the Spaniards helped careen and repair the keel of the British ship.

While this was going on, a party of Makah canoes arrived to trade their dentalia shells for furs. Maquinna promptly dispatched his own trading party overland, presumably to barter the shells with, among others, Cheslakees. Maquinna had drawn a sketch map to explain to Fidalgo which route the party would take; the leader had learned, and now used, the tool of cartography.

After leaving Hawaii, *Discovery* had again made landfall near Cape Mendocino and battled slowly north along the coast, arriving at Nootka a few days after *Chatham*'s departure. Vancouver, already a month behind schedule, soon followed to join the survey. One of *Discovery*'s boat parties, under Vancouver, just missed another British explorer. The fur trader Alexander Mackenzie, coming "from Canada, by Land," arrived at tidewater below Bella Coola on July 22, 1793. He learned from locals that "Macubah and Bensins" (presumably Vancouver and Menzies) had only recently left these waters. Neither group had been aware of the other's presence in the region.

To start their third season on the coast, in 1794, *Discovery* and *Chatham* headed directly from Hawaii to Cook Inlet in

Alaska—the northern limit of Vancouver's survey mission. They arrived in mid-April, still a time of storms and freezing conditions. They charted the coast of Alaska and the archipelago, now part of the Panhandle, and had completed their survey at Port Conclusion by the middle of August. After taking possession of the country, Vancouver granted all hands a double ration of grog and a thoroughly deserved one day's holiday. Once more, Vancouver's ships headed south for Nootka.

Their arrival was met with the news that their friend, Bodega y Quadra, had died that March. He had been a gentleman universally admired and respected—by Vancouver, his officers and the lower deck, by Maquinna, and even by the hard-boiled Boston fur traders. Today, the City of Victoria commemorates that gallant officer, inaccurately, by Quadra Street (see Fig. 37, page 84), and by a memorial bust in Quadra Park on Belleville Street, unveiled by King Juan Carlos and Queen Sofía of Spain in 1984 (see Fig. 38).

In December, still lacking word from his superiors, Vancouver sailed for England. In his final report, after recounting the completion of his survey, Vancouver summed up the major achievement of the project:

> I trust the precision with which the survey of the coast of North West America has been carried into effect, will remove every doubt, and set aside every opinion of *a northwest passage*, or any other water communication navigable for shipping, exists between the North Pacific, and the interior of the American continent, within the limits of our researches . . . making the history of our transactions on the north-west coast of America, *as conclusive as possible*, against all speculative opinions respecting the existence of a *hyperboreum* or *mediterranean* ocean within the limits of our survey.[6]

FIG 38 Victoria also remembers Spanish explorer Captain Bodega y Quadra by a bronze bust in Quadra Park, near the legislature building. His Majesty King Juan Carlos I of Spain dedicated the monument on March 17, 1984, to commemorate the spirit of cooperation between Captain Vancouver and Bodega y Quadra. [Photo by author]

FIG 39   Captain William Henry McNeill, known in Chinook Jargon as "Ma-ta-hell," was a highly experienced fur trader out of Boston. The Hudson's Bay Company chose him to captain the SS *Beaver*, and he advanced through its ranks. [Courtesy of the Royal BC Museum and Archives, Victoria]

CHAPTER SIX

"A CONVENIENT SITUATION FOR AN ESTABLISHMENT"

MA-TA-HELL, THE MOST SUCCESSFUL TRADER ALONG THE COAST William Henry McNeill was the archetypal "Boston man." This was the term the Mowachaht—along with other First Nations and tribes along the coast from Alaska to California—used for the Americans who came to trade for furs. They were readily distinguishable from "King George's men," their British counterparts.

McNeill was born in Boston in 1801, and went to sea at age 11. A dozen years later he gained his ticket as a master mariner, and took command of the brig *Convoy* on a trading voyage to the Sandwich Islands and the Queen Charlottes. By 1832 he had made many such voyages, and gained an intimate knowledge of the intricacies of the coastline and its resident peoples. He was fluent in Chinook Jargon—the trading *lingua franca* along the coast—as well as in Haida and other local languages, and his natural ability as an astute trader was reinforced by marriage to two high-status local women: first to Mathilda, of the Kaigani Haida, and later to Martha, of the Nass nation.

In his own vessel, the brig *Lama*, "Ma-ta-hell," as the Indigenous peoples pronounced his name, became the most successful trader along the coast, posing serious competition for the Hudson's Bay Company. Local HBC officers, well aware of the value of McNeill's superior knowledge, discussed recruiting him. One of them, Duncan Finlayson, observed:

> [McNeill's] greater experience on the NW Coast, from cruising thereon for the space of 12 years, will give our people an insight into the nature of the trade & a knowledge of the Bays, Inlets, Harbours & trading stations of that Coast, hitherto unknown to us & which cannot fail to give us a footing & promote our interests in that quarter.[1] [See Fig. 39, page 86]

In 1834 McNeill showed his mettle in an incident noteworthy for its relevance to the history of early Asiatic contact with these shores. News had reached Fort Vancouver that a Japanese junk had foundered off Cape Flattery; the Makah had captured the crew and were pillaging the wreck. McNeill immediately set sail in *Lama* to rescue the unfortunate mariners. When he arrived, several Makah warriors boarded his vessel, but he quickly overcame them, and held them to ransom for the Japanese prisoners. Sadly, by then only three remained alive, but the exchange was effected, the survivors were brought back to Fort Vancouver, and the HBC sent them home via England.

Evidently, a typhoon had struck the junk, causing damage that rendered it uncontrollable, then the Kuroshio Current had swept the vessel across the Pacific to make a tragic landfall upon the rocks of Cape Flattery. This is just one of an untold number of similar cases of inadvertent exploration that must have occurred over the previous millennia.

When the chance came to buy McNeill out, the HBC responded quickly. They purchased *Lama* and, despite the company's reluctance to break the law by employing a foreign captain for a British-owned vessel, they added him and his two mates to the payroll, to continue operating in their service. They even concocted a cover story if the Royal Navy were to intercept the Boston-registered *Lama*: another HBC employee aboard, James Scarborough, a British national, was to declare himself captain, and he carried papers to support this charade. This devious arrangement was continued when, in 1837, McNeill took command of the recently arrived steam paddlewheeler *Beaver*.

George Simpson, governor of the HBC, originally proposed the adoption of steam-powered vessels in 1832, for use on the many rivers, inlets, and sounds of the northwest coast. He anticipated that the main advantage would be independence from the vagaries of wind and tide. Two years later, the company ordered construction of a 101-foot (30.7-metre)-long sidewheeler, of 20-foot (6-metre) beam and 8-foot, 6-inch (2.6 metre) draft, of 187 tons (170 tonnes), powered by dual, 35-horsepower steam engines, fuelled by wood or coal. The cost was £2,992 for the hull plus £4,500 for the machinery. *Beaver* was built at Blackwall on the Thames, just east of London.

Escorted by her sister hull *Columbia*—rigged as a 310-ton (281 tonne) sailing barque—the two-masted *Beaver* departed Gravesend at the end of August 1835. With her machinery laid up and twin wooden paddles of 13-foot (4-metre) diameter stored in the hold, *Beaver* performed better under sail than did *Columbia*. After rounding the Horn and reprovisioning in Honolulu, the two ships arrived at Fort Vancouver in April 1836. A month later, *Beaver* was ready for operation as the first steam-powered vessel to operate anywhere in the Pacific Ocean (see Fig 44, page 100).

The coastline survey of George Vancouver and the overland expeditions by Alexander Mackenzie had together definitively disproved the existence of the fabled Northwest Passage. Afterward, the government showed little interest in this remote region. One exception to this apparent neglect was a brief visit in 1836 by two Royal Navy ships, *Sulphur* and *Starling*, under Captain Sir Edward Belcher. They came first to the Russian posts of Etches and Sitka and, after stopping at Nootka to verify Vancouver's astronomy, headed south as far as Panama. They returned two years later to call in at Fort Vancouver, which Belcher seemed to consider an outpost of the British Empire, although at that time, it was not.

For some years, Simpson and other directors of the HBC had felt increasing concern about the growing flood of American settlers across the Rockies and into the Willamette Valley, and they recognized the need to replace Fort Vancouver as their principal west coast depot. Not only was this for political, safety, and strategic reasons, but the treacherous currents and sandbars at the mouth of the Columbia River had already taken a heavy toll on their annual supply ships and cargoes. They needed a more accessible harbour, one that the British government would be more inclined to defend once the border had been negotiated.

After considering and rejecting possible ports in the Fraser River, the Strait of Juan de Fuca, and Puget Sound, in 1836 John

McLoughlin, chief factor and senior regional officer, issued this instruction:

> The Captain of the steamer *Beaver* should also be directed to examine on his way to Nisqually next summer the south end of Vancouver's island for the purpose of selecting a convenient situation for an Establishment on a large scale, possessing all the requisites for farming rearing of Cattle together with a good harbour and abundance of timber, in short containing every advantage which is desirable such a situation should furnish.[2]

The following year, McNeill duly carried out that mission and probably submitted a written report, but the original has never been found. In fact, McLoughlin may have lost it deliberately: He opposed the concept of an alternative to his very comfortable Fort Vancouver. The next official progress report to Simpson, however, written by James Douglas—standing in for McLoughlin, who had been summoned to the London office—included a detailed reference to McNeill's reconnaissance.

> The survey, strictly speaking, commenced at Nahwitti [the region around today's Port Hardy] near the north end of the Island and proceeded through Johnstone Straits and the Gulf of Georgia to Pt. Gonzalo [today's Ten Mile Point] . . . On reaching the South end of the Island, a decided improvement was observed in the appearance of the Country. Three good harbours of easy access, were found west of Point Gonzalo, at two of which, Captain McNeill passed a few days. The land around these harbours is covered with wood to the extent of half a mile, interiorly, where the forest is replaced by more open and beautifully diversified Country presenting a succession of plains with groves of Oaks and pine trees, for a distance of 15 or 20 miles. The most easterly of the harbours 10 miles west of Point Gonzalo is said to be the best on the Coast and possesses the important advantage, over the other, of a more abundant supply of fresh water furnished by a stream 20 Yards wide, which after contributing to fertilize the open Country, flows into it. The plains are said to be fertile and covered in luxuriant vegetation; but judging from the sample of soil brought here, I think it rather light and certainly not the best quality, admitting even this disadvantage, I am persuaded that no part of this Sterile & Rock bound Coast will be found better adapted for the site of the proposed Depot or to combine, in a higher degree, the desired requisites, of a secure harbour accessible to shipping at every season, of good pasture, and, to a certain extent, of improvable tillage land.[3]

The three harbours Douglas referred to are now known as Sooke, Esquimalt, and, the most easterly, Victoria. The name used at the time for this favoured location was Camosack, a Salish name associated with the camas plant, an important food source. McNeill had also inspected Becher Bay and Metchosin, but does not appear to have considered the harbours at Comox, Nanoose, Nanaimo, or Cowichan.

As soon as McLoughlin returned to Fort Vancouver the following year, 1839, he went with McNeill and John Work, another HBC officer, on a short visit of inspection to Fort Langley on the Fraser River, boarding *Beaver* at Nisqually. On their return to Nisqually, they took a cursory diversion to look at the place that McNeill had recommended. McLoughlin's next report, a few months later, mentioned, in passing:

> On the 12th [December] reached the plain on the South end of Vancouvers Island which Captain McNeill examined in 1837 and reported as a fine place for an Establishment. It is a very fine harbor, accessible at all seasons, but it is not a place suitable to our purpose; on the 14th arrived at Nisqually.[4]

Of his sole visit to the site that would become Victoria, this was McLoughlin's only mention of it in his letters to his superior, Simpson, or in his official dispatches to the company directors. His dismissive opinion, pointed silences on the subject, and prevarication were all to no avail with the company's decision makers. Eventually, Simpson issued some blunt instructions.

> [Y]ou will take the necessary steps to have the Southern end of Vancouver's Island very particularly examined in the course of the ensuing Summer [1842], in order that a proper place may be selected combining, if possible, all the advantages required . . . and as the selection of the locality is a matter of much importance, I have to beg [read "insist"] that it be made either by yourself or C[hief] F[actor] Douglas.[5]

Simpson and McLoughlin held radically different ideas on how the coastal fur trade should best be administered, including the number, location, and operation of trading posts. They also disagreed about the economics of sail versus steam for their supply fleet, and other issues. These differences grew wider until McLoughlin finally retired, on very poor terms with the company's leaders.

"WE HAD PASSED A MOST ANXIOUS TIME OF IT": SIMPSON'S VOYAGE IN *BEAVER*

Such was McNeill's high reputation in the HBC that when the crew of *Beaver* mutinied against him, the company upheld his authority and even promoted him to chief trader. In the autumn of 1841 he conveyed Simpson—by this time Sir George—from Nisqually to Sitka, Alaska, aboard *Beaver* (see Fig. 40, page 91).

> About seven in the morning we passed along the inner end of Fuca's Straits, the first of the numberless inlets of this coast

that was ever discovered by civilized man. The neighbouring country, comprising the southern end of Vancouver's Island, is well adapted for the cultivation; for, in addition to a tolerable soil and a moderate climate, it possesses excellent harbours and abundance of timber. It will doubtless become, in time, the most valuable section of the whole coast above California.

Simpson did not veer from the course that kept him close to the mainland and past the mouth of the Fraser, to anchor:

> in the snug little harbour [Blubber Bay] on the Island of Feveda [a transcription error by Vancouver's team for Texada on the Spanish charts] to take on wood and water. Captain McNeill generally preferred halting here on account of the superiority of the fuel . . . We were detained the whole of the next day by the same indispensable business of supplying the steamer with fuel. In fact, as the vessel carries only one day's stock, about forty cords, and takes about the same time to cut the wood as to burn it, she is at least as much at anchor as she is under way.

While Simpson goes on to justify his preference for steam over sail in these waters, he does not mention *Beaver*'s other disadvantage—that the need to carry so much wood for the furnace and water for the boiler left scarcely any room for cargo, either supplies or furs; sailing vessels could carry more payload. He continued, discussing Vancouver's depiction of:

> the intricacy and ruggedness of the line of the coast. We found Vancouver's charts so minute and accurate, that, amid all our difficulties, we never had to struggle with such as mere science could be expected to overcome; and, in justice to our own navigator and to one of his successors on the same path [a reference

perhaps to Alcalá Galiano], I ought to mention, that Commodore Wilkes [of the US Exploring Expedition], after a comparatively tedious survey from the mouth of the Columbia to that of Frazer's River, admitted that he had required to make but few and inconsiderable corrections.

Later on, they transitted Seymour Narrows.

In the afternoon we passed another village, near the narrowest point of Johnstone's Straits [on Vancouver's chart, the channel was called Discovery Passage]. Here we were greatly impeded by deep whirlpools and a short sea, which were said generally to mark these narrows, and to be caused by the collision of tides or currents flowing around the opposite ends of Vancouver's Island from the open ocean. [See Fig. 95, page 201]

Simpson liked the look of the people who came aboard at McNeill's Harbour (later Port McNeill) to trade their furs.

Both men and women were well grown, with regular and pleasing features; indeed, the girls were exceedingly pretty, and looked quite healthy. In fact, besides living well on the best of fish and the best of venison, these people have comparatively few diseases among them. They have been exempted from the smallpox, though their brethren, both from the south of the Columbia and in Russian America, have suffered severely from that terrible scourge.

When Simpson made an offer to the local leaders to vaccinate their children, they declined. He noted that the "Quakeolths" (Kwakiutl, or more correctly, Kwakwaka'wakw people) were very tricky traders, needing constant watching, but he also saw that the veteran McNeill was more than a match for them.

FIG 40 Sir George Simpson, governor of the Hudson's Bay Company, was a man of humble origins, small in stature, but of enormous energy, ability, and authority—known as the "Emperor of the North." [Courtesy of the Royal BC Museum and Archives, Victoria]

Simpson seemed impressed with the furs available,

amounting in value to about five hundred pounds sterling, consisting of martens, raccoons, beaver, bears, lynxes, and both kinds of otters; while the equivalents were blankets, tobacco, vermillion, files, knives, a small quantity of cloth, and only two guns, with a corresponding allowance of ammunition . . . During the preceding two years, the absence of competition in this quarter has enabled us to put the trade on a much better footing, by the entire disuse of spirituous liquors, and by the qualified interdiction . . . of the sale of arms and ammunition. These changes, however unsatisfactory to the parties interested, may, nevertheless, be considered as a great blessing to the whole of the native population, arresting the process at once of the sword and of the pestilence.

Beaver then carried Simpson north from Vancouver Island, up the Inside Passage and on to Sitka, where he reviewed the trading agreements with the Russian-American Company. He returned in early October.

[W]e succeeded, on a second attempt, in crossing the grand traverse [Queen Charlotte Sound] . . . the only exposed part of this coast, to Shushady Harbour [Shushartie Bay] in Vancouver's Island. As the swell of the ocean was here met by a high wind from the shore, no fewer than ten of our crew were laid up with seasickness. During the squalls, the paddles made seventeen revolutions per minute; but during the lulls they accomplished twenty-two. The proportions of actual speed, however, were very different—two or three miles per hour in the one case, and six or seven in the other. The northern end of Vancouver's Island would be an excellent position for the collecting and curing of salmon, which being incredibly numerous in these waters, might easily be rendered one of the most important articles of trade in this country. The neighbouring

Newettees [Nahwitti], a brave and friendly tribe, would be valuable auxiliaries, not only in aiding the essential operations of the establishment, but also in furnishing supplies of venison.[6]

Retracing their outbound course down Johnstone Strait and Discovery Passage, they faceed difficult conditions. In Simpson's subsequent report to the governors, he described the experience.

On coming through Johnstons Straits [Johnstone Strait] we were suddenly enveloped in a dense fog, in part of these Straits not exceeding two miles in width, where there was a tideway of 12 to 14 knots an hour, of which we were the sport for 13 hours. During this time the vessel was quite unmanageable. As we could not see the land, lost the best bower anchor, disabled the small bower and we were unable from the strength of the current to take soundings with two deep-sea lead lines fastened together, in places where at the slack of the tide, we afterwards ascertained the depth of the water was from 25 to 30 fathoms. In the course of these thirteen hours, the current hustled the vessel up and down the Straits with incredible speed, but fortunately there was an offset from the land, which kept her in deep water until the fog dispersed, when the steam was got up and enabled us to escape from this extraordinary tideway, without any other loss than the anchor in question, as the injury to the other has since been repaired.[7]

In his *Narrative*, Simpson provided more details of the harrowing episode.

About three in the afternoon, we entered the whirlpools of Johnstone's Strait, the water being tolerably smooth, and had got down nearly abreast of Point [now Cape] Mudge, when we became enveloped in a fog, which in density surpassed anything of the kind that I ever saw in London. Under these circumstances, to advance along a channel of only two miles in width was impossible; accordingly, slackening the speed of the engine, we endeavoured to grope our way out of the strength of the current to an anchorage on the shore of Vancouver's Island . . . We then dragged over a rocky bottom . . . while the tide was running up from twelve to fourteen knots an hour . . . We now plucked up courage to take tea, supposing ourselves secure for the night; but about nine, the vessel again began to drag for an hour or so, till the tide slackened.

Many worried hours later, they drifted into deep water.

[W]e caught a glimpse of land, supposed to be Point Mudge, while we were reeling wildly out into the gulf, the mere sport of the whirlpools. About six in the evening, the wind, shifting from north-east to south-east, dispersed the fog; and, after our poor fellows had been toiling at the windlass for nearly an hour and a half, they verified our fears, by bringing up the chain without the anchor, leaving us in no enviable condition at this boisterous season. Getting up steam, we hoped to reach the anchorage between Sangster's and Feveda Islands.

It seems probable that by "Sangster's" he meant Lasqueti and by "Feveda," Texada. Their intended anchorage sounds like Tucker Harbour on Lasqueti, and the glimpse of land could have been Mitlenatch Island. They had been carried—during at least three changes of tide, at night, in dense fog, and bereft of anchors—quite some distance south. They were not, however, out of trouble yet.

[B]ut our south-easter soon began to blow so hard as to make us bear away for Beware Harbour [Blubber Bay] at the north end of Feveda; and there we rendered ourselves as snug as possible for the night . . . We had passed a most anxious time of it, driving helplessly, as we were, in the midst of impenetrable darkness, with a current almost equalling the speed of a racer, with a bottom where no tackle could find holding ground, and with a coast where a touch would have knocked the stoutest ship to pieces. Nor was man likely to be more hospitable than nature. Even if we survived the perils of shipwreck, we should have had to enter a fearful struggle for our lives with savages, whose cruelty had never yet acknowledged any check but that of power and force.[8]

After this narrow escape, their fortune changed and a few days of fine weather brought them once more to Nisqually.

Simpson considered his adventurous journey aboard *Beaver* to be "the most extraordinary course of inland navigation in the world." He remained convinced of the value of steam-powered vessels over sail, and this "raised my estimate of Vancouver's skill and perseverance at every step of my progress." Also, he had carefully noted the impression that *Beaver* had made on the populations they visited. The locals—bold and highly skilled seafarers themselves—were clearly in awe of this large, noisy, fire-breathing craft that was able to defy any condition of tide, wind, or current.

"SO MANY ADVANTAGES": DOUGLAS AT CAMOSACK

While deputizing for Chief Factor John McLoughlin, who was away on business in London, James Douglas made an extended visit to Sitka related to the recently signed agreement with the Russian-American Company. Douglas took official possession of Fort Stikine, and built a second post he called Fort Taku. As he returned south, he thought about the question of another new trading post to serve the region around Queen Charlotte Sound. This region was known to be productive not only for peltry but especially so for two new potential trade items: salmon and whale oil. He made his recommendation to McLoughlin.

The place which I consider, in all respects most suitable for this purpose, is the neighbourhood of Neweeté [Nahwitti], near the north end of Vancouver's Island, where there are several good harbours accessible to Shipping at every season, and which is almost directly in the centre of the Native Population.[9]

Simpson's own visit to Shushartie the following year probably reinforced this opinion, but for strategic reasons, the govenor still preferred that the new establishment be located at one of the harbours identified at the southeastern tip of Vancouver Island. It would be called, in theory, Fort Adelaide, after the consort to the current King William IV.

After Simpson returned from his trip to Sitka aboard *Beaver*, he set out to return to London via California, the Pacific, and Asia. In early March, from Honolulu, he wrote to the Governor and Committee.

The Southern end of Vancouver's Island forming the Northern side of the Straits of de Fuca, appears to me the best situation for such an establishment as required. From the very superficial examination that has been made, it is ascertained that there are several good harbours in that neighbourhood no place however has yet been found combining all the advantages required, the most important of which are, a safe and accessible harbour, well situated for defence, with Water power for Grist and Saw Mills, abundance of Timber for home consumption and Exportation and the adjacent Country well adapted for tillage and pasture Farms on an extensive scale. I had not the opportunity of landing on the southern end of the Island, but from the distant view we had of it in passing between Puget's Sound and the Gulf of Georgia and the report of C.F. McLoughlin and others who have been there, we have every reason to believe there will be no difficulty in finding an eligible situation in that quarter for the establishment in question.

He added a note of caution.

There is a very large population of daring fierce and treacherous Indians on, and in the neighbourhood of the Southern Shore of Vancouver's Island, so that a heavy establishment of people say from 40 to 50 Officers and men, will be required for its protection in the first instance; but with the occasional presence of the Steamer [*Beaver*] whose power and ubiquity, has done more in my opinion to tame those daring hordes, than all the other means to that end that have ever been brought into action by Whites, not only the new depot but every other establishment on the Coast may in due time be reduced in point of numbers to as many only as are absolutely required to accomplish the work.[10]

Accepting that further resistance would be futile, McLoughlin delegated to Douglas the task of following up on McNeill's reconnaissance of five years earlier, by going to Vancouver Island to select a site for the new establishment. The plan was that, in order to staff the new depot at sufficient strength for its unassisted defence, Douglas would relocate men from the northern posts of McLoughlin (Bella Bella), Stikine, and Tanu. Regular visits by *Beaver* would enable trading for the furs brought to these outposts.

In early 1842, *Beaver* was still undergoing maintenance following its expedition with Simpson a few months earlier, so it was not available to convey Douglas and his small team from Nisqually to Vancouver Island. Instead, the party travelled aboard the HBC brigantine *Cadboro* (see Fig. 41, page 95). In all probability McNeill would have briefed Douglas before his departure, but he was unable to accompany the expedition because he had gone to England seeking citizenship.

This would be a return visit to Camosack for Captain William Brotchie and *Cadboro*; they had been, in 1837, the

FIG 41 Hudson's Bay Company's trading vessel *Cadboro*, seen here rigged as a topsail schooner, was 56 feet long, carried a crew of twelve and four guns, but was considered vulnerable to attack by larger ocean-going canoes of the northwest coast. [Courtesy of the Royal BC Museum and Archives, Victoria]

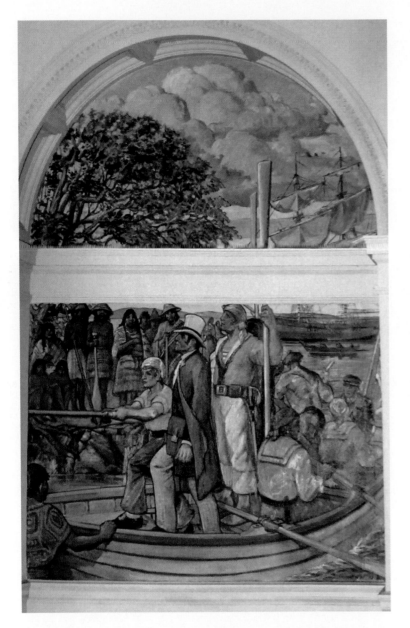

FIG 42 *Enterprise*, one of George Southwell's four controversial murals painted in 1932 and 1933 in the rotunda of the new BC Legislature buildings, depicts James Douglas's landing from the *Cadboro* at Clover Point in 1842. Sensitivities over the portrayal of Indigenous people caused the paintings to be covered over. [Courtesy of the Legislative Library of British Columbia]

second ship on record to enter the harbour. During that same visit, they had also found and named Cadboro Bay. Brotchie's own name is best remembered for his having "discovered"— with his keel—the reef or "ledge" just outside the entrance to Victoria harbour, off Dallas Road.

Cadboro was named after the hamlet Cadborough near Rye in southeast England, where it had been built for the HBC and launched in 1824. The small-but-speedy, two-masted vessel, with a standing bowsprit and rigged either as a brigantine or a topsail schooner, measured 56 feet (17 metres) in length and 17 feet (5.1 metres) in the beam. It drew 9 feet (2.7 metres) and registered at 72 tons (65.3 tonnes), was armed with six guns, and manned by a crew of 12. *Cadboro* had arrived at Fort Vancouver in May 1827, and that same year became the first vessel to enter the Fraser River. Despite its limitations, it served the company well for the next 30 years.

DOUGLAS FOLLOWS UP MCNEILL'S RECONNAISSANCE

Later called The Father of British Columbia, Douglas was born in British Guiana, the son of a Scottish plantation owner and a woman from Barbados, probably herself of mixed race. Douglas had joined the HBC at 15 years of age. Fluent in English, French, and Chinook Jargon, he had already acquired a wide range of practical, operational, and leadership experience in the northern fur trade. Douglas cut an imposing figure, as described in Simpson's confidential appraisal, written in the early 1830s:

> A stout powerful active Man of good conduct and respectable abilities . . . has every reason to look forward to early promotion and is a likely man to fill a place at the Council board in course of time.[11]

With his own background, and the reliable force that was *Cadboro* and its crew to support him, Douglas had few qualms about taking just a handful of men to explore inland, notwithstanding Simpson's warnings about the ferocity of the people he might meet there (see Fig. 42, page 96). The six-man exploration team he assembled included two millwrights, reflecting the importance that a water-powered mill would have for a new, major establishment. Needed for both grinding grain and sawing lumber, the mill could be on a freshwater stream or at a location to exploit tidal power.

He also included a draftsman-clerk, Adolphus Lee Lewes—the son of a fellow chief factor—who had recently returned from "a regular apprenticeship in [England] in the land surveying business . . . and in nautical surveying." Lewes and Douglas surveyed the area surrounding the selected site, and their map, called a Ground Plan, accompanied Douglas's subsequent report (see Fig. 43, page 98). They had brought two horses, and it is evident from the extent and detail shown on the map that the pair was able to cover considerable ground during their few weeks on site, and that they employed the services of local guides.

It is not clear in which order Douglas inspected "several Forts and harbours" along the coast between Point Gonzalo (Ten Mile Point, not today's Gonzales Point) and Sy-yousung (Sooke), nor where he landed. It would seem that he coasted beyond Sooke.

> [T]he south west point of the Island [perhaps San Juan Point] opposite Cape Flattery, and running westward from it . . . there are no safe harbours for Shipping and the country is high, rocky and covered in woods, presenting in its outline the almost unvarying characters of the coast of North west America, to which unfortunately it bears a too faithful resemblance.

However, the shore to the east was more promising.

> [The coast] from Port Sy-yousung to Point Gonzalo, is less elevated, more even and diversified by wood and plain; the coast is indented with bays and inlets; there are several good harbours, with anchorage at almost every point where vessels may bring up in calms.

Douglas's report described the positive and negative aspects of each of the five harbours he considered: Sy-yousung (Sooke), Whoyung (Becher Bay), Metcho-sin, Is-whoy-malth (Esquimalt), and Camosack (Victoria). As well as a good, all-weather harbour suitable for ocean-going shipping, he was seeking a reliable source of fresh water, and a "tract of clear land sufficiently extensive for the tillage and pasture of a large agricultural establishment." This last requirement effectively ruled out all of them except Camosack, even though the harbour itself was not as good as its neighbouring Is-whoy-malth: "one of the best harbours of the coast, being perfectly safe and of easy access." On balance, Douglas decided in favour of:

> the decided superiority of Camosack over the other parts of the Island, or of the continental shore known to us, as a place of settlement. The situation is not faultless or so completely suited to our purposes as it might be, but I despair of any better being found on this coast, as I am confident that there is no other sea port north of the Columbia where so many advantages will be found combined.[12]

From the amount of cartographic detail depicted on the Ground Plan, it is clear that the major part of the expedition's effort must have been devoted to the area surrounding the Canal of Camosack, known today as the Gorge, and the quantity of text in the report confirms this. The banks of the harbour and the "canal" were mapped very carefully, and particular attention

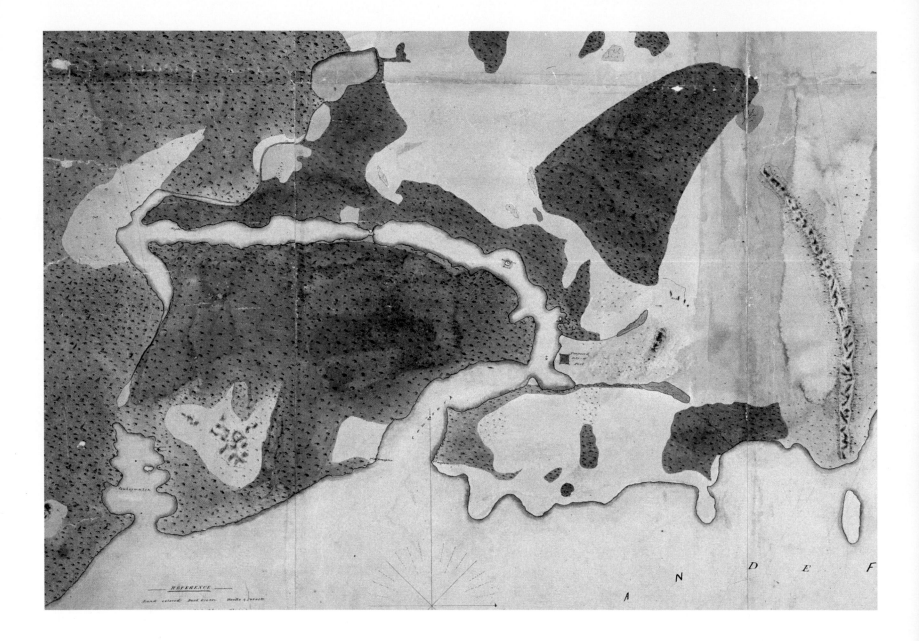

FIG 43 Central portion of the *Ground Plan . . . for New Establishment* surveyed by James Douglas in 1842, and drawn by Adolfus Lee Lewes. The red square by the "Camosack" waterway indicates the proposed site for the new fort. [Courtesy of Hudson's Bay Company Archives, Archives of Manitoba, Winnipeg]

was paid to sources of fresh water. Areas of plains or prairie, woods, and rock outcrops were differentiated.

A dotted line indicates that Douglas—probably accompanied by Lewes and a guide—followed a trail departing from the proposed site of the new fort, curving east then northward, crossing a line of rocky hills (about today's Oak Bay Corners), and then on to a place intriguingly marked "Battle Field," (about today's commercial centre of Oak Bay). No evidence or reports have surfaced of any battle ever having taken place there, and it seems probable that this was a linguistic misunderstanding. At best, Douglas would have been trying to converse with the Lekwungen guide in the very limited vocabulary of Chinook Jargon. One possibility is that the name derived from a nearby village at today's Gonzales Point, Kukleeluk, which roughly means "place of conflicting waters," referring to the fierce tidal rips between the point and Trial Island.

Douglas noted in his report that the tract of clear land crossed by the trail he had taken (today's Fort Street and Cadboro Bay Road) and running inland for some six miles, was "the most picturesque and decidedly the most valuable part of the Island that we had the good fortune to discover."

Lewes drew the coastline of Cadboro Bay quite well, indicating an "Indian Fort" at the northern end by some representative houses. The only other signs of Indigenous habitation on the map are a similar "Indian Fort" at the head of Is-whoy-malth, and a few patches of cultivation—probably camas—along the Gorge, around Beacon Hill, and near McLoughlin Point. Subsequent archeology confirms the impression gained by the boat parties of the Eliza expedition a half-century earlier, that many villages populated the coastline, so their omission on Lewes's map is a mystery. The houses at Cadboro Bay are now known to have been Sungayka, the fortified, principal village

of the Chekonein people, also called Samas or Samose, which became Songhees.

The team discovered no freshwater stream in the vicinity of the site selected for the fort with sufficient flow for a water mill; however, the two millwrights in the party examined the narrowest part of the Gorge, and advised that constructing a wheel to generate power from the tidal flows would be feasible "at a moderate expense."

Douglas, despite the circumspect wording of his recommendation for the Port of Camosack as the site for the new establishment, was most impressed with the delightful location. As he wrote in a well-known letter to a friend:

> The place itself appears a perfect "Eden," in the midst of the dreary wilderness of the North west coast, and so different is its general aspect, from the wooded, rugged regions around, that one might be pardoned for supposing it had dropped from the clouds into its present position . . . The growth of indigenous vegetation is more luxuriant, than in any other place, I have seen in America, indicating a rich productive soil. Though the survey I made was somewhat laborious, not being so light and active as in my younger days [he was, at the time, 39 years old], I was nevertheless delighted in ranging over fields knee deep in clover, tall grasses and ferns reaching above our heads, at these unequivocal proofs of fertility. Not a mosquito that plague of plagues did we feel, nor meet with molestation from the natives.[13]

The team reboarded *Cadboro* and returned to Nisqually and to Fort Vancouver, thus concluding the first serious land exploration anywhere on Vancouver Island. A small index map accompanied the Ground Plan. It demonstrated that the HBC (and any non-Indigenous person) possessed virtually no knowledge of the physical geography of the interior of the island.

FIG 44 *Fort Victoria* shows the company paddlewheel steamer SS *Beaver* at anchor opposite the wharf of the fort, with Coast Salish canoes in the foreground. [Painting by Harry Heine]

CHAPTER SEVEN

FORT VICTORIA:
EARLY VISITORS' IMPRESSIONS

THE FOLLOWING YEAR, 1843, JAMES Douglas returned to the Port of Camosack, his recommendation approved. He came to begin building the new fort, now graced with the name of Britain's newly crowned monarch, Victoria (see Fig. 45, page 102). Initially, the only people at the new location were company officers, a few "Canadian" (mixed-race) employees, and local people contracted to supply timber, fish, or game, or who were just generally curious about the antics of the strange newcomers with many interesting things to trade.

The fort took shape, wells were dug, and surrounding lands cleared for farming (see Fig. 46, page 103). The man in charge of getting the fort up and running, the veteran Charles Ross, was charmed by the ambiance of the spot.

> Nothing can be finer than the climate and scenery of this place. The former, especially surpasses anything I have ever before experienced—for from the month of June up to the present moment [mid-September], we have scarcely yet had four & twenty hours of consecutive wet weather.[1]

Soon, however, there came a trickle of non-Hudson's Bay Company visitors, most of whom kept journals, or prepared reports on various aspects of the burgeoning community. These were true explorers in the broad sense: fresh eyes seeing and recording first impressions of a locale scarcely known to Europeans.

The Oregon Territory, the region west of the Rocky Mountains between latitudes 42° and 54°, had been the subject of an agreement of dual sovereignty since 1818. The British authorities, alerted by the HBC, continued to keep a wary eye on American settlers travelling overland into the Oregon Territory, using the route pioneered by Meriwether Lewis, William Clark, and the Corps of Discovery in 1805. These newcomers changed the situation, tensions mounted, and Fort Victoria was one result. The government needed to assess the strategic implications of these developments: how could British interests be reinforced or defended if necessary? And, would the cost and effort of doing so be justified? They were not prepared to take just the company's word on this.

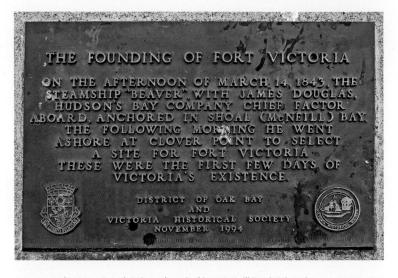

FIG 45 A plaque on Beach Drive, where it skirts McNeill Bay in Victoria, commemorates James Douglas's second visit to the place he selected for the new establishment. [Photo by author]

MILITARY MISSION OF INSPECTION

While the Royal Navy was to evaluate the question of harbours, the army would report on the ground aspects of the proposed new fort. The commander of the British military contingent in Upper Canada selected two young officers to make a covert, overland reconnaissance. He chose his nephew and aide-de-camp, infantry Lieutenant Henry Warre, and Lieutenant Marvin Vavasour of the Royal Engineers. They were to travel in the guise of young, sporting gentlemen out on a sightseeing jaunt.

The governor of the HBC, Sir George Simpson, accompanied the two as far as Fort Garry (now Winnipeg), and briefed them. Peter Skene Ogden, another HBC official, with six men, escorted them on a nine-week journey on horseback and by canoe as far as Fort Vancouver.

There they met James Douglas, who accompanied them to Port Discovery, where the British warship HMS *America* lay at anchor. Two Royal Marine officers serving aboard "just happened" to be visiting Fort Vancouver at the same time, and were due to rejoin their ship, so they, too, travelled with Douglas and the military men. Engaged on the same intelligence mission, the four officers got on extremely well with each other and, maintaining their cover, they compared insights.

Leaving Port Discovery in an open launch, Vavasour and Warre sailed across the stormy Strait of Juan de Fuca to Fort Victoria—then just two years old—where they spent the next few days before returning to Kingston. They submitted a joint report to the Governor General of Canada, Lord Metcalfe, who forwarded it to London. Later, Vavasour also submitted his own report to his direct military superior, Colonel Holloway, RE.

The joint report concerns the whole of the HBC's Columbia District, but does include some details related to Vancouver Island.

FIG 46 *The Birth of Victoria, British Columbia* painted by John D. Kelly in 1942, shows James Douglas supervising the early construction of the new fort in March 1843. The man by his side is probably Roderick Finlayson. [Courtesy of the Gallery of Canadian History]

The island is somewhat intersected by high mountain ranges, but the soil is said to be fertile, and well adapted for cultivation . . . [At Fort Victoria the HBC have established] a farm of several hundred acres, on which they raise wheat and potatoes, and a depot for provisions, supplies &c. for the different trading posts to the north.

They added a "Census of the Indian Tribes in the Oregon Territory, from Latitude 42° to Latitude 54° derived from the Trading Lists of the HBC, and from the best obtainable Information." [2]

The HBC's estimated total Indigenous population in the area was 86,947, but the soldiers considered this to be "rather under their numerical strength."

A year later, Vavasour's report to his colonel added more detail.

Fort Victoria is situated on the southern end of Vancouver Island in the small harbour of Cammusan, the entrance of which is rather intricate. The Fort is a square enclosure of 100 yards, surrounded by cedar pickets, having octagonal bastions, containing 6 six-pounder iron guns at the north east and south west angles. The buildings are made of squared timbers, 8 in number, forming 3 sides of an oblong. This Fort has lately been established; it is badly situated with regard to water and position, which latter has been chosen for its agricultural advantages only.

About 3 miles [5 kilometres] distant and nearly connected by a small inlet is the Squimal harbour, which is very commodious and accessible at all times, offering a much better position, and having also the advantage of a supply of water in the vicinity.

This is the best built of the Company's Forts; it requires loopholing and a platform or gallery to enable men to fire over the pickets; a ditch might be cut around it, but the rock appears on the surface in many places.

There is plenty of timber of every description on Vancouver's Island as also Limestone which could be transported to Nisqually, or other places in the territory, where it may be afterward deemed necessary to form permanent works, barracks, &c. [3]

Warre, a talented artist, left a delightful series of sketches and watercolours of scenes, characters, and incidents. Among them were several related to Vancouver Island, including one of the first pictures of Fort Victoria. To both of his reports, Vavasour attached well-executed plans of HBC forts and other places of strategic significance. These included copies of a map of Victoria harbour, the fort, and the Gorge from an original prepared by the HBC's Captain James Scarborough, who had run lines of soundings through the outer and inner harbours.

"NO FLY, NO FLY!" NAVAL DISMISSAL OF THE PLACE

That same year, 1845, the Honourable John Gordon, RN, captain of the 50-gun naval frigate *America*, summoned the senior HBC officer at Fort Victoria to come and meet with him at Port Discovery. Gordon, whose brother, the Earl of Aberdeen, was Foreign Secretary in London, carried confidential orders to evaluate the strategic and maritime factors linked to the location and the impending decision about the international border. All company officers were aware of the policy to offer every support and encouragement to the Royal Navy, as evident agents of the government. Chief Factor Roderick Finlayson—then in charge of the fort, having replaced the ailing Ross—took great pains to be accommodating to Captain Gordon, but all did not go as well as hoped, as was revealed in Finlayson's memoirs.

Proceeding to the vessel I went aboard accompanied by the officers sent for me, remained three days and during that time I gave the commander all the information I could about the country. The object of the vessel coming here was to obtain full information concerning the country & report to the English Government previous to the settlement of the boundary line . . .

Capt. Gordon crossed with me to Victoria in a launch, where he remained some time. We had some fine horses for the use of the Captain & his officers & we paid them every attention. We went out on one occasion to Cedar Hill [Mount Douglas] to shoot about the first of June. The country looked beautiful, carpeted as it was with beautiful wild flowers. [See Fig. 47] Capt. Gordon was a great deer stalker. We met a band of deer & had a chase after them on horseback. The deer ran for the thicket into which the horses with their riders could not penetrate and of course no deer were had.

The Captain felt very much disappointed & was anything but happy. I said to him that I was very sorry we had missed the deer &c, and also remarked how beautiful the country looked. He said in reply—'Finlayson, I would not give the most barren hills in the highlands of Scotland for all I see around me.' We went back to the fort. I was then a bachelor, had a cot slung in the bare walls which I handed over to the Captain, whilst I and the officers slept on the floor. In the morning we had a nice salmon for breakfast. The Captain seemed somewhat surprised & asked where the salmon was had. O! We have plenty of salmon, was the reply. Have you got any flies and rod, said the Captain. We have lines & bait was the answer & sometimes the Indians take them with the net &c. No fly, no fly, responded our guest. So after breakfast we went out to fish with the line, from a dingey. When we came back we had four fine salmon, but he thought it an awful manner in which to catch salmon.[4]

FIG 47   A seasonal carpet of blue camas lilies adorns the slopes of Beacon Hill. The sight that enchanted James Douglas exists today. [Photo by author]

After he had prematurely concluded his voyage, Gordon was court-martialed for disobeying orders by so doing, severely reprimanded, and "retired" from the service. Nonetheless, his trivial, dismissive opinion might have had some influence on his elder brother. Fortunately, it was countered by the more positive reports of the two Royal Marines, one of whom happened to be the son of Sir Robert Peel, the prime minister. They had formed their opinion during campfire discussions with their military counterparts and friends, Warre and Vavasour, and also, probably, Douglas.

The men appreciated that the region encompassing the Willamette and lower Columbia rivers, and with it Fort Vancouver, would be impossible to defend against the rising tide of American settlers and a sabre-rattling presidential candidate, James Polk. They felt it would be in Britain's best interest to accept a negotiated boundary that ran from west of the Rockies to the Pacific, along the 49th parallel, provided that the whole of Vancouver Island would lie to the British side of the line. For several years, Sir George Simpson had suspected this would be the outcome, hence his insistence on the new depot.

In light of the situation on the Pacific coast and the Americans' growing bellicosity—they had already taken Texas and were about to attack Mexico, including California—the British government instructed the Lords of the Admiralty to take counter measures. They issued orders to Rear Admiral Sir George Seymour, senior officer on the Pacific Station (renamed a few years earlier from the South American Station), to increase the British naval presence and visibility in the Juan de Fuca sector, and they dispatched additional ships to his squadron.

Captain John Gordon's unsatisfactory performance of his orders meant that the admiralty needed a second assessment. In addition, accurate hydrographic surveys of key harbours were required.

THE ROYAL NAVY RECONSIDERS

The first of the four Royal Navy ships to enter the Strait of Juan de Fuca in the eventful year of 1846 was the splendid 46-gun frigate, HMS *Fisgard*, ship-rigged on three masts, under the command of Captain John Duntze, RN. Aboard was a group of 14 midshipmen-in-training and their instructor, Robert Inskip. *Fisgard* anchored first in Port Discovery, then Nisqually, and teams in ship's boats visited Fort Victoria, Esquimalt, and Puget Sound. Duntze learned from the HBC men that at Victoria, although the company had successfully established a 50-head dairy herd, they had been unable to do so with sheep. "Sheep had at different times been imported from Puget Sound, but there was no keeping them on account of the wolves which infest the adjacent woods."

The next vessel of Admiral Seymour's squadron to round Cape Flattery was a hybrid: the paddlewheel sloop, first class, HMS *Cormorant*, under Commander George T. Gordon, RN. Launched and readied for sea at Sheerness in 1843, *Cormorant* was ketch-rigged on two masts and also powered by twin, coal-fired engines driving 26-foot diameter sidewheels, and capable of nine knots. Six pivoted guns provided the armament.

Gordon, soon to be promoted captain, and no relation to his recently disgraced namesake, was described by Seymour as "one of the best steam officers in her Majesty's Service." Gordon's orders were to stand by at Neah Bay and await the arrival of two more of the squadron. *Cormorant*'s general role would be to provide support as tug and tender to the squadron's sailing ships when wind and tide conditions were unfavourable. Gordon also carried orders to investigate any potential sources of steam coal in the region. An accompanying freighter had brought a cargo of fuel sufficient for the mission, but it was important to identify local sources for the future.

Two specialized hydrographic surveying vessels soon arrived, and were taken in tow across the strait, bound for Fort Victoria. They were HMS *Herald*, Captain Henry Kellett, RN, commanding, and as tender, HMS *Pandora*, under Lieutenant James Wood, RN. Both of these officers were highly experienced hydrographers. Their ships had sailed from Sheerness almost a year earlier. Just before departure, the crews had manned the yardarms to cheer and bid bon voyage to HMS *Erebus* and HMS *Terror*, leaving on Sir John Franklin's ill-fated expedition in search of the Northwest Passage.

Herald, a frigate of 680 tons converted into a surveying vessel, was 113 feet (34 metres) long and armed with 8 guns. *Pandora*, a speedier, 319-ton (289-tonne) packet-brig, also converted, was 90 feet (27 metres) long, of shallower draft, and carried 4 guns. The conversions for survey reduced the number of guns, to provide more space for charting tables and to carry additional ship's boats. Space was also made available aboard *Herald* to accommodate a civilian naturalist, Berthold Seemann, and his scientific impedimenta.

A few years earlier, Kellett had commanded the cutter *Starling* while accompanying Captain Sir Edward Belcher. Kellett had charted the Columbia River from its estuary as far as Fort Vancouver, and also had checked the longitude of Nootka. However, neither he nor anyone else aboard the three ships had ever visited Fort Victoria, or even entered the Strait of Juan de Fuca. The best chart available to them was Vancouver's, which incorporated the very hasty Spanish sketch of the southeastern sector of the island's coastline. Not surprisingly, they overshot Gonzales Point and anchored in today's Cordova Bay. A helpful local on the beach understood their mistake and guided them back around to Ogden Point at the entrance to the harbour.

The official *Narrative* of the voyage records the first impressions of a young officer aboard *Herald* as they landed and strolled to the settlement.

> The harbour of Victoria is little more than a winding and intricate creek . . . In walking from Ogden Point round to Fort Victoria a distance of little more than a mile we thought we had never seen a more beautiful country . . . It is a natural park; noble oaks and ferns are seen in the greatest luxuriance . . . One could hardly believe that this was not the work of art. We were astonished at all we saw. About 160 acres [65 hectares] are cultivated with oats, wheat, potatoes, turnips, carrots and other vegetables. Barely three years had elapsed since the settlement was made, yet all the necessities and most of the comforts of civilized life already exist in what was wilderness . . . Victoria may be the farm, but Esquimalt will be the trading post. At present, however, subsistence being the chief object, Victoria no doubt is the most advantageous site for a settlement.[5]

The naturalist Seemann had not joined the expedition until after it had left Juan de Fuca, but he accepted, reluctantly, the duty of compiling the *Narrative of the Voyage* from various sources, including the journals of midshipmen and junior officers. One of those diaries was also published, entitled *Euryalus; Tales of the Sea*. The anonymous author was probably the 18-year-old midshipman Bedford Pim (who would go on to a stellar career: the rank of rear admiral, a queen's counsel, member of parliament, and a knighthood).

> We passed up to Victoria, the Hudson Bay Settlement of Vancouver Island, and lay in a calm and peaceful bay, surrounded by a dense forest with shrubs and evergreens down to the water's edge . . . and in passing through the wood of Vancouver and the smaller islands, we could not but be struck at the lofty

and magnificent cedar, pine, oak, and cypress trees, and the blossoms of yellow laburnum scenting the air; every slope and undulation was a lawn and natural garden studded with the wild plum, gooseberry, currant, strawberry, and wild onion. Long grass and clover intermingled the soil, rich in the extreme, and would grow anything and everything.[6]

Kellett began his survey work after brief protocol meetings with the HBC's officer in charge, Chief Factor Roderick Finlayson, and the senior naval officer on station, Captain Duntze. Leaving Wood and *Pandora* to chart the harbour of Victoria and nearby Race Rocks, Kellett took *Herald* back across the strait to survey the harbours of the southern shore: Townsend, Discovery, and Dungeness. Prolonged dense fogs impeded his work all along that coast, but *Pandora*'s crew made good progress. In charting Esquimalt Harbour, they were assisted by Inskip, the instructor from *Fisgard*, and his class of midshipmen, who left their mark on the survey by naming several local features after their own captain and fellow officers, such as Duntze Head and Rodd Hill.

Wood continued charting the anchorages westward along the island's southern coast—Becher and Pedder bays and Port San Juan—before heading south for the winter. Kellett, frustrated by the fogs, returned to the northern shore, arriving at the anchorage to which *Cormorant* had towed them. This they charted and named Cordova Bay. They were probably unaware that the Spanish had earlier used the same name for what later became Esquimalt, but the place reminded them of the bond formed between George Vancouver and Bodega y Quadra. Seemann's source praised the gesture made by the former to honour his Spanish friend.

[B]ut it should not be forgotten that in this distant part of the world commanders belonging to rival nations joined in acts which tended permanently to benefit mankind; and it is to be hoped that the name given to this island will be maintained, and that Quadra and Vancouver may remind future ages when and how to agree.[7]

Sadly, neither the HBC nor the Lords of the Admiralty shared that sentiment; Quadra's name was soon dropped from British maps and charts of the island.

Kellett, fully intending to return the following season to make an accurate chart of Haro Strait, called in again at Victoria briefly before continuing, with some difficulty, to Sooke. This he dismissed as a potential naval harbour since it would provide no shelter from southwesterly gales. He gave the name of his clerk, John Whiffen, to the long spit guarding the entrance. Despite hindering fogs, *Herald*'s crew continued survey work for the season, concluding at Neah Bay before returning to pay respects to Finlayson.

On the 2nd September we bade adieu to Victoria and Mr. Finlayson, the company's officer in charge of the fort, to whom we were so much indebted for his uniform hospitality and kindness.[8]

Herald followed *Pandora* southward to spend the winter surveying the intricacies and anchorages of Central America's Pacific shoreline.

Since 1835, HBC officers at Forts Victoria and Vancouver had known of coal measures on the northeastern coast of Vancouver Island, the region they called Chislakus—a name very similar to Vancouver's Cheslakees. Although this was before *Cormorant*'s arrival, they were fully aware of the developing technology of coal-fired steamships, and had realized that mining and selling coal to such vessels would be another potential area of business for the company. McNeill in *Beaver*, with Finlayson aboard (see Fig. 44, page 100), verified the deposits in 1836, and at various opportunities had purchased coal from the locals to fire his ship's boilers. Duntze learned from Douglas of the discoveries, and knew of Gordon's orders to investigate such reports.

Accordingly, in late September 1846, *Cormorant* steamed north to assess the quality and quantity of the coal found in the vicinity of Beaver Harbour. The HBC's Captain James Sangster guided Gordon there. As they transitted the most constricted part of Discovery Passage, Gordon sounded the depth at 23 fathoms (42 metres) and named it "Sir George Seymour's Narrows" in honour of his admiral. At Beaver (or, as he called it, M'Neil's) Harbour they were able to explore.

> During our stay I proceeded on shore . . . We found a seam of coal just below high-water mark, which appeared to descend at an angle of about 30° towards the land . . . It is impossible to form any opinion of the extent of the field in any direction; but from the appearance of the country, I am of the opinion that it is very considerable . . . The natives are a fine race of men, and appear industrious and friendly, but much addicted to thieving.[9]

With Sangster's assistance, Gordon negotiated with the local Nahwitti people, who dug the coal using hatchets and wooden wedges, then ferried in their canoes the 62 tons of it that Gordon reported to be of "steaming quality, at least equal to the best Scotch coal." The coal he had collected worked out to cost, in the value of trade goods he exchanged, about four shillings a ton, significantly cheaper than the nearest alternative source, Antofagasta in Chile.

Gordon's report also pointed out the advantageous location of Beaver Harbour, which provided a good anchorage, easily accessible for ocean-going steamships entering by way of Cape Scott rather than Juan de Fuca. Duntze in *Fisgard* at Nisqually, upon receiving the report together with ten tons of the Vancouver Island coal, commented that this discovery would have a major impact. It would change the economics of a rail link "from Canada to the West Coast," which, in turn, would facilitate a trans-Pacific steamship link with China. The cost of freighting coal from Chile or Peru to Vancouver Island was prohibitive; the availability of a local source of fuel for both ships and trains would prove the key link in "an excellent and praiseworthy scheme."

While *Fisgard* was a wooden frigate of traditional design, it had been fitted with an innovative device: Sir William Snow Harris's conductors. Lightning strikes had long been a matter of great concern, causing severe damage to, and even loss of, ships of the Royal Navy and the merchant fleet. *Fisgard's* masts now carried strips of copper connected from their tips to the copper sheeting of the hull via the metal bolts holding it in place.

In a dramatic demonstration immediately following a gunnery practice, the new system proved its worth.

> [W]hen laying off the Nisqually River, a violent thunder-storm came on about six p.m. accompanied by heavy rain and approaching lightning. As I was speaking to one of the men about the connecting pieces of the lightning conductor, the electric fluid burst immediately over our heads, striking the main-mast, passing down the conductor within three yards of my body; the seaman, almost touching me, was temporarily blinded by the vivid light, and thrown down. The electric fluid passed clearly off to the sea, with an explosion beyond all description: it almost stunned everyone on board. Thanks to Mr. Snow Harris's Conductors, with which every mast is fitted, not the slightest damage was sustained.[10] [See Fig. 48, page 110]

FIG 48 HMS *Fisgard*, while at anchor off Nisqually in October 1846, experienced a direct lightning strike. Fortunately, the ship was fitted with an innovative system of copper conductors that protected it, and the crew, from harm. [*Illustrated London News*, February 27, 1847]

This confirmation of its effectiveness led to the Royal Navy's immediately adopting Snow's device for all its ships.

Meanwhile, in Washington, DC, British and American negotiators suddenly reached agreement in mid-June 1846 on the boundary between US and British territories west of the Rockies. It would follow the 49th parallel as far as the saltwater channel between Vancouver Island and the mainland. This meant that the whole of the island would be on the British side, while Puget Sound and the southern shore of the Strait of Juan de Fuca would be American—just as Simpson had predicted.

This important news was slow in reaching the people directly affected. Admiral Seymour learned the decision late in August in a note from a consular official in Mexico, and he relayed a summary to Duntze and to senior local HBC officials. He inferred that the settlement and the new border would lessen the need for a visible British naval presence in the theatre, and therefore he would no longer have to hazard his vessels negotiating the treacherous sandbanks of the Columbia bar. *Fisgard* sailed south in mid-October, but *Cormorant* stayed for another month before joining the admiral at San Blas.

Douglas lamented the fact that he had not been officially told about the decision, and viewed it as unfavourable to the company's interests. When the naval ships had all departed, he wrote: "It appears to us highly imprudent to leave the Country, without protection at this critical time when excitements are most likely to prevail."

Duntze delivered samples of the coal acquired by Gordon to Seymour, who forwarded them for further evaluation to the Admiralty in London, along with his opinion about the find.

The coal-mines, will add very much to the future value of the British possessions on the north-west coast, and contribute the means to extend their commerce, and to facilitate their defence . . . On these grounds it may, however, be worthy of consideration of Her Majesty's Government whether any steps may with propriety be taken to secure these mines for the public interests.[11]

PAUL KANE, THE WANDERING ARTIST

During the following year, 1847, no Pacific squadron ships came to the waters off Vancouver Island, but a most unusual visitor did arrive, by canoe from Nisqually. He was the artist-explorer Paul Kane.

Born in Ireland and coming to Toronto as a boy, Kane taught himself to paint, then honed his skills during a four-year study tour of European masterworks. In London, American artist George Catlin inspired him with his journeys throughout the Great Plains, painting Aboriginal peoples and scenes. Kane—then aged 35 and concerned about the impending loss of wilderness and native culture due to the westward expansion of Europeans—set out on a similar quest to create his own pictorial record.

At Lachine he impressed Sir George Simpson, who granted him the support of the HBC's extensive network of trading posts and brigade trails. Simpson provided a letter instructing company officers to provide the artist with free board and onward transportation. By late November 1846, Kane had reached Fort Vancouver, escorted on his travels by a succession of the company's fur brigades. After resting for a month, he met and drew portraits of tribal leaders in Oregon and the Willamette Valley.

Kane's technique was to make many swift sketches on site, then later work those sketches into more artistic renderings in his studio. He captured images of leaders and tribal people, exteriors and interiors of habitations, canoes, masks, and other ceremonial artifacts, and cultural structures such as gravesites, totems, and house posts. While the individual sketches were accurate, his subsequent composite scenes, and their captions, could be misleading, as he employed a measure of artistic license.

In early April, Kane visited the company farms of Cowlitz and Nisqually, where he boarded a canoe propelled by six stalwart paddlers—mixed-race and local—accompanied by James Sangster, the man who had piloted *Cormorant* to Beaver Harbour. The voyage of 90 stormy miles (167 kilometers) to Fort Victoria took over 30 hours of continuous paddling, helped by a scrap of a sail and cooperative tides.

Roderick Finlayson welcomed Kane to Victoria and provided him with a room in the fort for two months while he explored and sketched in the vicinity.

[The] communal lodges, sixty or seventy feet [18 or 21 metres] long . . . the largest buildings of any description that I have met with amongst Indians. [They were] well built, considering that the boards are split from the logs with bone wedges; but they succeeded in getting them out with great smoothness and regularity.

He found such buildings in different sites around the harbour. Confused, and confusingly, he called the people in them Clallams but they were mainly Songhees with some Klallams, intermarried with locals, who were visiting from across the Strait of Juan de Fuca. He also called their main village, across the harbour from the fort, Esquimalt. It was, in fact, the area now called Songhees in Victoria West. He reported that the residents claimed they could "turn out 500 warriors, armed chiefly with bows and arrows."

Kane did not venture inland, but commented on it.

The interior of the island has not been explored to any extent except by the Indians, who represent it as badly supplied with water in summer . . . The appearance of the interior, when seen from the coast, is rocky and mountainous, evidently volcanic; the trees are large, principally oak and pine. The timbers of a vessel of some magnitude were being got out.

He did travel with a Songhees leader he called Chea-clach on a trip by canoe to a large summer fishing encampment on the north side of Haro Strait, on San Juan Island. There he saw two medicine men, wearing masks carved and painted to portray fearsome, powerful denizens of the netherworld, ceremonially treating "one of the handsomest Indian girls I had ever seen. She was in a state of nudity." After an hour of chanting and vigorous drama, the younger shaman, having appeared to suck out the chunk of malign tissue from the girl's abdomen, "got up perfectly satisfied with himself, although the poor patient seemed to me anything but relieved by the violent treatment she had undergone."

Kane continued his canoe journey around the eastern end of Juan de Fuca by visiting Whidbey Island and Dungeness. There he heard about, and sketched, a recent raid by the Makah, who were looking to recover a whale they had hunted, killed, and lost. Then, crossing back to the island shore, he entered the basin at Sooke and watched people spearing a huge quantity of salmon that was ascending the river but impeded by an elaborate trap of stakes and woven willow stems. He also reported how, of an evening, they would snare many ducks by stringing a fine net between two posts 30 feet [nine metres] high and obscured by a smoky fire below. On the last leg of his circuit, a strong wind blew up.

> [It] increased to a perfect gale, and blowing against an ebb tide caused a heavy swell . . . The Indians on board now commenced one of their wild chants, which increased to a perfect

yell whenever a wave larger than the rest approached; this was accompanied by a blowing and spitting against the wind as if they were in angry contention with the evil spirit of the storm. It was altogether a scene of the most wild and intense excitement: the mountainous waves roaming round our little canoe as if to engulph us every moment, the wind howling over our heads and the yelling Indians, made it actually terrific. I was surprised at the dexterity with which they managed the canoe.

After this 11-hour ordeal, they arrived soaked, exhausted, and ravenous at the fort to a "cheerful fire and hearty dinner." Some days later, Kane had another notable experience.

> [I] visited the lodges of the Eus-a-nich Indians, who were on a visit. The chief was very rich and had eight wives with him. I made him understand . . . that I wished to take his likeness. This was, however, opposed so violently by his ladies, that I was glad to escape out of the reach of their tongues . . . A few days afterwards, I met the chief some distance from his camp, and alone, when he willingly consented to let me take his likeness upon my giving him a piece of tobacco.

During his stay at Fort Victoria, Kane chatted with company officers. He heard about "the characteristics of the different tribes inhabiting these regions," including a remarkable account of company communications.

> The gentlemen in charge of the various posts, have frequent occasion to send letters, sometimes for a considerable distance, when it is either inconvenient or impossible for them to fit out a canoe with their own men to carry it. In such cases the letter is given to an Indian, who carries it as far as suits his convenience and safety. He then sells the letter to another, who carries it until he finds

an opportunity of selling it to advantage; it is thus passed on and sold until it arrives at its destination, gradually increasing in value according to the distance, and the last possessor receiving the reward for its safe delivery. In this manner letters are frequently sent with perfect security, and with much greater rapidity than could be done otherwise.

Kane returned to Fort Vancouver in the canoe of an elderly leader from Nisqually, carefully carrying a package of mail from his hosts, and grateful for the chance to repay their hospitality. Over the next 18 months, he made his way back to Edmonton, Sault Ste. Marie, and Toronto. The account of his three-year, solo quest concludes: "the greatest hardship I had to endure, was the difficulty I found in trying to sleep in a civilized bed." [12]

Paul Kane's monumental body of artwork consisted of more than 700 sketches and 100 large-format oil paintings based on them. These, and his book *Wanderings of an Artist among the Indians of North America*, are of great significance, notwithstanding some confusion over names. They constitute one of the greatest records of First Nations' peoples and their diverse cultures at the crucial time of their early contact with European settlers, and before the fundamental changes this brought about—and just before the advent of photography (see Fig. 49, page 114).

CAPTAIN COURTENAY'S CONCERNS ABOUT COAL

During the year 1848, the new farming and trading establishment of Fort Victoria saw brief visits by two ships of the Pacific squadron, now under the command of Rear Admiral Phipps Hornby, who had replaced Seymour.

Lieutenant Commander James Wood in *Pandora* returned to continue his work of two years earlier, particularly the charting of Haro Strait. This season *Pandora* arrived alone; Kellett, in

Herald, had left on an urgent mission to search for signs of the ships of the Franklin Expedition in the Bering Sea, since no word had been received of their progress, fate, or whereabouts. After six weeks, Wood had charted as far as the northern tips of Sidney and San Juan islands.

Two weeks before *Pandora*'s arrival, a newly launched hybrid warship steamed into Esquimalt harbour to drop anchor. This was the 50-gun screw frigate *Constance*, Captain George Courtenay, RN, commanding. Copies of the chart prepared earlier by Wood, Inskip, and the midshipmen-trainees of *Fisgard* reassured Courtenay about the safety of the anchorage. Wood, in a courteous gesture to his senior colleague, added the name Constance Cove to the chart.

Courtenay was a traditional naval officer with, by then, 20 years' seniority as a captain. He was not a hydrographer, nor was he prepared to expose his splendid new command to the hazards of uncharted waters. He carried orders from Hornby concerning the coal deposits around Beaver Harbour, charging him with taking measures to secure these deposits for the British Crown. He hoped to meet with James Douglas to discuss this matter, but the latter was away on business in Hawaii, not due to return before Courtenay headed back south. This failure to meet, and a document drafted by Courtenay, annoyed Douglas, who thought it infringed on the HBC's exclusive right to trade in the region.

Historian Allan Pritchard has corrected earlier accounts, pointing out that Courtenay did not, in fact, go to Beaver Harbour. He merely drafted a proclamation claiming the area for the Crown, which he gave to Finlayson, requesting that it be posted at Beaver Harbour. News of the coal had reached other ears, and a private steamship operator was already negotiating to purchase fuel from the HBC. The Lords of the Admiralty were worried that rascally, independent American speculators

FIG 49 Itinerant artist Paul Kane compiled *The Return of a War Party* from a number of sketches he made during his visit to the region during 1847. He depicts two Makah canoes improbably heading west in Victoria's Inner Harbour. [With permission of the Royal Ontario Museum, © ROM, Toronto]

might attempt to stake their claims, notwithstanding the newly agreed-on boundary. Douglas, despite his many pleadings for a British naval presence in the area, took exception to Courtenay's request. He felt that this was a company matter and that he had it well in hand and under control.

Leaving *Constance* at anchor, Courtenay and his ship's master made a three-day sortie in the launch into Haro Strait. The potentially fatal combination of swift and unpredictable tides, fog, rocky shores, and unreliable charts soon deterred them. Pronouncing the passage "perfectly unfit for anything but steam vessels," Courtenay returned to the safety and comfort of Esquimalt. He went nowhere near the river and community that were later given his name.

He quizzed Finlayson about the geography and peoples of Vancouver Island, quickly deducing that the company men knew precious little of the interior or the eastern coastline and harbours, other than what was shown on Vancouver's chart. Had he been able to talk with Captain McNeill, he would have learned a great deal more.

FIG 50   James Douglas entrusted the stalwart and personable Joseph McKay with several missions of exploration and negotiation with the Indigenous peoples of Vancouver Island. [Courtesy of the Royal BC Museum and Archives, Victoria]

CHAPTER EIGHT

THE NEW COLONY IS PROCLAIMED AND EXPLORATION BEGINS

THE 1846 TREATY THAT ESTABLISHED the new boundary between British territories and those of the United States also affected the relationship between the Hudson's Bay Company and the British government. The company's grant from the Crown, of exclusive trading rights west of the Rocky Mountains, was due to expire in a few years, so the governors asked about the government's intentions. Of particular concern was the status of the company's settlement at Fort Victoria and its surrounding area.

After a few years of discussion, debate with a vocal opposition, and negotiation, the British government came to a decision on January 13, 1849. It issued a Charter of Grant to the HBC for the whole of the island for a period of ten years, and proclaimed that it was now the Crown Colony of Vancouver Island. The substance of the grant was that the company would stimulate, foster, and administer settlement. In effect, the government was "outsourcing" colonization.

The company had to carry out this plan according to a restrictive set of rules known as the Wakefield System. It was not to profit from the endeavour, but reinvest the bulk of all revenue from sales of real estate and mining rights back into the colony. What was more, the company was to be charged an annual "rent" of seven shillings for the privilege. The Colonial Office appointed an outside governor, Richard Blanshard, but until he could arrive, Chief Factor James Douglas acted as governor. This move created inevitable conflict between the two men.

The hapless Blanshard—young, inexperienced, and denied the essential support of the company—was doomed to failure, and he left after just one year. Douglas, reinstated as governor, now found himself having to serve two masters: the Crown and the company. This situation destabilized the young colony during its formative years.

Initially, the company was concerned only with the southeastern tip of the island, as a trading and agricultural base. However, responsibility for the entire island, coupled with the discovery of coal resources up-island, stimulated its interest further afield. Senior company men recognized that they had very little information about the greater part of the island: its topography, exploitable resources, and particularly its Indigenous peoples. They planned to rectify this lack of knowledge by mounting a campaign of systematic exploration and on June 30, 1849, George Simpson laid out the plan to his superiors.

> By my dispatch to [Douglas] of this date, you will observe that I have directed that the exploring party should be confined to the interior country, traversing it in every direction and noting accurately its features leaving the marine survey (except at the coal mines) to be performed by the "steam vessel and sloop of war" to be forwarded by the Admiralty, under an officer of scientific attainments, for the purpose of general survey and careful examination.[1]

At the time, negotiations were under way for the Royal Navy to deploy another specialized hydrographic survey team that would properly chart the coast and surrounding waters of the island and the nearby mainland. Regarding the land survey project, HBC Governor Sir John Pelly met with recently retired cavalry officer Walter Colquhoun Grant about his becoming the colony's first settler and the official surveyor. Only in his mid-20s, with the rank of captain in a prestigious regiment, Grant had recently lost his personal fortune and been obliged to sell his commission. This new financial reality had inspired his interest in a fresh—and civilian—direction for his life.

Little of the correspondence between Grant and Pelly has survived, but it would seem that Grant, a very persuasive fellow, convinced Sir John that he was well qualified for the position of surveyor. However, the type of survey Grant proposed differed from what was urgently needed by the company. His plan was for an exploratory reconnaissance, not detailed topographic mapping, nor the preparation of cadastral and property-subdivision documents required for managing an influx of settlers.

Grant's proposal, in principle, was reasonable: to gain an overview of the magnitude of the task of surveying Vancouver Island, prior to starting on its detailed, large-scale mapping, or establishing legal title to individual parcels of land. He seems to have been oblivious to the enormity of what he was proposing in terms of manpower, logistics, time, expense, and exposure to potential hazards.

Pelly rejected Grant's idea, not from its impracticability or cost, but from the company's pressing need to secure title to the lands that they had already cleared and were farming. Such technical work was beyond Grant's experience. Nonetheless, he appeared to be exactly the class of settler envisioned by Wakefield, so, despite Grant's evident lack of money, Pelly accepted him, forestalling Simpson and Douglas's plan to nominate a candidate from within the company.

Grant reached Victoria at the end of May 1849. He arrived penniless and already in debt to the company, burdened by the need to find and clear land, and build his own house. As well, he had to fulfill the company's urgent requirement to secure legal title to their own properties—termed the Fur Trade reserve—and those set aside for churches, schools, and the government. The HBC properties with their official reserves occupied 20 square miles (52 square kilometers), the major part of the area surrounding the fort. Grant, and any other settlers, had to locate themselves some distance outside the community and its associated facilities. Hoping to install a water-powered sawmill, Grant chose to settle in Sooke, whose only connection with the fort was by native canoe.

His situation proved totally impossible. His first priority, as Douglas acknowledged, was getting his own house built.

> I fear that Captain Grant has undertaken a duty, which the pressing nature of his own affairs, will not allow him time to attend to;

he has not been able as yet to make any surveys nor can he with prudence absent himself from his establishment until it is in more advanced state.

He went on to request that a full-time surveyor be brought on staff, recommending the man who had worked with him on the initial survey for the 1842 Ground Plan, Adolphus Lee Lewes.

Grant resigned in March 1850 after less than ten months in the colony, having done little surveying and no exploration, but he had gathered geographical notes about the island, and retained an interest in acquiring more. He had struck up a friendship with a company clerk, Joseph McKay, who helped with his brave attempts at mapping and, during their many years of correspondence, kept him informed of explorations and discoveries as they unfolded. Grant left for the goldfields of California, where he did well. He later returned to the island for a short while before rejoining his regimen and serving with honour in India, where he died of a fever.

TRAVERSING THE ISLAND IS BEGUN

The seed of Grant's original idea for a general exploration of the interior did take root, to appear later, unacknowledged, in Simpson's instruction to "traverse the island in every direction." Employees of the company were to carry out any such explorations.

These expeditions had several objectives: to locate and contact native tribes scattered throughout the island, in order to build trading links with them; to identify areas of potentially good agricultural land appropriate for settlement; and to discover deposits of minerals such as coal, limestone, gold, copper, and iron ore, and stands of valuable timber with access to water (for transporting logs to a sawmill). Most of the early traverses of the island employed local guides, and took advantage of the existing trading trails made and used by the mainly coastal local people, the so-called "oolichan" or "grease" trails.

The first recorded traverse of the island made by a European was not a general exploratory trip, but one specifically to determine the extent of a coalfield. Veteran company man John Work—by then a member of the triumvirate Board of Management for the HBC's Columbia District and in charge of the northern posts of Forts Stikine and Simpson—was supervising the construction of the new Fort Rupert near Beaver Harbour. This was to be the base from which the coal deposits would be exploited. During this visit, Work wanted to verify the extent of this potentially very significant new business opportunity for the company. His first-hand report on the findings no longer exists, but in early September 1849, Douglas summarized them in a letter to Archibald Barclay, the company secretary in London.

Chief Factor Work reports that the Coal Beds are fully as extensive as were supposed, and that he traced their course from McNeill's to Beaver Harbour, a distance of about 20 miles [32 kilometres]. He also traced them in a westerly direction about 12 miles [19 kilometres] across the island to the head of the Inlet of Quatsenah, where they again crop to the surface. This Inlet Communicates with the spacious harbour of Quatsenah, a fine Port for Shipping on the west coast of the Island to which point, it may, hereafter be found expedient to transfer the mining operations, as it is infinitely, more accessible to sailing Vessels, than Beaver Harbour, whose approach through the Strait of Galiano and Valdez [Goletas Channel] is, at some seasons, of the year difficult and tedious.[2]

It seems probable that Work, guided by the local Nahwitti people, followed a traditional oolichan trail leading to what is now Coal Harbour. It is intriguing that he and Douglas understood that the place was an arm of the complex and extensive

Quatsino Sound, which led out to the Pacific. The latest chart at that time was the recently published *Vancouver Island and the Gulf of Georgia*, incorporating Kellett's and Wood's work as well as the coaling trip of *Cormorant* two years earlier. The chart shows "Coal Measures" in the Beaver Harbour area, but no connection to an unnamed, short entrance at the correct location for Quatsino Sound. Apparently, Work had learned from his Nahwitti guides how much further the inlet extended.

The following year, John Muir retraced Work's overland route as "oversman," or leader, of a small team of Scottish coal miners recruited by the company to apply modern mining techniques to the Nahwitti coal measures. He did so to provide an expert opinion on the practicality of operating a mine, and reported that while he felt the area was rich in coal, he found no workable seams on the surface, so an expensive program of exploratory drilling would be needed.

The next mining expert deployed, Boyd Gilmour, did drill, but without success. He endorsed Muir's opinion. By this time, however, new and far more promising deposits had been found near Wentuhuysen Inlet (Nanaimo Harbour), so the company abandoned further efforts to develop the Nahwitti sector, although coal continued to be shipped from Fort Rupert for a few more years.

The man largely instrumental in identifying the new coal prospect was a young clerk in the HBC service, Joseph William McKay. The son and grandson of mixed-race fur traders, he had attended the Red River Academy in Fort Garry before joining the company at age 15. Posted to Fort Victoria in 1846, five years later he was second-in-command at the fort and a vigorous all-rounder; "a very active young fellow," wrote Dr. Helmcken, "who knew everything and everybody" (see Fig. 50, page 116). Douglas valued and used McKay's "uncommon degree of tact and address, in managing Indians" to help negotiate the series of

land deals with Indigenous peoples of the area surrounding the new establishment. These became known as the Fort Victoria, or Douglas, Treaties.

In late April 1850, a canoe arrived in Victoria from Wentuhuysen, filled with good quality coal brought by an elderly member of the Snuneymuxw tribe—the people whose name would be transliterated as Nanaimo. McKay's subsequent report of the next action has not survived, but was recounted 28 years later, in his "Recollections of a Chief Trader."

> I fitted out a prospecting party at once and about the first of May we landed near the place where the town of Nanaimo is built now. For several days we looked around and on the 8th of May I located the Douglass vein, which is still being worked [1878] at the place from which the old Indian had taken his specimen.
>
> On our return to Victoria I made a favourable and very circumstantial report on our discovery, but owing to the press of other business on hand the mine was not actually opened until August 1852.[3]

In the interim, McKay may have made a second exploratory trip to the Wentuhuysen deposits. By June 1852, Douglas was able to communicate important news to his superiors.

> A bed of surface coal of considerable depth was discovered by Mr. Joseph McKay of the Company's service at Point Gabiola [*sic*] [the Flat Top Islands], on the east coast of Vancouver's Island nearly opposite the mouth of Fraser's River. Mr. McKay who was sent with a small party to examine that part of the Island, describes the coast as abounding in Sandstone, and he observed in several places seams of Coal varying from 8 to 12 inches [20 to 30 centimetres] in depth; cropping out from the cliffs; but the principal bed is at Point Gabiola, where the seam measures

thirty seven inches [94 centimetres] in thickness; if so it will be immensely valuable, and I will take the earliest opportunity of having it carefully examined and secured for the Company.[4]

Douglas was as good as his word, and immediately set in motion a flurry of activity related to securing and developing the HBC's interest over this resource, which included making his own high-profile visit to the site.

RICHARD BLANSHARD ARRIVES, TRIES, AND ALSO QUITS

A few weeks before Walter Colquhoun Grant's ignominious departure, another ill-fated gentleman arrived from England. Richard Blanshard landed, and read aloud his document of appointment as Her Britannic Majesty's Governor of the Colony of Vancouver Island. Douglas pointed out to him the site allocated for the governor's residence, which had been cleared but construction barely begun. Most discourteously, Douglas did not offer the new arrival the hospitality of the company fort, so the governor was obliged to remain aboard HMS *Driver*—which had brought him to Victoria—as it visited forts Nisqually and Rupert.

During Blanshard's visit to the latter, a crisis was brewing: a clash of wills between the newly arrived contingent of coal miners and the autocratic rule of the company, embodied at that time by the fiery captain, William McNeill. The legally trained new governor listened sympathetically to the miners' case, which antagonized Douglas. The "Nahwitti affair" festered and involved the local people, resulting in a punitive visit by the gunboat *Daedalus* and the destruction of a village, for which the Colonial Office blamed Blanshard.

The government had placed him in an untenable position: no salary, no staff, no budget or means of generating revenue. He was totally reliant on the company store for food and supplies—at exorbitant rates—and on occasional visits by ships of the Royal Navy for enforcement of his authority and civil law. Not surprisingly, he formally requested his recall just eight months after his arrival. He departed in September 1851, *persona non grata* to Douglas and out of favour with the Colonial Office. They even made him pay for his passage home from San Francisco. Douglas was appointed governor.

COMPANY EXPLORERS SEEK LAND FOR FARMERS

Even while Blanshard was nominally the head of the colony, Douglas was the senior company man, responsible for the contractual requirement to stimulate and foster settlement. It was already evident that the types of settler targeted under the xenophobic and class-conscious Wakefield theory—yeomen farmers or men of substance, supported by their entourages of paid craftsmen and workers—were not being attracted to the island. The system was proving counterproductive.

While the Wakefield rule tied Douglas's hands in the choice of settlers, he could solve locally the lack of identified potential farmland and security of tenure. His team would have to develop a program of exploration and mapping, and to create a formal system of legal cadaster, so he needed competent surveyors. Grant was proving unsatisfactory, but Douglas did have men on staff fully capable of exploring for land that could be settled. The first who came to mind was Joseph McKay, whom Douglas had described as "an active and faithful servant."

Douglas had previously advised his superiors that early optimism about the farming capacity of the southeastern tip of the island had proved unjustified. While the existing allotment was ample for the company's original purpose, more was needed for the colony's settlers.

I am extremely sorry that I cannot make a very favourable report as to the capabilities of this part of the island for the immediate support of an agriculture population ... The great want, which will be felt hereafter is the absence of cultivable lands of sufficient extent, for a large agricultural population ...

The Cowetchen Valley is reported by the Indians to be much superior to this part of Vancouver's Island, in respect to the extent of cultivable land, and to the absence of hills and rocky ridges. It is traversed by a considerable river of the same name which discharges into the 'Canal de Ario' [Haro Strait] about 30 miles [48 kilometres] north of this place. This river is navigable for canoes, to its termination in a lake of some magnitude which extends to within 8 miles [13 kilometres] of Nitinat a spacious harbour and Inlet on the west side of the Island, Latitude 48°55' North ... The natives who having never been brought under our influence, have lost nothing of their naturally savage character.[5]

Douglas confused Nitinat—which is a river and long lake, but has no harbour—with the adjacent "spacious harbour and Inlet" of Barkley Sound.

In the spring of 1851, Douglas sent a report to Barclay.

On the 3rd, Inst. I sent Mr. Joseph McKay Clerk, and Thomas Cluamatany Interpreter under the protection of 'Hosua' chief of the 'Cowetchin' Tribe on a journey of exploration to the Cowetchin River ... having for the general objects to report on the character of the country and accessibility of the Coast to shipping: and specially to examine a bed of coal and a 'salt lake' said to be known to the 'Cowetchin' Indians, who state that a large quantity of salt is annually formed on its banks, through the natural evaporation of its water. I hope the Indian statement may turn out to be correct, in respect to the discovery of salt in particular, which will be of incalculable advantage to the country as a means of bringing the valuable fisheries of Vancouver's Island into full play.

McKay's interpreter was a most intriguing character. Thomas Omtamny seems to have been his name, but it enjoyed a wide variety of spellings; he is now generally known as "Tomo Antoine" and will be referred to here as Antoine. He participated in most of the major explorations of the island, up to and including the Vancouver Island Exploring Expedition of 1864. Graham Brazier has researched the many legends that have sprouted and spread about this fellow. One of the main sources of these was a series of detailed but fanciful yarns published in the *Ladysmith Chronicle* in 1963, penned by a W.H. Olsen, but with no reference to his informants (see Fig. 51, page 123).

Briefly, Antoine is believed to be the son of a high-status Chinook woman and a French-Iroquois mixed-race man, a renowned "voyageur" in the North West Company's employ who had paddled west with the fur brigades. Born at Fort Astoria on the Columbia River shortly after his father had been killed, Antoine spent his early years among the mixed-race children of the fort, and, for half of each year, with his mother's people.

He had a sharp brain and an aptitude for languages, as well as great physical strength. Unschooled, but exposed to many tongues from his earliest days, he learned to speak Joual (French Canadian patois), English, Chinook and Chinook Jargon, and several Indian dialects. He came to Fort Victoria in 1843 as an interpreter, after having served at Fort Langley, during which time he lost his right arm—Brazier suspects—in an accident during a ceremonial firing of one of *Beaver*'s cannons.

At Fort Victoria, Antoine mingled with several groups from up-island tribes who, attracted by the opportunities for trade and casual labour near the fort, set up camp among the Songhees. Having acquired their languages, he went to investigate their home territories of Chemainus and Cowichan. Sometimes referred to in company correspondence simply as "the Iroquois," Antoine respected and was devoted to Douglas, who in turn recognized his abilities and loyalty. His home was a cottage close by Douglas's residence. Antoine's extraordinary strength seems to have overcome his lack of an arm, and he became adept at handing a paddle, axe, or even musket with just his left hand.

McKay's report, sent shortly after he arrived in the Cowichan region, has not survived, but Douglas's letter continued with a summary of the exploratory visit.

> I received a note, by Indians yesterday, from Mr. McKay, dated the 5th inst. informing of the welfare of his party, and that the Natives were civil and obliging. He had just entered the Cowetchin River, which he discribes [sic] as a stream of some magnitude . . . The Valley of the River varies from two to three miles in breadth, beyond which the Country, on both sides, rises by a succession of acclivities and intervening table lands to a range of hills about ten miles distant. He has discovered two fresh water lakes, surrounded by 'beautiful Prairies'. One of these lakes is four miles long by about two miles broad. He was then about to start for the 'Salt Lake' continuing at the same time the examination of the country, the result of which I will communicate on his return.[6]

FIG 51 The one-armed, polyglot, mixed-race hunter and expedition interpreter, Thomas Omtamny, was known variously as "Antoine," "Tomo," or "the Iroquois." He was fiercely loyal to Douglas, but others found him hard to handle. No photograph of him is known. [Courtesy of the Chemainus Chamber of Commerce, *Water Over the Wheel*, page 13]

Douglas does not seem to have reported the subsequent events of McKay and Antoine's Cowichan expedition to his superiors.

HAMILTON MOFFATT MAKES THE FIRST MAJOR TRAVERSE OF THE ISLAND

During his visit to the village of Cheslakees at the mouth of the Nimpkish River in 1792, George Vancouver noted signs that a trading link existed with Maquinna, leader of the Mowachaht people of Nootka Sound (see Fig. 52, page 124). Maquinna subsequently sketched a map for Peter Puget to show the route a party of his traders would be taking to reach the mainland, via Cheslakees's village. In 1852 George Blenkinsop, senior trader

FIG 52 *Cheslakees' Reception*—John Horton's depiction of how, in July 1792, George Vancouver in *Discovery* anchored off a village with a "picturesque appearance" at the mouth of the Nimpkish River. In the afternoon he went ashore to visit the headman, who awaited him, while the rest of the villagers stayed close to their houses.

at Fort Rupert, sent his young subordinate, Hamilton Moffatt, to investigate this trail.

Moffatt, a nephew of the famous Arctic explorer Dr. John Rae, had joined the company and arrived at Fort Victoria in late March 1850 (see Fig. 53, page 126). Despite his uncle's reputation within the company, he did not impress Douglas, who, after watching him for only a few months, reported: "Moffatt has talent, but is lazy, conceited, careless and indifferent, and has yet to learn how to do things well." To help improve his attitude and work ethic, Douglas posted him to Fort Rupert to work under the guidance of the disciplinarian McNeill. While McNeill was temporarily absent, leaving Blenkinsop in charge of the fort, Moffatt received his orders to go exploring. Moffatt, some seven years after the event, sent a copy of his journal, with "a chart, unfinished, but pretty correct" to the colonial surveyor, Joseph Despard Pemberton. Pemberton published Moffatt's report of the first experience of exploring the wilderness of Vancouver Island's interior, and the first major traverse of the island by a European.

Thursday, July 1st 1852. About 10 a.m. left the Fort for the Nimpkish village, en route to the Nootka tribe . . . I procured guides and got everything in readiness for an early start in the morning.

Friday, 2nd. Left the village at daybreak in a canoe with six Indians; at 9 a.m. reached the Nimpkish ['Namgis] fishing village, on the borders of the T'sllelth Lake [now Nimpkish Lake] . . . The shores on either side at this end rise perpendicular from the water's edge to the height of some 1500 or 1600 feet [460 to 490 metres], and from 4000 to 5000 feet [1,220 to 1,520 metres] a little inland, and in many places capped with snow; the width of the lake at the entrance is about half a mile, gradually widening to one and a half miles; I endeavoured to ascertain the depth with a forty fathom line, but did not succeed. Our course through the

lake was about south-east, and the length I have since ascertained to be fully twenty-five miles [40 kilometres] . . .

Saturday 3rd. After passing a most unpleasant night, on account of the rain which poured down in torrents the whole time and until 10 a.m., we again embarked in our frail craft for the ascent of the River Oakseey [Nimpkish River] . . . The whole of this day was spent in working up the rapids, of which the river is one continuation; encamped in the evening at Waakash, the half way house to the second lake, a distance of twelve miles [19 kilometres]. The banks of the river are rather low, and abounding in splendid red pine and maple of all sizes, but not the slightest vestige of cleared land to be seen. The country a short distance inland from the river is very high.

Sunday 4th. Left encampment about 4 a.m. for another of the Nimpkish fishing villages . . . The river at this place branches off in two directions . . . [We] started for the Lake Kanus [Woss Lake] distant about six miles. The Indians having told me that this part of the river was very shallow, and that the country through which we had to pass to reach the lake pretty open, I started on foot with a portion of my crew, and arrived at the lake after a very pleasant walk; the country through which I passed was clear, with occasional belts of wood and brush, and abounding in partridges, of which I shot a good many. I also noticed a pond of cold spring water, of great depth without an outlet, similar to what at home are called blow-wells.

During my walk I was informed of a tribe of Indians living inland, having no canoes or connection with sea coast whatsoever. I have since learned that these people sometimes descend some of the rivers for the purpose of trade with the Indians south of Nootka . . . the name of the tribe is Säa Käalituck; they number about fifty or sixty men, and were only discovered a few years back, by one of the Nimpkish chiefs while on a trapping expedition . . . I have not the least doubt that a road might with little difficulty be discovered from here to Victoria, through the very centre of the island.

After passing through this lake, which is probably ten miles [16 kilometres] long, we encamped at the base of a snow-capped mountain, two very fine cascades falling several hundred feet from its summit; and the streams which they form abound in trout of excellent quality and great size, numbers of which we caught.

Monday 5th. Early this morning I started, accompanied by an Indian, for the summit of this mountain [Rugged Mountain], [See Fig. 54] which I named Ben Lomond, but did not succeed in reaching any further than the second tier of snow, on account of the ascent being so steep; so having been disappointed with my walk, I returned to the camp at 9 a.m., and set out for the walk across the portage (which was a succession of mountain defiles), to the head waters of the Nootka River [Tahsis River].

The first ascent of Rugged Mountain, 6,152 feet (1,875 metres) high, was not achieved until 1959, more than a century later, and then only by a team of three expert and properly equipped mountaineers, led by a man who had honed his skills in the Dolomites and Alps. Young Moffatt had been rather naïve and optimistic that morning. His journal continued:

The [Tahsis] river, during its course of three or four miles from its source, disappears three different times . . . [we] arrived in Nootka Sound at 7 p.m., after passing over sixteen or eighteen miles [26 or 29 kilometres]. I have not however, reached my destination for the night yet, the Indians wishing to camp further down the sound, on account of some superstitious fear of ghosts. Stopped for a short time at the fishing village, where I saw the wheel of a ship. The Indian houses here [probably Maquinna's winter village of Tahsis] are very large, in fact more so than those of the Indians near Fort Rupert.

FIG 53 (TOP)   Hamilton Moffatt, a less-than-impressive nephew of a renowned Arctic explorer, made one of the earliest recorded crossings of the island. [Courtesy of the Royal BC Museum and Archives, Victoria]

FIG 54 (BOTTOM)   Woss Lake, looking south toward Rugged Mountain. Moffatt called the peak "Ben Lomond," and attempted to climb it during his traverse of the island in July 1852. [Courtesy of Panoramio gymg1939]

Tuesday, 6th. Having passed a very comfortable night under cover of a large quantity of salmon frames, we started early for the Nootka village in Friendly Cove, passing through a long inlet [Tahsis], that runs about south-east, surrounded by lofty mountains covered to the very top with timber, but of stunted growth. We arrived at our destination at 4 p.m., having occupied five days on our journey from the Nimpkish village.

Upon entering Friendly Cove, we were received by a discharge of cannon from the chief's house; until we were about to land scarcely an Indian was to be seen, but at a given signal the whole tribe darted from their houses and commenced a grand dance in honour of the arrival of a white man to visit them, after which a sea otter was presented to me by the chief, and we landed amid the welcome shouts of the Nootkas. In the evening a grand fancy dress ball was given, and a large quantity of blankets and other property distributed.

Wednesday 7th. Nothing strange or new; time mostly spent in feasting and smoking in the houses of different chiefs, all of whom seemed to be on the highest terms of friendship.[7]

Moffat provided no details of his return journey, either in the journal or in the accompanying Remarks, which were probably added later. In these, he enthused about the timber available in the interior and how it might be brought to the coast by river. He also offered some praise for the abundance of fine salmon and halibut on the coast. His map, copied by Pemberton, was not very accurate—as might be expected from a man of his limited exploration or survey experience—but it added some important detail to the knowledge of the interior. However, he was not sent to explore the island again (see Fig. 55).

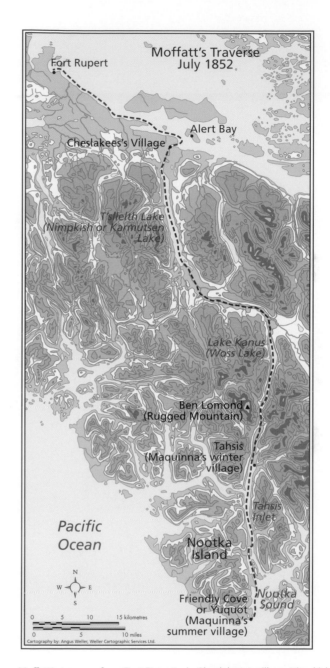

FIG 55   Moffatt's traverse from Fort Rupert, via Cheslakees's village, Nimpkish, and Woss lakes to Tahsis and Yuquot (Friendly Cove). This was the first recorded crossing of the island using an established oolichan trail. [Map by Angus Weller]

FIG 56 *Homeward*, Gordon Miller's dramatic painting of a 64-foot Haida canoe riding a wave off Haida Gwaii. That canoe is on display at the American Museum of Natural History in Washington, DC. The green creature at the prow represents *Wasgo*, the mythical sea wolf.

CHAPTER NINE

EXPLORATIONS NORTH TO COMOX AND ACROSS TO ALBERNI

"A FEELING OF EXULTATION:" DOUGLAS'S CANOE JOURNEY
James Douglas welcomed Joseph McKay's encouraging report of May 1850 on the prospects for coal at Wentuhuysen (today's Nanaimo), but was unable to follow it up for two years. As soon as he could, he organized a personal visit to inspect the reported outcroppings.

Rather than make the journey in the paddlewheeler *Beaver*, the schooner *Cadboro*, or any other vessel of the company's fleet, he opted to travel in two northern canoes, renowned for their seaworthiness and speed, and probably obtained from the Haida (see Fig. 56, page 128). He paddled through Arro Canal (later known as Haro Strait and Satellite and Stuart channels) along what was known by then to be the true coastline of Vancouver Island. He arranged for *Cadboro* to sail the more usual course—east of the archipelago, into the open Strait of Georgia—and meet them at Wentuhuysen.

Accompanying him were Joseph Pemberton, his chief surveyor; Richard Golledge, an apprentice clerk, recently appointed Douglas's personal secretary; and John Muir, the veteran coal-mining expert, now released from his original contract but brought along as a consultant. Completing the expedition was a six-man escort—probably mixed-race employees, and almost certainly including Tomo Antoine, Douglas's loyal and most trusted aide—and "a few Indians."

Pemberton was one year into his first three-year contract, and had focused on two tasks—recording the land holdings of the Hudson's Bay and the Puget's Sound Agricultural companies, and mapping the "South-Eastern Districts." These activities involved only the area that surrounded the fort and the growing village of Victoria, from Sooke to the Saanich Peninsula. During that year, he had established an excellent working relationship with Douglas, sharing the obligation of simultaneously serving two masters—the company and the Crown (see Fig. 57, page 130).

As the party passed the estuaries of the Cowichan and Chemainus rivers, they landed to meet and parlay with the local peoples. They met with success at the former, but found no one at home at Chemainus. Apparently without identifying the secondary chain of Thetis, De Courcy, and Mudge islands, and after transiting perilous Dodd Narrows, they arrived at the northern tip of yet-unnamed Gabriola Island where *Cadboro* awaited them. They met the Snunéymuxw people, who directed them to the outcrops of coal they had previously shown McKay. The locals dug and loaded 50 tons [45 tonnes] of coal aboard *Cadboro* in a single day, receiving trade goods valued at £11 in payment. Afterward, the canoe party returned by their same route to Victoria.

Douglas immediately reported his findings to Archibald Barclay, his corporate boss in London, in his usual reserved and formal style, but with emotion bubbling under the surface.

> This discovery has afforded me more satisfaction than I can express and I trust the Company will derive advantages from it equal to the important influence it must necessarily exercise on the fortunes of the Colony.[1]

As well as sending Pemberton back to Wentuhuysen for mapping, Douglas also sent the reliable McKay to take charge of establishing a new fort and mining settlement there. His instructions were to make it clear to any arriving ships that this was now the property of the company, but they were welcome to buy coal. The Muir team of miners would also be there, and McKay was under orders to deal only with John Muir on matters related to their activities.

Douglas deliberated for over a week following his return before sending a report to his other set of superiors, the Colonial Office. During that time, he recognized that the discovery of a rich source of fuel provided him with an opportunity to press his case with the government. Several times in the recent past he had pleaded for the continuous presence of Royal Navy gunboats to deter unwanted American incursions into this remote

FIG 57 Joseph Despard Pemberton, first surveyor general for the colony of Vancouver Island; he was an avid horseman, a highly accomplished theoretical and practical surveyor, a farmer, and an astute businessman and politician. [Courtesy of the Royal BC Museum and Archives, Victoria]

British outpost. As the Royal Navy converted from sail to steam power, it would need coal, and he could use this to reinforce his requests for more tangible, imperial support for his nascent and vulnerable colony.

He seized on Pemberton's new and more accurate survey of the island's true coastline (see Fig. 58), while downplaying his own prior knowledge of the shortcomings of John Arrowsmith's latest maps. He emphasized that the discrepancies showed the urgent need for proper hydrographic charting of this now strategically important region. Douglas included Pemberton's map of their "discoveries" with his report to Sir John Pakington, the colonial secretary.

I have carried out the project which I have long entertained, of a canoe expedition through the Canal de Arro, and along the east coast of Vancouver's Island, for the purpose of examining the country and communicating with the native Tribes, who inhabit that part of the Colony . . .

In our passage through the Canal de Arro, we were struck with the extreme incorrectness of Arrowsmith's Map of Vancouver's Island. The line of the coast is well delineated, and could be traced upon the map, as far as the promontory named "Cowetchin head," but from that point, all resemblance to the coast ceases; the multitude of Islands forming the Arro Archipelago, which extend as far as, and terminate at "Cala Descanso," being laid down as an integral portion of Vancouver's Island, whereas the true line of the coast runs from 15 to 20 miles [24 to 32 kilometres] west of its position as laid down, on that map, the intermediate space being occupied by Islands, and channels of various breadths, generally navigable, but probably inconvenient for sailing vessels, on account of the strong currents and frequent calms, which occur in those waters. A correct survey of those channels will remove many of the difficulties,

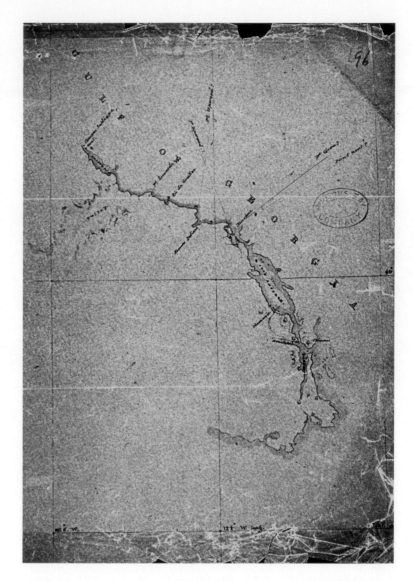

FIG 58 Pemberton's manuscript sketch of the southeast coastline of Vancouver Island as revealed during his 1852 canoe trip with James Douglas to inspect the newly found coal deposits at Wentuhuysen (Nanaimo.) [Courtesy of the Hudson's Bay Company Archives, Archives of Manitoba, Winnipeg]

that would at present be experienced by sailing vessels navigating those straits, and should Her Majesty's Government, at any time direct surveys to be made in this quarter I think the Arro Archipelago will be found to have peculiar claims to their attention, as there is the prospect of its soon becoming the channel of a very important trade.

While Douglas's comments on the inaccuracies of Arrowsmith's map were justified, he dissembled about the extent of his knowledge of them prior to his somewhat theatrical expedition. Company staff at the time included capable mariners such as McNeill, Stuart, Dodd, and Brotchie. They all had access to local peoples' intimate knowledge of the waters of what is now the Salish Sea, and had already investigated the many channels of the archipelago. In fact, Douglas had provided a very detailed depiction of the islands of Haro Strait as far north as Wentuhuysen to his Russian fur-trading counterpart at Sitka, Captain Mikhail Teben'kov, and the latter had incorporated the details into his map of the island drawn in 1849—three years before Douglas's report to London.

Arrowsmith's 1849 map of *Vancouver Island and the Adjacent Coasts* had been based on the Admiralty chart *Vancouver Island and the Gulf of Georgia* dated that same year. While this chart included some information acquired two years earlier by Kellett and Wood, the coastline in question remained largely as Vancouver had represented it. He, in turn, had copied the configuration from Spanish charts, based on hasty sketches made during the latter stages of the Narváez boat exploration of 1791.

Douglas went on to describe his meeting with the Cowichan tribe:

On our route through the Canal de Arro we touched at the Cowegin River which falls into that Canal, about 20 miles [32 kilometres] north of Cowegin Head, and derives its name from the Tribe of Indians, which inhabit the neighbouring country . . . The Cowegins are a warlike people mustering about 500 fighting men, and the total population is about 2100 Souls.

They were extremely friendly and hospitable to our party, and gave us much information in regard to the interior of the country; which by their report appears to be well watered, and abounding in extensive tracts of arable land.

Douglas's perception of the Cowichan people as warlike came from the opinion of their traditional rivals, the Songhees, who inhabited the region around Fort Victoria. Cowichans were occasional visitors to the fort, where noisy, sometimes violent, disputes erupted with the Songhees. The contrast between their reputation and the reception they afforded Douglas and his party must have been both surprising and welcome.

About 10 miles [16 kilometres] north of the Cowegin, the Chemanis River enters the Canal de Arro, it is altogether a smaller stream, than the former, and is navigable to a short distance only from the coast. It is inhabited by a branch of the Cowegin Tribe, whom we did not see . . .

The Promontory of Cala Descanso is the northern point of the Arro Archipelago, beyond which is the Inlet of Wentuhuysen, to which point my attention was particularly attracted, through a report of coal having been seen by the Indians in that vicinity. These people are called "Nanymo", and speak nearly the same language, but have not the reputation of being either so numerous or warlike in their habits, as the Cowegin Tribe. We entered into immediate communication and found them very friendly and disposed to give every information we desired, in regard to all matters concerning their own affairs, and the country which they inhabit.

The favourable impression the "Nanymo" (Snunéymuxw) people made on Douglas matched that of the Spaniard Captain Galiano, just over six decades earlier. Besides, McKay had acted as a good emissary during his visit two years earlier, and had established an atmosphere receptive to cooperation.

At this point, the tone of Douglas's report changed from his customary formal tone into, for him, almost euphoria.

> The reports concerning the existence of coal in that place, were I rejoice to say, not unfounded; as the Indians pointed out, three beds, cropping out in different parts of the Inlet . . . One of those beds measured 57¾ inches [1.47 metres] in depth, of clean coal, and it was impossible to repress a feeling of exultation in beholding, so huge a mass of mineral wealth, so singularly brought to light by the hand of nature, as if for the purpose of inviting human enterprise, at a season when coal is a desideratum in the Pacific, and the discovery can hardly fail to be of signal advantage to the Colony . . .
>
> There is every reason to believe from the appearance of the country, and its geological phenomena, that Vancouver's Island about Wentuhuysen Inlet, is one vast coal field, and if that conjecture be correct the progress of the Colony, will be rapid and prosperous . . .
>
> It is therefore of the very greatest importance to the trade of this Colony that the Canal de Arro, should be explored, and a correct survey prepared as soon as possible . . . Her Majesty's Government, would thereby render an essential service not only to this Colony, but to the general interests of trade and navigation . . .
>
> The harbour is safe and accessible to vessels of any class, and the coal is within 2 cables [2 times 100 fathoms = 1200 feet or 366 metres] length of the anchorage, so that every circumstance connected with this valuable discovery is suggestive of success.[2]

Various senior functionaries at the Colonial Office appended comments to Douglas's report and request. One official, a Mr. Blackwood, noted,

> This is, I think the most favourable report the Govt. have recd. concerning the products of Vancouver's Isld . . . Send copy Admiralty, and Geographical Society; and Land Bd. Shew this to Mr. Arrowsmith, who has of course, had very limited means of acquiring geographical knowledge concerning the part of the world explored by Governor Douglas . . . I think for the sake of British interests . . . the Admiralty should be desired to make the Survey.

Another, simply initialed "D," added:

> [T]he possession of coal in "Vancouvers island"—a solitary instance along the long line of the coast of the two Americas (as far as we have yet discovered), together with its favourable position as regards Pt Francisco & the whole Western coast of N America ought to make it the centre of the Pacific Commerce.

Pakington, the colonial secretary, had the final say: "Communicate as proposed by Mr. Blackwood, & I think a suggestion should be made to the Admiralty as to surveying the navigation."[3]

Responding to the copy of Douglas's "interesting communication," Sir Roderick Murchison, president of the Royal Geographical Society, expressed his gratitude. He said that it "will be read at an early meeting of our body." He was as good as his word and the following February, it was duly presented. The society later published it in their *Proceedings*, accompanied by a map of the new coastal configuration engraved by John Arrowsmith, based on Pemberton's manuscript. Arrowsmith also used the new data to correct his own regional map and published a revised edition of it in 1853.

The Lords of the Admiralty graciously thanked the colonial secretary for the suggestion to allocate a charting vessel to the "Georgian Strait." Most unfortunately, they regretted, their budget was fully committed. If, however, a special grant were to be made available . . . Thus, the project withered in an all-too-familiar issue over funding, to be quietly shelved, but not for long.

THE COUNTRY OF THE SIKLAULTS: COMOX RECONNOITRED

Joseph McKay followed up on James Douglas's canoe expedition to the newly found coalfield at Wentuhuysen Inlet. Accompanied by a few miners and a team of company tradesmen and labourers, he landed on September 6, 1852, and set up their camp near the mouth of the Millstone River. He called the new establishment Colville Town, after a senior administrator of the Hudson's Bay Company. They were to make clear to any arrivals that this area was under the control of the company. Mining began straight away, while Joseph Pemberton surveyed the surrounding area, preparing to lay out a townsite for what he called Nanaimo, his version of the name of the local people.

A few weeks later, following reports of more coal being found further up the coast, "in the country of the Siklaults," McKay made a quick visit to what is now Comox, and wrote to Douglas.

> I accordingly started on the tenth in a well-manned canoe with a strong S.E. wind. After pushing on all night, I arrived at Siklault at 11 a.m. on the 10th. I there hired another canoe and dispatched her with the Express. The weather being very rainy, wind strong from the S.E. I could not return, and in the meantime stood up in the bay inside of Point Holmes [Point Lazo], towards the Puntlitch [Puntledge], a river about the size of the Nanaimoe. 2 miles [3 kilometres] up the River are some large prairies . . .
>
> As I necessarily made a very short stay there, I could not examine the Country sufficiently to make a sketch of it, and merely made

a short excursion to the prairies, which in their general character much resemble those at Sanetch, being undulating, studded with oak on the ridges and rows of poplars in the valleys. The bottoms along the course of the River are very rich, the Black mould in some places being more than Two feet [60 centimetres] thick.[4]

In his daybook, or log, McKay recorded:

> Visited the Pentlitch River where there are extensive prairies studded with oaks. Most of the country between Nanaimo and Sihlault is level, thickly wooded, and intersected by numerous streams supplied by lakes in the interior. Half way between Nanaimoe and Sihlault is the village of Sahlum from which there is a path through a continuous valley leading to a large lake in the interior of the Island inhabited by the Nitinat and Tchis-a-tue who fish on the streams which run from the east side of the lake. This lake is reported to be very extensive extending from Sahlum to the Ucult ah River. The south side is bordered with prairie land. South of this lake is another of equal extent which supplies the Nanaimoes, Cowichin, Chemanis, Nitinat and several other streams. No authentic accounts can be gained from the Natives of this quarter regarding the country which surround these lakes as they are at various [sic, variance?] with the inhabitants thereof. All the streams along the coast abound with salmon, trout and wild fowl. At the mouth of each stream immediately on the sea coast are small plains very fertile yielding when cultivated large crops of potatoes . . . The Sihlault village is situated on an island [Denman] which commences at Valdez Inlet and terminates at Point Holmes. The shores of the island are composed principally of claystone and the natives report coal at three places on the island and several places on the opposite shores of Vancouver Island. Being pressed for time and the weather being very blustery I deferred examining these places for the present.[5]

McKay's reference to a valley and trail leading inland from a village called Sahlum (probably Qualicum) to a large lake appears to indicate local awareness of Horne and Cameron lakes. However, the hazy topographic and ethnographic detail McKay recorded seems to show just how limited was his ability, and that of his companions, to understand the local languages and cultural subtleties.

The name of the people at the source of the rumour of more coal deposits, the Siklault, provides another example. The K'omocks name Sálhlhtwx refers to the Island Comox subgroup, who shared a relationship with the Pentlatch within the Coast Salish, but spoke different languages and had been historical enemies. The former had gradually taken over the traditional villages of latter, but at the time of McKay's visit, the villagers at the northern end of Denman Island were still Pentlatch. A decade later the smallpox epidemic affected them badly, enabling the Island Comox, or Siklaults, to occupy the site and eventually absorb the few remaining Pentlatch people.

McKay's report to Douglas continued:

> I returned homewards, with the intention of examining the Siklault Coal which according to the Indian reports crops up on both sides of the Valdez Inlet [Comox Harbour and Baynes Sound] owing to neap tides I was obliged to defer the examinations to some future period.
>
> Valdez Inlet extends from the Valdez Inlet, Vancouver Chart to Point Holmes and separates the Siklaults from Vancouver Island.[6]

Douglas swiftly responded:

> I have to thank you for the very interesting description of your excursion to the Sihlault Village. We shall have the Coal seam, in the District Carefully examined in a fitting time and I trust that further valuable discoveries will be made in that quarter.[7]

In contrast to his delayed follow-up to McKay's earlier report on the coal prospects at Wentuhuysen, Douglas reacted swiftly to the hints of potentially rich farmland—and possibly more coal—at Valdez. He had Pemberton retrace McKay's route north along the coast from Nanaimo as far as Comox, and continue identifying various landmarks shown on the earlier map, already known to be considerably in error. In September 1852, Pemberton had advised London that:

> with proper chronometers I hope to be able to correct a good deal of the Coast line of Vancouver's Map, which in many places as to form and position does not bear the least resemblance to the land.[8]

The company in London responded to his request, and sent out some more timepieces. The following March, now equipped with a newly arrived pair of chronometers, Pemberton calculated latitudes and longitudes for seven places: Cowitchen, Nanaimo, "Q" (Icarus Point, Lantzville), "X" (wildlife sanctuary, Dashwood), Rio de Grullas (Parksville), Valdez Lagoon (south end of Baynes Sound), and "d" (Sandy Island, northern tip of Denman Island). His results differ significantly from their modern coordinates, primarily because of the irregularity of the new chronometers.

A land surveyor requires great precision in his timekeeping for measuring longitude, far more so than does a maritime navigator. Since one hour of time equates to 15 degrees of longitude, it follows that one second of time represents 15 arc-seconds in longitude, or about 300 metres on the ground at this latitude. The instruments sent to Pemberton were designed for use on board ship and, moreover, were in poor condition. It is not necessary for a chronometer to indicate the exact time, but a steady rate of variance from the true elapsed time is critical.

Pemberton reported that his latest results differed from his earlier calculation for Nanaimo. He also identified an apparent valley leading from "the Bay N. of Pt Leonardo [mouth of the Little Qualicum River] within 20 miles [32 kilometres] of the waters of Nitinat, if the latter be correctly laid down." This was the same place that McKay had earlier noted as the village of the Sahlum people. Pemberton recognized that Valdez Inlet was, in fact, a passage between a large island (Denman) and the main island, and he found more signs of coal there. The letterbook copy of his report to Barclay in London continues:

> It would have been useful to find Pt Holmes [Cape Lazo?] where Vancouver joins the Spanish Survey, but might have occasioned detention as just then Equinoctial winds prevailed. From a few <s [angles] taken to coast opposite, I should conjecture that it is generally drawn 8 miles [13 kilometres] or so too far E.—Islands are wrong in no. [number] and position . . . Between Nanaimo & Valdez Inlet there is a considerable extent (5 to 15 miles?) [8 to 24 kilometres] of flat land looking thickly wooded before we reach the foot of the Mts which are covered with pines. At the Rio de Grullas several small streams form a delta [Englishman River], the place does not seem important. Geese abundant.[9]

He accompanied his report with a map he termed "a tolerable correct outline of the s.e. coast of V.I.—about 100 miles [160 kilometers] from Victoria" (see Fig. 58, page 131).

"A FINE AGRICULTURAL DISTRICT": THE GOVERNOR COMES TO COMOX

A few months later, Governor Douglas boarded the company's new sail-steam vessel, ss *Otter*. After spending a few days at Nanaimo to inspect the progress of the year-old settlement and mining operation, he headed northwest along the coast.

Wed. 24th. Proceeded this morning to examine the coast between Point Holmes and Valdez Inlet [the north side of Comox Harbour]. Some Indians residing near Point Holmes [probably K'omocks people], accompanied us as guides. Pulling round Point Holmes on the Valdez Inlet side we came to a deep bay running N.W. that is parallel with the coast, and entered a river named Puntlatch [now Puntledge] which we ascended about half a mile in the Boat. Finding it difficult to proceed further on account of the shallowness of the stream, we landed there and proceeded further on foot through a fine open country sloping from the higher tableland which divides the river from the coast, and is covered with trees chiefly of the pine, into the valley of the stream.

We travelled about 8 miles [13 kilometres] in a north westerly direction, to a higher point of land commanding an extensive view of the valley—which is really beautiful and contains a large quantity of arable land free of rocks and stones.

To the westward is a range of mountains capped with snow [Forbidden Plateau, Mount Washington, and the Comox Glacier] [see Fig. 59, page 137], where it is reported the river takes its rise out of a large lake [Comox Lake]. This valley is a fine agricultural district and contains more arable land than is found in any other known district of Vancouver's Island.

The river abounds with salmon; observed pieces of coal brought down by the River, as we discovered no outcrop, but found the lime, sandstones and shales which mark the coal measure on the sea-coast at the entrance of the Puntluch. It is evidently a coal district, and could not be more advantageously situated. A chalbeate [chalybeate, or therapeutic mineral water] spring was pointed out by the Indians. The woodland is level and of good quantity—so that this district is well adapted for a settlement . . .

Thurs. 25th. Ran and anchored at Point Mudge. A number of Layculta [Ligwildaxw or We Wai Kai] exceeding one hundred hung about the vessel all day; a circumstance which detained me on board to prevent difficulties with the natives.

The land from Point Holmes to beyond Point Mudge appears level and covered with trees principally of the Pine order. The Indians say there is very little clear land north of the Spuntlatch [*sic*] [Puntledge] on the South side of the Island. On the West Coast they speak of large prairies about Nitinat and Clayoquot, but their accounts are evidently derived from hearsay—and consequently little to be depended upon. The Indians brought in specimens of a mineral resembling white quartz, but much softer, interspersed with sulphurate of iron.[10]

In contrast to his effusive report on his canoe journey to Nanaimo the previous year, Douglas's dispatch to the Colonial Department following his Comox expedition returned to his more formal style:

I devoted a part of the month of August last to the exploration of the east coast of Vancouver's Island, being also desirous of seeing and entering into closer discourse with the native Tribes residing in that part of the Colony.

In course of that excursion it was ascertained that the settlements may be extended in that direction with great advantage, there being much valuable land, with timber of the largest dimensions and decided indications of the existence of Coal, and other minerals in almost every part of the coast between Point Mudge & Nanaimo.

We also observed that the Natives had an abundance of fish, and appeared to live in the midst of plenty, and comparative comfort. They still retain much of their natural ferocity of disposition and dishonest habits . . . They were very communicative . . . and gave a flattering account of the beauty and fertility of the country they inhabit, with the view of prevailing upon us to form a white

FIG 59 An early postcard showing the Comox glacier and valley with the Beaufort Range, viewed from the water off Cape Lazo. [Author's collection]

settlement there, from which they would commercially derive much advantage.

> The native population of the District we visited which includes 70 miles [113 kilometres] of Coast, numbered as nearly as we could ascertain about 2,200 souls.

> One of the Tribes the "Laculta" [Ligwildaxw] have acquired the reputation of being the greatest marauders on Vancouver's Island and are consequently with good reason dreaded by all their neighbours.[11]

The McKay and Pemberton reports and the Douglas diary all indicate that the expedition members were aware of an island lying offshore (later called Denman) as they travelled past. It is clear that in getting to Valdez Inlet, McKay and Douglas took what is now Baynes Channel, close to the Vancouver Island shore, as did Pemberton. They still consulted versions of Vancouver's chart, based on the Narváez boat expedition of 1791, on which the existence of three islands, called Llorena, was indicated close by "R[ada = anchorage] Valdez."

"THE MOST PRETTY AS PLACE IN THE WORLD AS EVER I SAW AS YET." ADAM HORNE'S MYSTERIOUS CROSSING TO ALBERNI

From his home base at the new Fort Nanaimo in the mid-1850s, Adam Horne made a series of expeditions into the interior of Vancouver Island. There are various reports linked to these journeys, whose details have since become confused by the passage of time, fallible memories, and the colourful imagination of popular writers. This is yet one more attempt to unravel those sometimes-contradictory reports of a most intriguing episode.

Adam Grant Horne was born in 1831 in Edinburgh, Scotland, but raised in Orkney. The Hudson's Bay Company recruited him from there as a labourer, and he arrived in the new colony in 1851 aboard *Tory* (see Fig. 60, page 139). A veritable giant of a man for those times—6 feet, 3 inches (1.90 metres) tall and weighing over 200 pounds (91 kilograms)—he was, as Walbran recorded, "a man of fearless, daring disposition, whom the Indians seemed to admire as well as dread for his intrepidity." After two years at Fort Rupert, he was transferred to Nanaimo, where Joseph McKay put him in charge of the company store. However, he sought more challenging activity. He probably met, and impressed, Governor James Douglas with his physique and keenness for action.

Captain Charles Stuart, who had replaced McKay as chief factor, kept the sketchy journal of Fort Nanaimo for 1856. In it, there are brief mentions of comings and goings by Horne on trading sorties to the west coast.

> Saturday May 10th 1856 Toma Ouatomy [Tomo Antoine] left here on an expedition across the Island accompanied by three Indians and one Indian woman—Mr. Horne also left with him with instructions not to proceed further than a high mountain situated a little beyond the large lake in the interior but if the interior tribes be peaceable he may proceed to Alberni Canal.

This is puzzling, in that it seems to have Antoine leading the expedition, with Horne as supernumerary. It also indicates that Stuart already had some prior knowledge of the island's interior.

> Sunday May 18th 1856 Mr. Horne and Toma Ouatomy returned from their expedition to the other side of Vancouver's Island having crossed to the Seaboard, which appears as far as we have hitherto examined to be an inlet near Port Cox in Claiacut or perhaps an inlet to the south of it but not as far as Netenat—they traded a quantity of Beaver and Martin furs.

From this, it is clear that the location of "the Seaboard" or tidal salt water, was still uncertain. "Claiacut" is most likely today's

Clayoquot Sound, well to the northwest of Alberni. "Netenat" was the supposed name for the area around today's Bamfield, and not Nitinat Lake, the separate body of water to the south. This name continued to confuse later explorers.

> Saturday, September 20th 1856 Mr. Horne returned after a successful expedition across the island bringing with him numerous skins and accompanied by seaboard Indians of the tribe Seashaad.
>
> Tuesday September 23 As the Saatlam Indians conveyed the seaboard Indians up the coast, Capt. Stuart accompanied them in order to take the latitude of the point whence Mr. Horne started from this side of the island.[12]

So, what happened during those two journeys, in May and September? No other reports or records related to Horne's overland explorations can be found in the company's journal or correspondence in Fort Victoria; and the *Colonist* newspaper was yet to be published. Two hearsay versions of Horne's recollections of his first crossing do exist, although they differ in some important details.

The editor of a small community newspaper, the *Victoria Standard*, published the first of these accounts in 1914. He was W. Wyndham Walkem, a physician and collector of tales from the early colonial era. He reported that, 31 years previously, in May 1883, an elderly Adam Horne had recounted a story that "had never before been told." It began: "In 1855, or thereabouts," (another 28-year time span), and continued with how he had been called to Fort Victoria by Roderick Finlayson and briefed for an expedition.

He then went on to tell, in considerable detail, of his journey to explore a reputed grease trail across to the island's west coast. The account began with the description of witnessing a gruesome massacre of a village of Qualicum people. The

FIG 60 Mr. and Mrs. Adam Grant Horne, in an 1855 portrait, probably on their wedding day. He wears the uniform of an officer of the Hudson's Bay Company. [Courtesy of the Royal BC Museum and Archives, Victoria]

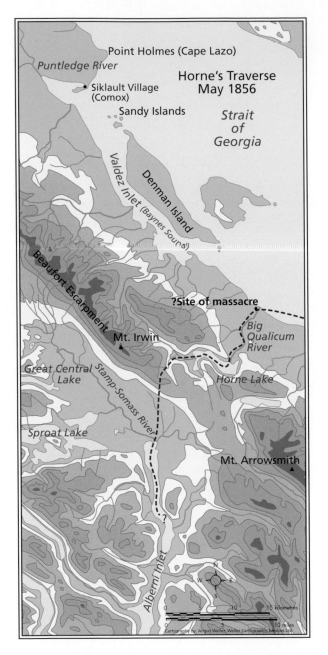

FIG 61 Adam Horne's probable route across the Beaufort Range to the head of Alberni Inlet in 1856. There is some doubt about the recorded details of his journey. [Map by Angus Weller]

victims, according to Finlayson, were probably a sub-group of the Wc Wai Kai tribe of Cape Mudge, but more likely, they were the few remaining Pentlatch people, related to the Coast Salish of Comox. The killers had been a large "Haidah" raiding party.

Horne's small group, now without guides, found their way past a large lake and across mountains to the head of a saltwater inlet. After a nerve-wracking exchange with the local people, including bartering for the release of a young Songhees captive, Horne and his party went back the way they had come. He reported his findings to Finlayson in Victoria (see Fig. 61).

Olga Blanche Owen, the eldest granddaughter of the eldest son of Adam Horne, wrote the second account of Horne's story in 1980. She relates that her grandfather had told it to her "several times when I was young [and] based on verbal accounts to [Adam's] family and friends." Her account, dating the trip at May 1856, had even greater detail than the Walkem version, but different specific elements. It also described their witnessing of the murderous raid by a large war party of Haida on the village at the mouth of the Qualicum River. In both versions, Horne told of finding a sole survivor of the carnage: an old woman, badly wounded, who managed to utter a few words before she died.

The narrative as reported by Owen continues with finding a large, placid lake, later named Horne, for its discoverer. After climbing a large mountain (probably the southeastern spur of Mount Irwin in the Beaufort Range), they "could see many lakes and another long arm of water which was later found to be salt water." After a difficult descent of the steep and densely forested scarp face, "and a long trek westwards we came across salt water." This could only have been the head of the Alberni Inlet. The account continues with Horne's first encounters with the locals, their mutually nervous attempts at trading, including the barter for the Songhees slave, who proved his gratitude by warning Horne of the locals' plan to attack their camp, and by guiding him to an easier ascent of the escarpment.

On their return trip they found that their caches of food and their carefully hidden seagoing canoe had not been disturbed. There were no signs of life in the ravaged village of the Qualicum people. After reporting to Stuart at Nanaimo, Horne and Antoine continued on to Fort Victoria to convey their findings. No mention is made of what happened to the young Songhees man they had freed. This is a curious omission, since his knowledge of the geography and the peoples of the region around the head of the Alberni Inlet could have provided important information for Douglas and his surveyor, Joseph Pemberton.

As if the discrepancies between the two versions of Horne's recollection of his first traverse were not enough to raise questions about what actually transpired, new documentation surfaced subsequently to throw much of the story even further into doubt.

In June 1953, George Horne discovered, in a secret drawer of his late father's desk, two diaries that seemed to refer to early days at Nanaimo, when his father, Adam, was the company store man and fur trader. The originals of the diaries have since disappeared, but someone, probably George, typed transcripts of them. One further aspect only adds to the mystery: In her account, Olga Owen makes no mention of her grandfather George's discovery of these diaries 27 years earlier. Nor does she comment on the differences between them and the Horne family's version of the trip.

The spelling and grammar in the diaries, particularly in the first one, reveal a semi-literate writer, but the transcripts appear faithful to their originals. The bulk of the first consists of miscellaneous notes about everyday business life at the new HBC establishment of Nanaimo: furs traded, coal shipped, and construction work, etc.

Then, on page 40, the style changes radically. Headed "Our road from the sea at the other side," the entry lists—

exclusively—undated, rough survey notes, including crude sketch maps of two lakes. It concludes with a list of "Good[s] required for trad[e]" and a list of peltry, presumably obtained during the trip. The rudimentary survey notes were made sometime after March 12, 1855, and the two sketch maps clearly depict Horne Lake and nearby Spider Lake.

The second diary is dated, initially without the year indicated, but evidently recording a period between May 11 and 18, 1856, and from September 10 through 19 of the same year. These periods clearly cover two separate journeys across the island, and the entries in the Fort Nanaimo Journal kept by Captain Stuart support both of them.

The transcript of this diary starts abruptly with "We walked 2 mills [presumably miles] and camped . . ." apparently on the evening of May 11, a little to the east of Horne Lake. This entry would have been made soon after the horrific events they witnessed at Qualicum at the beginning of their trek, as reported in subsequent, second-hand accounts. The mood of the writer, however, is not one of someone in shock. The next day, camped on the southern shore of Horne Lake, Horne recorded:

Tuesday 13th [May 1856] Beautifull morning the wind from the West the Trout and Beavers sporting all round. The most pretty as Place in the World as ever I saw as yet . . .

Here, the text ends abruptly, in mid-sentence, and the next page continues, probably a day later, at a completely different location, and again, mid-sentence:

Can go out and tak as meny salmon as they please at any time they are large and fat and read as [word illegible] This lake has got three lakes on the [word missing?] th Indians say that thare is one much larger then this one . . .

It would seem that Horne's party had by this time crossed the ridge of the Beaufort escarpment, descended to near the eastern end of Sproat Lake (see Fig. 62, page 143), and met the local people, probably the Opetchesaht (see Fig. 84, page 179). The larger lake could be Great Central Lake or even the Alberni Inlet. In this version, Horne's relationship with the locals was not one of mutual suspicion, but of friendship:

> The Head Cheff Brought me up the lak in his own canoe and says that he would like iff the White People would come and Stop on his ground There was one womon that Knowed me whin she saw me on the other side of this stream and called my name I was more than Thunderstruckd all together . . .

After some brisk trading of blankets and guns for some of the "Hunders of skins of Different Kinds which they want me to trade," the people's leader conveyed them downstream (presumably the Stamp and Somass rivers) to arrive "whare the tid Ebbs and flows," and further down the tideway, looking for more settlements. Finding none inhabited, Horne decided to return, travelling almost non-stop for two days, to arrive once more at the lake he had found on his way out.

Evidently, it was during this latter part of the trip that Horne used the first notebook to record some compass bearings and estimate—inaccurately—distances travelled and landmarks, such as "a large mountain covered [in snow?] from top to about the middle" [(Mount Arrowsmith) (see Fig. 63, page 143),] "High mountain above the lake whare the Indians stop" (Mount Irwin), Mount Mark, and a back bearing to "the End of the sea whare the Tid comes up" (the head of the Alberni Inlet).

The party made an uneventful return to Nanaimo, probably late on Sunday, May 18. Nowhere in the diaries does Horne mention the massacre of the Qualicum, the purchase of the Songhees captive, or the threat of attack on his camp. Nor is there any indication that this was not his first journey along this route.

The diary restarts on September 10, with a larger trading party out from Nanaimo to "a qualchem river," past Horne Lake, and "arrived at the top of the mountain where we spied the sea at the other side." This, presumably, was the same crest of the escarpment where he had camped on the earlier journey. After a night of gunshot sounds, a group of heavily armed locals arrived in camp. Horne recognized none of them but they proved friendly enough, and they escorted the visitors down to the main villages on the river, where they were ceremoniously welcomed and offered a feast. The headman made it clear that the locals wanted to establish an exclusive trading relationship with the company.

> [They] took me by the Hand and put me in a canoe the largested canoe that I ever saw as yet & mead me a present of his to me to cum dun the strates to trad all thar Furs.

There followed seven hours of ceremonial dancing.

> The pritested site that I ever saw in my life thay ware Dancing with thar Guns & Knives & Darts of ever kind so all was settled.

Horne eventually persuaded the reluctant leader, High-pinuilth, to return with him to Nanaimo, despite the leader's embarrassment that he had no sea otter pelts to bring. The diary concludes:

> Saturday 20th started at 7 Oclock & arrived at Nanaimo at 9 oclock a.m. all in Safty & in good health &c.[13]

Curiously, on the same coast during that summer there occurred an event much like that described in both versions of Horne's

FIG 62 (ABOVE)   The Beaufort escarpment and Stamp River valley seen from near the eastern end of Sproat Lake. The valley at centre is Hal Creek, with Mount Irwin centre-right. Horne and Pemberton would have first seen the head of Alberni Inlet as they crossed the ridge at right. [Photo by author]

FIG 63 (RIGHT)   Early postcard of a snow-covered Mount Arrowsmith. [Author's collection]

recollection of his first sortie. Douglas, in a dispatch to the colonial secretary, reported that in late July 1856:

> A gang of Queen Charlotte Islanders . . . attacked and nearly destroyed a native "Cowegin" village situated about 50 miles [80 kilometres] north of this place. The "Cowegins" few in number fought desperately and were all slaughtered on the spot; and the assailants made off towards their own country with a number of captive women and children.[14]

While this would seem to be the same incident that Horne reported having witnessed, there are some significant disparities: the timing does not fit with the diary and the station journal; the victims were not "Cowegins" (presumably Cowichans), but Pentlatch, or Island Comox; the location of the Qualicum village is two and a half times as far from Victoria as Douglas's "50 miles" and, in both versions, Horne reported that the raiders headed south after the event, as opposed to northward toward Haida Gwaii. Horne's vivid story provides enough detail to show that he could have witnessed such a horrific event, but he seems to have confused the time and place.

The plausible evidence of the diary transcripts, with the corroborating entries in Stuart's journal, contradicts the two later versions of the story. This could indicate that the elderly Horne and also his son embellished the yarn to amuse and spellbind the family. An alternate interpretation might be that the many adventures from his early fur-trading days had become muddled in his ageing memory. Nonetheless, Adam "Trader" Horne fully deserves to remain high on the list of pioneer explorers of Vancouver Island.

PEMBERTON SENT TO VERIFY THE ALBERNI REPORT

As soon as Douglas learned, perhaps verbatim, of Horne's explorations westward, he responded. He welcomed the possibilities of an ongoing trading relationship with the Tseshaht and other peoples of the Alberni region, so he sent his newly returned chief surveyor, Joseph Pemberton, to investigate the route and this important part of the island.

Accordingly, Pemberton assembled a team of seven axemen, packers, and paddlers to retrace Horne's steps. No record of the names of those assistants remains, but he had earlier expressed strong preference for "Canadians"—mixed-race woodsmen, veterans of the company's fur brigades. He found them to be hardy, self-reliant, and wilderness-savvy, especially when compared with more recent arrivals from Europe. It seems probable that Antoine would have been included as a guide.

By this time, Pemberton himself had three years' hard-earned experience of the hazards and difficulties entailed in surveying in the unbroken, primary rainforest of southern Vancouver Island. He had covered, on foot and in all weathers, all the coastal lands from Sooke to the Saanich Peninsula, Cowichan, and Nanaimo, and had mapped them. He had travelled by canoe as far as Comox. In so doing, he had far exceeded all expectations of his superiors, both Douglas and those in London. He had just returned from a year's home leave with a substantial bonus and a generous new contract.

During the first contract, Pemberton had focused his time primarily on preparing the cadastral, or property, mapping of the company lands and those intended for settlement. He had now received written confirmation that he was to expand the coverage of his exploratory surveys.

> It is the Governor & Committee's desire that you will take an early opportunity to examine the other parts of the Island beyond those now in course of Survey, more particularly the harbours on the West coast and the country between those and the Settlements on the East coast, and ascertain the practicability

and probable cost of making a road across the Island, reporting to the Governor & Committee the facts, and your opinion to the expediency of doing so.[15]

The weather in mid-October was not conducive to proper survey observations, but Pemberton was able to determine the latitude and longitude of nine places, including the mouths of the Saaltum (Englishman) and Qualicum rivers and along his journey as far as Cape Beale, on the open Pacific. Evidently, they returned to the head of the Alberni Inlet and explored up the Somass River—"broad, say 80 yds. [73 metres] And shallow"—to the village of Opochesalth (today's Klehkoot Reserve). From there they ascended the Stamp River.

> Exceedingly rapid, several waterfalls, 40 or 50 yds [36 or 46 metres] wide and contains 2 or 3 times as great a body of water as the Nanaimo River does at the same time of year . . . The scenery about Opochesalth and head of Inlet is often very beautiful but there is no great extent of valuable or open land.

They ventured ten miles (16 kilometres) along "Central Lake" (most likely Sproat Lake) and learned that "the ice was very thick on it in the winter." As he crossed the pass of the escarpment, Pemberton noted: "A ridge of mountains (some snow on them) occupying the middle of the island in the direction of its length, but not unbroken." He attached a sketch map to his summary report to Douglas (see Fig. 64), and concluded by endorsing the precautionary advice the governor had given him about the seaboard's inhabitants: "Your opinion that no confidence is to be placed in them is quite correct." [16]

FIG 64 Joseph Pemberton retraced Horne's route across to Alberni late in 1856. He noted the Beaufort Range and the Somass River valley on this manuscript sketch map attached to his report to governor Douglas. [Courtesy of the Hudson's Bay Company Archives, Archives of Manitoba, Winnipeg]

FIG 65   HMS *Satellite* in Victoria in a photograph by Richard Maynard. This small but well-armed warship provided Governor Douglas with crucial support during the Fraser River gold rush and the dispute over San Juan Island. [Courtesy of the Royal BC Museum and Archives, Victoria]

CHAPTER TEN

MESACHIE, THE HAUNTED FOREST: PEMBERTON AND GOOCH IN THE COWICHAN VALLEY

IN EARLY SEPTEMBER 1857 GOVERNOR James Douglas made his fourth expedition to the lands of the "Cowigins." Five years earlier, en route to Wentuhuysen by canoe, he had stopped briefly to see for himself the fertile valley reported by Joseph McKay, and to meet the resident people. The next two visits were much more solemn affairs, meant as salutary demonstrations of the authority and power of the new tribe in the region—the colonial forces now based at Fort Victoria.

Both were massive, ship-borne excursions, with armed naval ratings and marines. They came to help apply colonial justice to separate incidents of the murder of white people by Cowichan men. Both cases, one in 1853 and the second three years later, entailed the apprehension, swift trial, and public hanging of the perpetrators. Douglas reinforced the message with stern lectures on the severity with which any further crimes of such a nature upon the newcomers would be treated. He impressed upon his naval escort that strict discipline was essential, and both expeditions took place without a single shot fired, the two guilty men being the only people killed.

Douglas was well aware of recent bloody incidents in the new states immediately to the south and in New Zealand. These had shown the ineffectiveness of retaliation against tribes for acts by individual miscreants. His predecessor, Richard Blanshard, had tried to do the same to the Nahwitti people. Not only had retaliation proved counterproductive, that expedition had almost escalated into warfare. Douglas spent much time explaining to the Somenos leaders that it was his earnest wish that relations between his people and the locals would continue to be friendly, and he felt he had successfully set the foundation for that.

The main purpose of Douglas's fourth visit to the valley was to continue the diplomacy and strengthen the relationship with the resident tribes. It had become clear by this time that there was not enough arable land to support a self-sustaining British colony around Victoria and the neighbouring inlets, and on the Saanich Peninsula. Much more, and better, land would need to be brought under cultivation and cleared for rearing livestock. The deep, rich, well-watered alluvial soils of the

Cowichan Valley offered by far the most attractive prospect, and Douglas had come to prepare the locals for an influx of British agricultural settlers.

Douglas's party was once more escorted by a 50-strong, armed detachment of officers, ratings, and marines from the 21-gun screw corvette, HMS *Satellite*, commanded by Captain James Prevost, RN (see Fig. 65, page 146). The civilians had been conveyed there in the company steamer *Otter*, which also carried several ponies and ample camping gear and provisions. In addition to "a motley crowd of Canadian *voyageurs* and Indians" accompanying Douglas, Joseph Pemberton had his own entourage of two young "Americans" (mixed-race) and an Iroquois—Tomo Antoine again. Pemberton was on a confidential mission for the governor to "Examine & report upon the Country between Cowitchen Harbour and Nitinat of the Indians (not the Nitinat usually marked on Maps of Vancouver's Island in Barclay Sound)."

The orders had a covert requirement, to keep an eye open for indications of gold in any streams they crossed. Sizable placer deposits of the metal had already been found in the Thompson River, but this was still, they hoped, a company secret.

Once the contingent had ascended the river as far as the ship's boats could manage, they landed and took an easy trail along the left bank for three miles to a large Somenos village. There, Douglas gave a brief speech in the local (Huḻqumíńuḿ) dialect, which delighted the villagers. The leader of the village led them two miles further to an extensive plain covered in six-foot (two-metre) tall grass, where they were to set up camp. The naval officers were well entertained by the governor, and were served a "capital claret, [making] it difficult for us to believe that we were in a young and remote colony, and in the immediate neighbourhood of savages." The following day, Douglas spent the morning receiving the surrounding leaders,

and the afternoon riding with the captain and his officers across the plain to a prominent hill, which the surveyor named Mount Prevost.

PEMBERTON'S PARTY SETS OUT

Pemberton initially planned for his survey crew to discreetly slip away from the second night's ceremonies and entertainment. With several Somenos guide-packers, they would investigate a new route across to the Pacific coast. Changed circumstances soon obliged him to modify that plan.

Pemberton, in his usual laconic style, omitted from his report any details of the expedition, which he considered trivial.[1] Fortunately, an observant and articulate participant left an record of their eventful traverse. The account describes the difficulties, hazards, and sheer physical effort required in undertaking an unguided, exploratory expedition through the interior of the island (see Fig. 66, page 149).

The men left the camp as planned, but Pemberton returned a few hours later, explaining that their porters had deserted for fear of being massacred by the Indians on the west coast. Another factor in the porters' desertion could well have been their foreboding about entering the deep forests, regarded as *mesachie*—evil or haunted. No replacements were forthcoming, so at the request of the governor, Prevost called for volunteers from the naval escort to accompany the team as porters. Every man offered his services. Two ratings and two marines were chosen, and one officer also requested permission to participate "as an amateur."

A Royal Navy policy, at the time, encouraged junior officers to undertake overland journeys of exploration while serving at sea. Such trips were understood to provide a valuable element for one's chances of promotion, and the officer's request was granted. In his report, Pemberton described 25-year-old Lieutenant Thomas Sherlock Gooch, RN, as having proved himself to be "of much service in every emergency" (see Fig. 67, page 150). Some 30 years later, Gooch published his account of their adventures in Colburn's *United Service Magazine*.

The governor, captain, and escort cheered the five new members of the exploration party as they and Pemberton left to rejoin Antoine and the other two men, camped several miles away. Each man carried just a blanket, a flannel shirt, and a rifle. Their route took them northwest through head-high grassland into the forest (see Fig. 68, page 150). After a few miles they passed the large village where, the previous year, the attacker of a white squatter had been hanged. It was deserted, but they saw bones, which they presumed were those of the miscreant, carefully placed in a canoe in a tree. A few miles further, in another small prairie, they found the camp and dinner awaiting them.

Gooch reported that the supplies carried by the expedition, in addition to Pemberton's survey instruments, consisted of a number of different firearms, axes, a sack of trade goods, an inflatable rubber boat, meat, flour for biscuits, tea, and shag tobacco, but no alcohol. The leader took responsibility for carrying the instruments, and the men divided the remainder of provisions and stores equally among themselves. As they started, each man carried, as well as a rifle or shotgun, a pack weighing about 70 pounds.

It had become clear that they would be the first Europeans to venture into this territory. The Somenos seemed to know very little about the interior, other than the vague existence of a large lake. The travellers nursed a faint hope of finding other local people along the river who might be employed as porters and guides. They spotted occasional signs of human presence, but saw no one.

They broke a trail on a course roughly northwest. Hacking through dense undergrowth, and clambering over fallen trees while heavily laden, they made a din that must have scared away

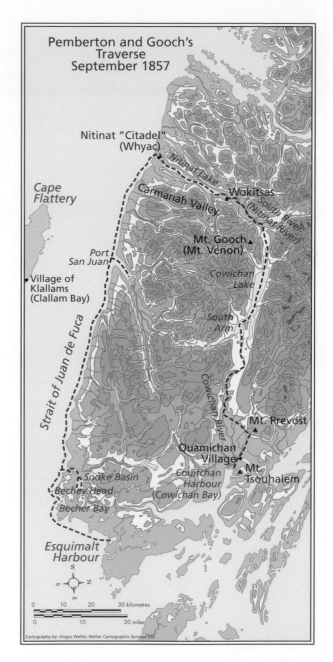

FIG 66 In the fall of 1857 Joseph Pemberton, accompanied by Lieutenant Sherlock Gooch, RN, and a small party of naval volunteers crossed the island from Cowichan Bay to Nitinat on the Pacific coast. [Map by Angus Weller]

FIG 67 (LEFT) The grim-looking officers of HMS *Satellite,* by an unknown photographer. Captain James Prevost, RN, stands in front while Lieutenant Sherlock Gooch leans nonchalantly on the massive gun. [Courtesy of the Royal BC Museum and Archives, Victoria]

FIG 68 (BELOW) Italian merchant and photographer Carlo Gentile took this *View on Vancouver Island* in early 1866. Recently identified as looking west over the lower meanders of the Cowichan River from Tzouhalem Road in Comiaken. [Courtesy of Greene Frogge Press]

any game in their vicinity. While they did see tracks of bear, elk, and deer, none came within range. Their path crossed several dry, steep-sided ravines; footing was dangerous and progress slow. The weather had been pleasant: "a Devonshire summer at its best," noted Gooch, but after a few days it turned stormy, making the trek even slower and more laborious.

While crossing fallen timber, Pemberton and the others slipped several times. Such accidents damaged the delicate chronometers and other instruments, preventing him from accurately fixing their position. The stock of meat soon ran out, and Antoine the hunter was unable to replenish it. Rations became sparse, limited to tea and biscuit "dampers" (roasted dough); however, tobacco was plentiful, so morale remained high.

On the third day, their path brought them to the left bank of the Cowichan River, and they descended the brush-filled, rugged slope to fling down their burdens and plunge gratefully into the water. The river at this point was some 200 metres wide and two metres deep, winding swiftly through a steep-sided gorge some three kilometres wide.

After resting a couple of hours, they resumed their march, following the river upstream. When the valley narrowed to a canyon and the forest closed in, they scrambled on hands and knees up the nearly perpendicular cliff to find themselves on a plateau covered in the aftermath of a vast and evidently recent forest fire.

> But the destruction of the trees did not assist our progress, for the ground, in addition to its being strewed with masses of charred timber, was densely covered in sallal-bush, forming a thick net-work which required constant use of the axe in order to force a passage through. This bush, however, ought to be spoken of gratefully by every member of this expedition, for it produces a blue berry about the size of a large black currant, containing a sharp and not unpleasantly flavoured juice, which we found extremely refreshing when other refreshments were unpleasantly scarce.

Gooch recorded their joy when Pemberton managed to shoot a young buck; by then they had been without meat for three days.

> The prospect of venison for supper was invigorating. The deer was soon skinned and cut up in six pieces, and then, after a readjustment of loads, the tramp was renewed. To avoid tedious repetition, this day's work may be shortly summarized as alternately stumbling and scrambling over spurs of mountains, in thick forest with matted undergrowth . . . and walking across pleasant intersecting valleys, our guide being the windings of the Cowichin, which tended generally to the west-north-west, the river gradually becoming narrower and rapids more frequent as its supposed source, the lake, was approached. At five o'clock the pioneers, whilst on the ridge of a high spur, had their eyes gladdened by the sight of a large sheet of water glistening in the rays of the setting sun.

NAVIGATING COWICHAN LAKE

They camped and feasted on venison broth and stew. The inflatable boat *Pioneer* was prepared, and Antoine set out to reconnoitre. He returned, having found the basin that formed the headwaters of the river that also led into the main lake. They would explore the lake on a raft, which they needed to build. Gooch, the naval officer, was most interested in its construction.

> A large cedar was felled, cut in half, each half split in two, making four lengths each 30 feet [9 metres] long. Nine feet [2.7 metres] was then cut off two of these lengths, and the shell or hull of the raft was then formed by lashing with cedar withes the two

9-feet lengths across the ends of the two 30-feet lengths. Eight more 9-feet lengths of cedar were then lashed at equal distances across the 30-feet lengths. These, as well as sufficient wood for shaping out nine good stout paddles, were obtained by cutting down a second cedar-tree. Little time as it takes to describe its construction, eleven hours' hard work were required to put together the Saucy Jack, as the raft was named by her builders on its being launched.

After a successful sea trial, and waiting a day for the invaluable, but exhausted and feverish, Antoine to recuperate, all personnel and stores were loaded aboard. The inflated *Pioneer* was lashed on top, amidships, with the arms, ammunition, and provisions placed in it for safekeeping, should the raft come to grief. Paddling against the wind, they progressed at about one knot along what is now known as the South Arm. With water up to their knees, Gooch imagined that from the shore, they would seem to be mermen. "Happily, the weather was fine and the lake delightfully warm."

Passing with some difficulty through the Narrows,

The paddlers were fully repaid by the wild grandeur of the view that presented itself on the other side. Before us lay a vast expanse of water surrounded by an amphitheatre of lofty hills over 2000 feet [610 metres] in height, their summits crowned by dark forests of pine [Douglas fir], and their bare and gloomy sides descending precipitously to the water's edge . . . Mr. Pemberton judged that so far as from this sheet of water being the termination of the lake, it was only one of a series of similar basins connected by narrow straits, that probably extended through the interior from southeast to north-west.

Well before dawn on the seventh day of their expedition, Pemberton took Antoine in *Pioneer* to reconnoitre the western end of the lake. There he discovered two feeder streams, one from the northwest and the other from the southwest. Time and the shortage of provisions did not permit exploration of the former, and the latter presented the better chance of leading to their destination of Nitinat.

The lashings on the raft were working loose and the weather worsening, so they were obliged to find shelter and camp in a "snug-looking cove" to wait out the storm. They noted that the lake "abounds in fish, but by an unfortunate oversight there was not one hook amongst the whole party." While the crew relashed the timbers of the raft, Pemberton took his double-barreled rifle in search of game on the nearby hillside.

He returned after dark to announce, to everyone's delight, that he had shot a bear. A party went to recover the precious meat, and after a 45-minute "sharp scramble up the forest," found the corpse, which Antoine expertly skinned and butchered. They had to carry the joints of bear meat back down the mountain to their camp—a "difficult and breakneck affair."

Despite this welcome addition to their stock of food, they recognized they would need to go on half-rations to make it last for another ten days. Pemberton had originally brought supplies for ten to twelve days, and they had already been out for ten. Nonetheless, Gooch recorded that "everyone was in good spirits, and confident of soon reaching some friendly tribe on the coast."

At the western end of the lake, they discovered a recently occupied Indian camp and, nearby, a distinct trail. Leaving the *Saucy Jack*, and following the trail northwest for six hours, across torrents and ravines, and through "a somber, damp forest of hemlock-spruce and cedar . . . several of them measuring from 24 to 27 feet [7 to 8 metres] in circumference," they came upon "a broad and rapid river flowing from the northward." Pemberton called this the South River and they followed a trail along its right bank. They saw clear signs that this was the hunting territory of a west coast tribe. Pemberton named a nearby peak Mount Gooch, to honour his naval companion, but the toponym was later changed, for reasons unknown, to Mount Vernon.

The next morning the party faced a new challenge:

> a deep gorge, through which there rushed with great violence a considerable body of water to join the South River. The depth of this chasm must have been 100 feet [30 metres] and its width about 70 feet [20 metres] . . . It was decided to make a bridge of a large pine that had fallen from cliff to cliff . . . it presented a smooth and slippery surface. The transit along it was therefore a ticklish undertaking to weak and heavily-laden men, as a false step would have resulted in falling headlong into the boiling waters a hundred feet beneath.

The going got no easier as they progressed down what would be named the Nitinat River, having to choose between hacking through dense salal and scrambling over huge, rotting, fallen tree trunks. After a five o'clock breakfast of a three-ounce biscuit and a gulp of water, they battled their way southward for 14 hours.

> Some of the men dropped to the ground when the order came to camp was given, and were with much difficulty persuaded to eat their "ha'penny buns." To add to our discomfort the rain came down viciously, and everything was so soaking wet that it was a long time before a fire could be made.

The next morning, they discovered and followed a trail to a deserted lodge, which had a small plot of potatoes, with a few plants not harvested. They fired a salvo of shots to alert the owners. They planned to construct another raft from the poles and planks of the hut, but in response to the shots, a small canoe with an elderly man, a woman, and two children appeared, and paddled hard toward the visitors. These were the first people they had met since leaving the plain of Somenos.

"Firmly but civilly" they commandeered the canoe, loaded everyone aboard, and set off downstream, but after half a mile, they came to "long and dangerous rapids, which would have severely tried the lashings of our proposed raft." All except Pemberton and Gooch, with the flour and trade goods, landed to bypass the rapids on foot. The old man skilfully shot the rapids, and came to place where he had hidden a much larger canoe.

The expedition, with the old man as pilot, transferred to the large canoe, leaving the woman and children to follow in the smaller one. During this process, the wily fellow managed to purloin Antoine's rifle and drop it overboard, to be recovered by him later. Its owner's "grief and rage were great," and he sulked for the rest of the day. Thereafter, the rapids gradually diminished and the valley became more level and open. At one o'clock the pilot steered to a sandy beach and signalled to the team that they should wait here while he alerted his village to their arrival. Pemberton issued a double allowance of biscuit, since they should not appear too eager for food, and thereby raise the price asked by the villagers for salmon and potatoes.

Before they had finished their token lunch, a large group of villagers, many armed and not at all welcoming, surrounded them. Gooch was unimpressed with their appearance, noting that all were dirty and many of the men "were studies for the nude." They were evidently astonished to see white men approaching from inland. They led the way to the village [perhaps today's Wokitsas Reserve], where Pemberton set up camp under constant curious scrutiny. Flanked by his armed companions, the surveyor laid out a selection of trade goods, and, with Antoine leading things—mostly by gesture—the haggling began. After three hours, rates were agreed and Antoine "secured ten large salmon and ten measures of potatoes." Both sides retired to enjoy the proceeds of their negotiation.

The following morning, negotiations resumed, the visitors seeking to buy a canoe to take them to the coast. It became apparent that one of the locals had a smattering of the pidgin trade language, Chinook Jargon. As a result, Antoine was able to learn that this group was subservient to the Nitinat leader, whose village was at the far end of a long, saltwater lake.

The surly headman demanded the exorbitant price of 20 new blankets, up front, for a canoe barely big enough for the party. Pemberton offered a "paper"—an IOU that would be honoured by the Hudson's Bay Company in Victoria, a standard process used and trusted in all places trading with the company—for 12 blankets, double the going price for such a canoe. The headman, thinking perhaps that he had the travellers at his mercy, denied any knowledge of such a system. Matters seemed at an impasse.

Pemberton, deciding instead to build another raft, instructed Antoine to take *Pioneer* and seek out a suitable spot for the work. To the amazement of the locals, Antoine inflated the boat and, paddle in hand, stepped aboard.

The staggered headman, followed by the Chinook interpreter, rushed to the river's side and screamed out "Where are you going?" "To the Nitinat Chief to complain of your conduct," replied the Iroquois in Chinook, with great presence of mind but absence of truth. "Stop," shouted the other excitedly, "and you shall have a large canoe at once!"

A large canoe, powered by five young tribesmen, loaded with the laughing expedition members and their gear, set off downstream. But the crew had another card to play. After a mile, they suddenly beached the craft and jumped out, taking their paddles and blankets with them, to sit, sullenly, on a nearby bluff. Apparently they felt that the negotiation should start again. They renewed the demand for 20 blankets, but were now prepared to accept a "paper"; the crafty headman had clearly known all along what the system was.

Pemberton's well-armed team was capable of taking the canoe by force, but following company policy of treating their trading partners equitably, he tried bargaining, with little success. Again, impasse. Suddenly, the five paddlers gave a shout, leaped back into the canoe, and continued paddling furiously.

The reason for this change of attitude became clear when, after rounding the last bend in the river, they came to "a large, lake-like body of water" and saw approaching them "a large canoe under sail and containing several Indians in their war paint." This was a canoe sent by the leader of the Nitinat, who had just received word that some "King George's men" (British) had arrived at his vassal village and were purchasing salmon with ammunition and powder. The five paddlers were clearly in abject awe of the powerful party sent by the leader, although the new group was lighthearted and respectful toward the visitors. The senior of them invited Pemberton and his men to change canoes, and the surveyor dismissed the group of five with a token tip of a few charges of powder.

As they proceeded down the inlet, which Gooch calculated to be some 25 miles [40 kilometres] long and an average of 4 miles [6 kilometres] wide, he admired on the east side several magnificent waterfalls springing from "mountains covered in forests of gigantic pine." He was seeing the now-famous stands of trees in the Carmanah watershed. Toward its southern end, the inlet narrowed and habitations became more frequent.

[We saw,] rising from verge of a bold cliff . . . a large, stockade village, evidently the Nitinat citadel [Whyac]. But as yet no opening to the sea was visible, when suddenly, on rounding a point, the Pacific burst on our view through a narrow channel between high cliffs. Our young braves ceased their chaffing and became silent and grave as we rapidly approached the entrance. Each man appeared to be gathering himself up for a great effort, and every eye was fixed upon the steersman for directions, and good cause there was for having an experienced and attentive crew. The great body of water we were now leaving was struggling to escape through an outlet forty yards [37 metres] wide by a hundred yards [90 metres] long; this being met by a young flood-tide, a most dangerous, formidable and ugly race was produced, and the white men held their breath when they saw what was before them. Our fragile craft was shot straight into this boiling and seething whirlpool, the water curled up to her gunwales, and the canoe seemed to be dashed without control from side to side of the rocky channel, but her crew had been born and bred to this work, and although the odds appeared much against it, we were safely landed on a sandy beach to the south of the village . . . Altogether our surroundings were grand, striking and picturesque.

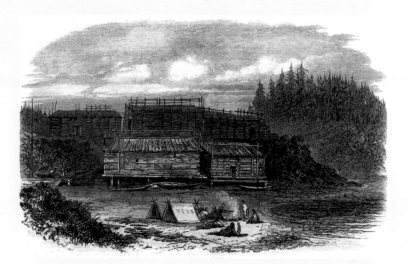

FIG 69 *Whyac*, the principal village of the Nitinat (Ditidaht) people, sketched by Frederick Whymper during an expedition only a few years after the visit by Pemberton and Gooch. The village was much larger than shown here. [*Illustrated London News*, November 24, 1866]

After setting up their camp, Pemberton, Gooch, and Antoine, escorted by the young leader who had led the reception party, climbed to the stockaded citadel (see Fig. 69). At the far end of one of about 25 longhouses, they were courteously received by "a short, stout old man of about sixty . . . in bearing and manner, he was every inch a chief." Pemberton, through Antoine, explained who they were and the purpose of their expedition. It soon became clear why the leader was so welcoming.

A war party from the Nitinat, explained the leader, had just returned from a successful raid against their arch-enemies, the Klallam people of Cape Flattery, where they had taken 20 human

FIG 70 Another sketch by Whymper, purportedly of a villager he saw at Whyac, but in fact, he copied it from a photograph by Carlo Gentile. [Courtesy of the Greater Victoria Public Library]

trophy heads. As a consequence, the leader was expecting retaliation at any moment. He advised the visitors that they would be far safer if they brought their camp into the stockade. In fact, if they were to join forces with him, they could stay in his own lodge.

Antoine relayed Pemberton's polite non-acceptance of the hospitality, explaining that he could not, as an official of the company, take sides against another tribe. This disappointed the Nitinat leader, and when asked to sell the visitors a canoe, he brusquely put off any further discussion (see Fig. 70). Pemberton's group returned to the shoreline camp to find that some of their gear had been stolen. The food initially promised by the leader amounted, in the end, to a single pot of potatoes.

Next morning, in an attempt to restore cordiality, Pemberton asked to see the Klallam heads. The leader granted the request, taking the visitors to the grisly sight of 22 poles, 12 feet [4 metres] tall, each with an impaled head or the heart of a Klallam leader. The warriors proudly recounted how, in the usual way of such raids, a party of Klallams out fishing had been surprised, capsized, and butchered while in the water. Disgusted, the Europeans returned to camp.

The leader reciprocated their diplomatic gesture by visiting their camp later that afternoon, and was now more amenable to negotiation. For the canoe that had collected them, he asked the reasonable price of ten new blankets and two trade guns. Pemberton explained that he while was prepared to give "paper" for that amount, he did not have the goods with him. The leader acknowledged that he knew the paper would be honoured, but he would not be able to collect on it for several months. He really needed the goods, now. Even the highly persuasive Antoine could not budge him, and the leader departed without an agreement.

Later, two young leaders arrived with a message that *their* leader had ordered no food be given to the visitors, except for direct payment in powder. But should they agree to an alliance, they would be given as much salmon, halibut, and potatoes as they might wish. Then, once any Klallam reprisal raid had been repelled, the Nitinat warriors would escort the Englishmen back to Victoria in triumph. This represented a serious problem for Pemberton, since his stock of powder was getting low. He ran the risk of their being starved out by the leader.

In desperation, Pemberton sent Antoine back with an offer to leave the two naval Tower rifles as deposit against ten new blankets, plus two flintlock trade guns for the canoe. Since the rifles were state-of-the-art, percussion-fired weapons, the team doubted if the leader would accept the new technology. The leader did accept, but on the condition that the guns were not the naval Towers, but the marines' long Enfield rifles. No mention was made of the necessary percussion caps, nor of instruction on their use. The two marines sorrowfully greased and wrapped their precious Enfields in oily rags and handed them over.

RETURN TO VICTORIA

Amicable relations restored, the parties began cheerful bargaining for food and nine paddles in exchange for thimbles, charges of powder, and a hand mirror. While this was going on, one of the locals brought some samples of local coal for Pemberton. That evening, with one of the Nitinat whalers steering them through the breaking surf, they paddled southeast for two hours alongside what would later be called the West Coast Trail. After a few hours' rest, they set out along the northern shore of the Strait of Juan de Fuca. In the afternoon, off Port San Juan, a favourable breeze enabled them to rig a mast with a sail from their tarpaulin, and make good progress before camping by a huge fire for the night.

They made similar progress the next day, which brought them by the evening into "Soohk Inlet." Before dawn on the 17th day of their adventure, and after collecting fresh water, they again set sail, hoping to reach Victoria that night. Their perils, however, were not yet over.

> Off Becher Head [Beechey Head] we were caught in one of those sudden south-westerly gales that make the Straits of Juan de Fuca so dangerous for open boats. Our canoe shipped a good deal of water and it was with difficulty that we managed to get her under the lee of the head and beached.

They watched as a second canoe, in similar difficulties, attempted to make the same landing. It was a much larger canoe, filled with warriors in full war paint, but it managed to overcome the adverse wind and tide to join them on the shore. It was, in fact, a war party of the Klallams. Their leader openly told the team that they had had a narrow escape that morning.

The Klallams had set up an ambush for the Nitinat, whom they expected to come along the coast to Victoria to acquire supplies of weapons and ammunition. In hiding, east of Sooke and in the dark before dawn, they had seen a Nitinat canoe leaving the harbour. As the canoe was about to enter their ambush and they were on the point of firing, "a gleam of light showed that the paddlers were palefaces. The delay occasioned in having to cross the inlet to obtain water in all probability saved our lives." The crews of the two canoes feasted and traded, and parted friends.

As the team left the shelter of Becher Bay, they spotted a launch from *Satellite* sent out to seek them, or news of them. "We were soon investigating the contents of a well-filled hamper which kind friends had thoughtfully provided for the possibly hungry and thirsty travellers." Gooch, his two ratings, and two marines rejoined *Satellite* at Esquimalt, and Pemberton's group carried on to Victoria.

Gooch concluded his gripping account with a comment on morale.

> Notwithstanding Lenten fare and hard work, one and all of the exploring party had thoroughly enjoyed their trip, and would gladly have followed their late leader [Pemberton had died before Gooch's account was published, some 30 years after the expedition] again over the same ground, but with the addition of native porters.

Gooch listed their accomplishments and noted that the marines' Enfields were later reclaimed, still in good condition.

In marked contrast, Pemberton made no mention in his report of the many hardships they faced, nor of the dramatic interchanges with the Nitinat and Klallam people. He merely commented on the size of the trees they had noted, and the southern end of the inlet, where there appeared to be a bar.

> I was not able to take soundings. The tide rushing out through this narrow entrance with great velocity & meeting the Tide coming in makes a Whirlpool which has a very remarkable appearance. Perhaps at H[igh] W[ater] a vessel of large size could be floated in as the water is then still.[2]

He does mention, as if an afterthought, "Gold bearing rocks are met with in the Mountains."

Pemberton's resulting map, *Sketch of a Journey of Exploration*, was remarkably accurate, considering that his instruments had been damaged beyond use by the rigours of the travel (see Fig. 71, page 159). He shows, in his spelling, the villages of Quamichin, Somenos, and Nitinat, the Cowichin and South rivers, and Mounts Tsouhalem, Prevost, and Gooch, as well as considerable shore detail of Cowichan Lake.

Lieutenant Gooch had one more brush with local history before *Satellite* returned home in 1860. He commanded a small detachment of marines in a longboat to provide visible, armed support to the collector of customs at Fort Langley—a position of considerable vulnerability at the time—during a particularly tense episode in the Fraser River gold rush. In August 1858 a conflict developed between rival factions of Californian prospectors at Yale. The local magistrate, Peter Whannell, exaggerating this as an imminent threat to British authority by American outlaws, pleaded for support. Governor Douglas felt this necessitated his personal presence, with Judge Matthew Baillie Begbie and a force of Royal Engineers and Royal Marines. Once colonial justice arrived, backed by a company of redcoats, no further shots were fired and the matter was resolved peaceably. The affair became popularly known as "Ned McGowan's War."

Gooch, having risen to the rank of captain and seeing action in the defence of Amoy, retired in 1870. He took command of the brigade of Royal Naval Artillery Volunteers guarding the Bristol Channel, and wrote the two articles recounting his adventure with Pemberton on Vancouver Island. He died in 1896.

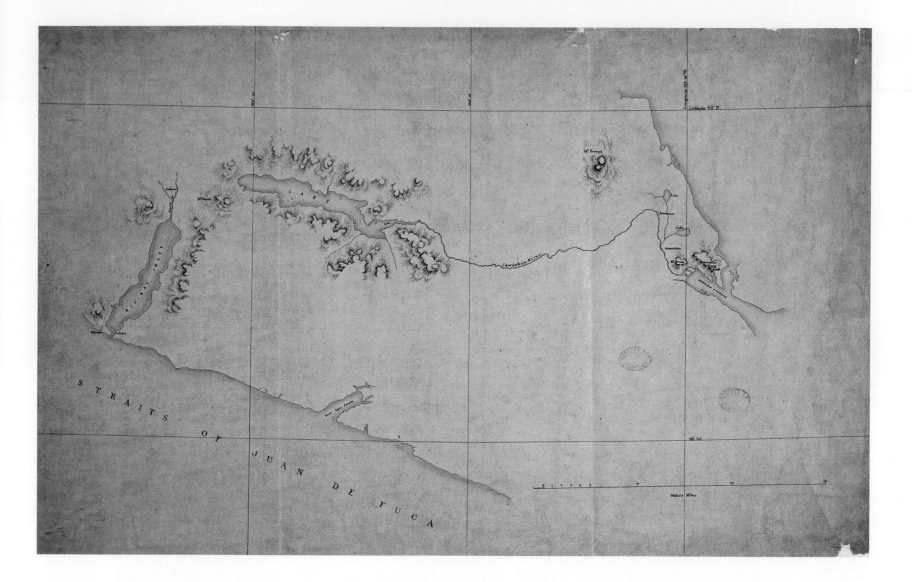

FIG 71 Joseph Pemberton's *Sketch of a Journey of Exploration* shows his party's route from Cowichan Harbour via Cowichan and Nitinat lakes into the Strait of Juan de Fuca. Note "Mt. Gooch" between the lakes, which someone later changed to Mount Vernon. [Courtesy of Hudson's Bay Company Archives, Archives of Manitoba, Winnipeg]

FIG 72 High on the north gallery of Christ Church Cathedral in Victoria is a series of painted window panels by Scottish artist James Ballantine. This one, *Exploration*, depicts surveyors working in "untamed and uncharted country." [Photo by author]

CHAPTER ELEVEN

THE NEW DISTRICTS

THE 1857 JOURNEY TO NITINAT with Lieutenant Sherlock Gooch was to be Joseph Pemberton's last overland expedition on Vancouver Island.

The following year, Victoria experienced a massive influx of prospectors on their way to the gold diggings of the Fraser River. London endorsed James Douglas's proclamation of authority over the goldfields by pronouncing British Columbia the second British colony on the west coast, with Douglas as governor and Pemberton as surveyor general for both colonies. These new duties on the mainland added to their burdens on the island. Pemberton had to expand his Victoria office to handle a surge of land claims from the flood of people into the town and the neighbouring, fertile peninsula of Saanich, and this work fully occupied his time until he retired in October 1864.

In 1859, Pemberton was obliged to sever his connection with the Hudson's Bay Company as a condition of taking an equivalent position with the colonial government, as were Douglas and Benjamin Pearse, Pemberton's trusted deputy, who had come to the colony in October 1851 as his apprentice.

By the end of 1853, Pemberton had established a structured system of districts for the colony, and had surveyed and marked their boundaries. He had kept Archibald Barclay, the secretary of the HBC in London, up to date on his progress with frequent reports and maps. Governor Douglas had similarly made the Colonial Office aware of Pemberton's advancing campaigns of reconnaissance, mapping, and land registration (see Fig. 73, page 162).

Once significant areas of potential interest to agricultural settlers had been identified, the next stage of exploration was to incorporate them into the land registry system. "Unsurveyed lands" were not available for settlement, although "squatters" or unregistered settlers had started arriving in the fertile Cowichan Valley.

Following the first-priority survey work related to the coal reserves of the Nanaimo area and the new settlement of Colville Town (see Fig. 74, page 163), Pemberton and Pearse explored the surrounding region, finding ample land well suited for farming.

As one of the first tasks following their change of status from company men to colonial servants, Pemberton delegated to

Pearse the creation of three new districts: Mountain, Cedar, and Cranberry (see Fig. 75, page 164). He was to delineate them, and prepare reports on characteristics with agricultural importance, such as topography, depth and quality of soil, tree cover, water resources, game and wildlife, climate, economic minerals—coal, limestone, salt, etc.—and the attitude of the local peoples. Pearse devoted the early summer of 1859 to this task.

Each new district contained up to 25 square miles (65 square kilometres) with rectangular sides (except along a coastline), aligned with the grid, and subdivided into square blocks of 1,000 acres (405 hectares). Each block could be further subdivided into 100-acre sections, as required. The work involved cutting lines through the bush along the divisions, measuring distances with a chain, and marking the intersections with cut posts. The surveyor needed a team of assistants, axemen, and packers in support, and by this time Pemberton and his men could call on a pool of men familiar with such fieldwork.

Pemberton had earlier written:

> There is a considerable number of lads in this country, of extraction partly native, who possess great natural intelligence and I believe it would be very desirable, if a Surveying Department should be . . . established here, to interest this class in its success.
>
> Two or three such lads might be taken young as pupils or apprentices, paying a moderate fee to cover trouble and expence [sic] until they could be of service . . . If any such plan were adopted, want of education would be the principal difficulty at first to be overcome.[1]

While no such formal training program was established, Pemberton had been building a cadre of such "lads"—not boys, but men in good physical condition and experienced in the forest—to be employed for seasonal fieldwork.

FIG 74 Nanaimo in 1859, painted by surgeon-lieutenant Edward Panter-Downes, of HMS *Tribune* (seen at anchor). It shows the chimney and winding wheel of the colony's first coal mine, the HBC bastion, storehouse, and loading pier. [Courtesy of the Royal BC Museum and Archives, Victoria]

FIG 75 The index map to show eight new districts around Nanaimo and the Cowichan Valley, surveyed and ready for settlement. Drawn in Pemberton's survey department and printed by the Royal Engineers on behalf of the Emigration Board in London. [Courtesy of Land Title and Survey Authority, Victoria, BC]

During that same season, 1859, Pemberton gave another surveyor, Oliver Wells, the task of establishing five more districts in the flat lands of the Cowichan Valley: Shawnigan, Cowichan (by this time the modern spelling had been adopted), Somenos, Comiaken, and Quamichan (see Fig. 75).

Wells is a rather mysterious person; little is known of either his background or subsequent life history. He appeared in Victoria during the gold rush of 1858 among the torrent of prospectors, associated merchants, service providers, and opportunists. He carried credentials sufficient for Pemberton to entrust him with laying out the proposed capital for the new province of British Columbia—the township of Derby, near Fort Langley.

Following that, Pemberton gave him responsibility for the crucial stage of bringing the Cowichan Valley into the district structure. To introduce Wells to the country he would be surveying, and to ensure that he understood the scope of exploration reports expected, Pemberton accompanied the newcomer while he surveyed the first of his new districts—Shawnigan.

In his field notebook, Wells recorded that the party consisted of himself, Pemberton, and five men: Olin Gates, John Hunter, Thomas Dooley, and William Kelly—from whose names, it seems likely they were recent arrivals rather than workers from the cadre of mixed-race "lads"—and "Louis." He was perhaps a local boatman who conveyed them between Victoria and their camps, and who sold them fish. They were well armed: "1 rifle, 1 musket, 2 Double barrel guns, 1 Colt revolver." They carried a bag of trade goods: "Powder & Flints, Balls, Shot, Tobacco & pipes, Calico, Shirts, Thread & needles, fishhooks, and Blankets."

They completed the Shawnigan district in three weeks, of which 14 days were spent actually surveying. Wells recorded that they had surveyed 29.75 line miles (47.9 kilometres)—subdividing 10,236.35 acres (4,143 hectares)—at a total cost of $268.82, or two-and-a-half cents per acre.

Having completed the district survey, the party returned to Victoria to restock their provisions. The group, except for Pemberton, then went back immediately to set up a new camp for the next district. Joining the team, according to Wells's next field book, was "Tomo"—presumably Antoine—who drew two trade blankets on account.

Pemberton returned to England on overdue leave, leaving Pearse to act in his stead. Wells, after fulfilling his assignment of the five districts and submitting a well-received report, also departed on a five-month leave, but failed, and without notification, to return.

Both Pearse and Wells made reference to the attitudes they had found among the local tribes. Pearse, reporting on those of the Mountain District around Mount Benson, wrote:

> The Indians, though numerous, are perfectly peaceful, and are made use of by the whites as ploughmen, servants, voyagers, in fact, labourers of all kinds of work. Their pay and rations amount to little, and, if kindly treated and properly superintended, the results of their labour are profitable to the employer.

Wells reported:

> Along the rivers there are nine Indian villages, as follows: three Clemclemaluts, two Comiaken, one Taitka, one Quamichan, one Somenos, and one Kokesailah . . . The Indians have shown throughout a perfectly friendly disposition, and a strong desire to see the white man settled among them. Their services may prove of utility to the early settler by way of cheap labour.[2]

From these observations, it would seem that Governor Douglas's earlier shows of force and summary justice, combined with his diplomatic talent, were having the desired effect, at least with the natives of that part of the colony.

Douglas dispatched the two sets of reports to London accompanied by detailed, finely drawn maps, the work of another recent arrival, a cartographer, Rudolph d'Heureuse, with the suggestion that they be lithographed and distributed. The dispatch pleased the officials at the Colonial Office:

> It is encouraging to receive such accounts of the natural capabilities of Vancouver's Island. It seems to be a very attractive region: & likely to prosper greatly, if the settlers can be secure against the Indians: at present (thanks to the Hudson's Bay Company management) these seem very tractable.[3]

They suggested that the Emigration Board publish the texts, and requested that the Military Topographic Office of the Royal Engineers print the maps.

In 1860, while on leave, Pemberton published *Facts and Figures relating to Vancouver Island and British Columbia*, a booklet summarizing "What to expect and how to get there" as a guide for prospective emigrants from Britain. In it, he provided a summary of knowledge about the two colonies, based on his near-decade of direct experience and responsibility. He included, as appendices, some reports of cross-island explorations, as well as four maps.

FIG 76 Captain Edward Stamp, master mariner and entrepreneur. He played a key role in the development of the community of Alberni by establishing a large-scale, commercial sawmill at the head of the inlet. [Courtesy of the Royal BC Museum and Archives, Victoria]

CHAPTER TWELVE

"A MOST ELIGIBLE AND HANDSOME LOCALITY": ALBERNI COLONIZED

IN LATE JULY 1848, CAPTAIN George Courtenay, RN, in command of HMS *Constance*, visited Victoria. During that six-week visit he had anchored in Esquimalt Harbour, pronouncing it "good and secure" with ample sources of fresh water and excellent spars, as well as supplies of potatoes and beef from the nearby Hudson's Bay Company farms. One of his crew at the time was a carpenter, William Eddy Banfield.

WILLIAM BANFIELD SETTLES ON VANCOUVER ISLAND

Few details are known of Banfield's early years. He was born on St. Mary's, one of the Isles of Scilly, off the "toe" of Cornwall's Land's End. The islands, often foggy, and exposed to ferocious storms sweeping in from the Atlantic, are notoriously hazardous for seafarers, so Banfield would have felt completely at home on the rocky, tempestuous, west coast of Vancouver Island. As a young man he learned skills in seamanship, carpentry, and boatbuilding, but, unable to find work, he joined the navy as a carpenter in 1846. Two years later, he was aboard *Constance* during the visit to Victoria.[1] While Banfield was busy cutting and trimming new spars for the ship, his shipbuilder's eye noted the impressive stands of fine timber throughout the region, and he recognized the potential that this remote outpost would hold for someone with his skills.

Records of Banfield's story for the five years after 1848 are scant, but it would seem that he took his discharge from the navy in good standing with Captain Courtenay, and returned to Scilly. From there, in 1851, he applied unsuccessfully to the HBC for permission to come to the new colony. Nonetheless, he got to Victoria somehow, for in 1853 he bought, and quickly resold, a town lot.

He was literate, and clearly of a curious and enterprising nature. Since he had little starting capital, his first few years ashore must have been both arduous and precarious. He traded with the various tribes on the island's west coast, eventually settling on a small creek just inland from Cape Beale, on the southern side of Barkley Sound, in the territory of the Ohiaht people, now called the Huu-ay-aht. He purchased a plot of land from the local leader, with whom he established a relationship of trust, and he drew up a document recording the transaction.

THE CARPENTER TAKES UP THE PEN

In 1854 Banfield joined forces with Peter Francis, who owned a trading sloop, *Leonede*, based in Ucluelet, and Thomas Loughton, another trader operating in Port San Juan. They traded with the "Native population" from Port San Juan as far as Cape Scott. A year later, Banfield began a long series of written reports, addressed initially to the governor, then to Colonial Secretary William Young, concerning various matters related to the region. Banfield said that the three men, all proud British subjects,

> deemed it our duty, to communicate to your Excellency, as much information relative to this part of the Island of Vancouver, as our simple means and poor ability will admit.

He proceeded to provide a paragraph on each of the tribes and villages: Nettinat, Oh-I-ata, She-Shata, To-qua-ata, You-cluel-Yet, Clayoquat, Ahouset, Moachat, Matchelat, Ehateset, Ki-You-Cut, Cheakleset, Koosh-Kema, Classet, Ko-uo-at, and Kot-seno, outlining the location and approximate numbers of people, and some details of their social structure.

For the Ki-You-Cut he noted:

> They are the most powerful on this side the Island they number in total about 3050, and send forth 1000 fighting men on an emergency; their chief is a young man, he has Complete Command over them, he is very desirous for white men to settle among them, and I stoped with him 10 days, and I felt as much at home and as safe as though I was at Victoria.

His first report continues with "General particulars relative to the aspect of places, their harbours, and facilities":

In the case of Nettinat,

[Francis] saw a narrow boat entrance, 4 feet water the utmost draft that it would admit—inside of which was a large piece of salt water, much larger than the interior harbour of "Soke," and with a small piece of prairie land at its bottom not adapted for agriculture to any extent, its harbour wholly unfitted for commerce.

This information would have preceded Pemberton and Gooch's experience by two years, although they made no reference to having known of it.

"You-cluel-Yet," he noted:

> [I]s a pretty little cove, when entered a mere reef of rocks outside, with a little piece of clear land about 2 mile from the village. We have not ascertained anything in the shape of minerals nor any thing, that would warrant Colonization.

Reporting on the peltry situation, Banfield related that:

> in the course of 12 months we have not seen above 4 sea otters skins and 20 others of different sorts . . . Those that have come here have been invariably traded by the Cape Flattery Indians. The Moachat and Mutchelat [*sic*] [Muchalaht] Tribes report [they] take the most skins their local situation would warrant me in thinking so, the Bay entrance to [Nootka] Sound is not adapted for oil or Dog-Fish. They have also a trail across the Country to the H.B.C. Fort [Rupert] from which circumstance I have presumed what skins they get are sold there they walk across in about 36 hours.[2]

In 1858, Banfield wrote a series of articles for the semi-official *Daily Victoria Gazette*, covering a wide range of subjects about life on the island's west coast. He pointed out the strategic location of the Alberni Inlet, noting that it provided sheltered, direct access to the Pacific, and that a short rail connection with

Nanaimo should be feasible. He extolled the great wealth of fishery—salmon, herring, and halibut—in nearby waters, and the potential for a whaling base, as well as the reserves of giant trees throughout the region. Victorians read his articles eagerly; many followed his example and came to settle along this hitherto little-known coast.

Young appointed Banfield government agent for the Alberni district in 1859, at an annual salary of £100. The following January Banfield, with the Ohiaht leader, Kle-shin, visited Victoria, where they were received by Douglas. The governor presented the leader with a new suit of clothes, and asked Banfield to find out and report, as accurately as possible, the numbers of people in the various west coast tribes.

Later that same year Banfield reported on the stands of timber that he had seen at the head of the Alberni Inlet:

> Although I had formally considered the timber there unable to compete either in quality or quantity with the timber on Puget Sound, I am now convinced that the stands in the district are both extensive and valuable . . . The places I have remarked merely at hazard, sir, will I think warrant me in stating that ere long it will cause Barclay Sound to be noticed and must eventually become an article of export and an important item in the prosperity and peopling of the Southern end of the Island.[3]

The following year, Banfield again travelled up the Alberni Inlet, noting many signs of copper mineralization as he went. At its head, he explored the Chee-tan-o-ass and Yu-cul-tat valleys. He reported:

> The Chee-tan-o-ass valley is the tract of country on the Nanaimo trail. Mr. Horn[e] the HBCo Clerk has long antecedent to this has no doubt given better information relative to it than I possibly can.

> It is a large tract of beautiful country alternate plain and wood land, but the wood land is so clear from under wood and such straight slender graceful red pine that it is nothing more than ornamental and no more than would be useful for farm purposes. I viewed it in dirty rainy weather when every thing looked gloomy, therefore I think I should not be guilty of exaggeration or high coloring to pronounce it by far the best tract of country on the Island. I was merely one day walk and for miles on either hand and before appeared the same, Sir, the soil was richer by far than about Victoria or Saanich. Where the trees have fallen they are broken and not uprooted. Some of the plains are covered in Sal-lal, I am not aware Sir of the proper name of this crop this common name is given to it by Canadians, or by Ferns and indigenous grass.

> On the following day I took a different direction, going up the Somass river intending to have gone a couple of days journey farther to the North towards Yu-cal-tat I got as far as the upper camp of the Opechesets' tribe on the border of a large lake which feeds the Somass River when my guides objected to go any farther alleging as an excuse that the weather was to [sic] cold to camp in the forest at night consequently I did not press them but they described a much larger tract of clear country in this direction than on the other. But Sir, I think before I forward this I shall make another visit and be able to give information from personal observation.[4]

While he was there, Banfield purchased a second small property "under rather than over 100 acres [40 hectares] of clear land at the mouth of the Somass River," from the locals, again drawing up a deed-of-sale document. He erected a small cabin, intending to stake a formal pre-emption claim once the area became duly available. He had moved his original cabin with the Ohiaht to another site nearby, later known as Port Desire, again making sure that the transaction was paid for and recorded. He was anxious to establish his claims with the authorities in Victoria, since he had heard rumours that a Captain Stamp had been given a large grant over the whole sound.

CAPTAIN STAMP PLANS A SAWMILL

This man, Captain Edward Stamp, had indeed secured from Douglas interim approval for a large lumbering operation in the area. The legal situation was then in limbo; the HBC was no longer responsible for creating and registering land titles, and the Colonial Office had yet to issue permission for Stamp to begin building. The entire district was still technically "unsurveyed land." Stamp would certainly have read Banfield's glowing articles and reports of the area's timber resources, and, actively seeking a suitable site for the location of a major mill, he moved quickly to exploit this serendipitous news.

Stamp, a master mariner and astute businessman, was born at Alnwick in England, on the North Sea at the border with Scotland, and had first come to the north Pacific coast in 1857 to collect a shipment of lumber bound for Australia. Impressed with the coast's potential, he contracted with London merchants for another voyage to obtain spars, ships' timbers, and lumber (see Fig. 76, page 166). He was in Victoria in 1858 when the Fraser River gold rush began, and immediately recognized the many business opportunities this would create.

He registered as an importer and commission agent. One of his ventures was an attempt to establish a steamer service between Victoria and San Francisco. This did not succeed, but he did manage to put together a London syndicate to establish an industrial-scale export lumber mill on Vancouver Island. This syndicate eventually came under the control of a family named Anderson, and the venture became known as the Anderson Mill.

SETTLING A SITE FOR THE MILL

In early 1859, Douglas, keen to see this development come about, granted Stamp temporary possession of 2,000 acres (800 hectares) for the mill and associated settlement, plus 15,000 acres (6,000 hectares) of timber rights, all subject to approval by the colonial secretary in London. The agreed sale price was not to exceed one pound per acre. The objects of the enterprise, in addition to milling and exporting lumber, were shipbuilding, commercial fishing, whaling, and mining—all activities suggested as possible by Banfield in his *Victoria Gazette* articles.

In April 1860, the armed commercial schooner *Meg Merrilies* docked in Victoria with a cargo of equipment and personnel for the new mill at Alberni. Aboard was a young executive from the syndicate backing the enterprise, Gilbert Malcolm Sproat, who carried a letter of introduction from the Duke of Newcastle to Governor Douglas. Sproat, the son of a farmer from Kirkcudbright in southwest Scotland, had excelled as a student while studying commercial law and being trained for the prestigious Indian Civil Service. He had, instead, joined the London merchants Thomson & Company, which acquired a major stockholding in what became the Anderson syndicate. Now, aged 26, he was to be deputy to Captain Stamp, the syndicate's manager on the west coast (see Fig. 77, page 171).

At the end of June, *Meg Merrilies* entered Barkley Sound, picking up Banfield to act as interpreter and local liaison adviser before heading to the proposed mill site at the head of the Alberni Inlet. Banfield reported to Young:

I accompanied the party up the canal to make every thing go as smooth as possible between them and the natives—the white men appear a decent class of men and have promised to abide by instructions that I furnished their leading man with.

Banfield had earlier drawn up a set of guidelines for settlers and visiting vessels on interacting with the local tribes. Young and Douglas had approved these guidelines, but Banfield felt that if they could be printed, and copies made available for distribution, they would carry more weight with newcomers.

> The natives have also promised not to annoy them, but Sir, I shall visit them at short intervals and use my influence with either party should any dispute take place which I do not at present apprehend.[5]

A second ship sent out from England by the syndicate, *Woodpecker*, arrived after a passage of 140 days, bringing more personnel, including some wives and children, machinery, and general merchandise. A week later, *Meg Merrilies* again pulled into port, with oxen, mechanics, and more merchandise. Also aboard were Stamp and Sproat, with Banfield acting once more as translator. By this time, the local Tseshaht people had surrounded the area with a temporary encampment, attracted by the construction activity.

There are two versions of the negotiations that ensued. According to Sproat, in his book *Scenes of Savage Life*, published eight years after the events:

> In August 1860, I entered Nitinaht; or Barkley Sound, on the outside, or western, coast of Vancouver Island, with two armed vessels, *Woodpecker* and *Meg Merrilies*, manned by about fifty men, who accompanied me for the purpose of taking possession of the district now called Alberni.
>
> Reaching the entrance of this inlet, we sailed for twenty miles up to the end of it—as up a natural canal—three-quarters of a mile wide and very deep, bordered by rocky mountains, which rose high on both sides almost perpendicularly from the water. The view, as we advanced up this inlet from the sea, was shut in behind

FIG 77 Gilbert Sproat, a bright and well-educated administrator, deputy to Captain Stamp at the Anderson sawmill, initially disdained Vancouver Island's Indigenous people, but later became a student, admirer, and defender of their culture and human rights. [Courtesy of the Royal BC Museum and Archives, Victoria]

and before us, making the prospect like that from a mountain lake. At the end of this singular canal, the rocky sides of which appear to have been smoothed by a continued action of moving ice upon their surface, and which gives the idea of having been the furrow of a mighty glacier moving downwards to the sea, the high land on the right receded from the shore, and a large bay or basin, with a river flowing into it through level wooded land, met our view. The range of hills which opened on one side formed an elbow about ten miles distant from the canal, and crossing in the direction almost at right angles to the course of the inlet, met a continuation of the other range, and thus shut in the district known to all the Indians as the famous berry land of Somass.

Near a pretty point at one side of the bay, where there was a beach shaded by young trees, the summer encampment of a tribe of natives was to be seen. Our arrival caused a stir, and we saw their flambeaux of gumsticks flickering among the trees during the night.

In the morning I sent a boat for the chief, and explained to him that his tribe must move their encampment, as we had bought all the surrounding land from the Queen of England, and wished to occupy the site of the village for a particular purpose. He replied that the land belonged to themselves, but that they were willing to sell it. The price not being excessive, I paid him what was asked—about twenty pounds' worth of goods—for the sake of peace, on condition that the whole people and buildings should be moved next day.

But no movement was then made, and as an excuse it was stated that the children were sick. On the day following the encampment was in commotion; speeches were made, faces blackened, guns and pikes got out, and barricades formed. Outnumbered as we were, ten to one, by men armed with muskets, and our communication with the sea cut off by the impossibility of sailing down the Alberni Inlet (the prevalent breeze blowing up it),

there was some cause for alarm had the natives been resolute. But being provided, fortunately, in both vessels with cannon—of which the natives at that time were much afraid—they, after a little show of force on our side, saw that resistance would be inexpedient, and began to move from the spot . . . two or three days after wards, when the village had been moved to another place [Somass], not far distant, I visited the principal house at the new encampment, with a native interpreter. [Presumably, this was Banfield. No one else at the time would have been capable of conveying such complex interactions between speakers of English and the local Nootkan dialect. Interestingly, nowhere in his book does Sproat refer to Banfield by name.]

"Chiefs of the Sheshaht," I said on entering, "are you well; are your women in health; are your children hearty; do your people get plenty of fish and fruits?"

"Yes," answered an old man, "our families are well; our people have plenty of food; but how long will this last we know not. We see your ships, and hear things that make our hearts grow faint. They say more King George men will soon be here, and will take our land, our firewood, our fishing grounds; that we shall be placed on a little spot, and will have to do everything according to the wishes of the King George men."

"Do you believe this?" I asked.

"We want your information." Said the speaker.

"Then," answered I, "it is true that more King George men (as they call the English) are coming: they will soon be here; but your land will be bought at a fair price."

"We do not wish to sell our land, nor our water; let your friends stay in their own country."

To which I rejoined: "My great chief, the high chief of the King George men, seeing you do not work your land, orders that you shall sell it. It is of no use to you. The trees you do not need; you will fish and hunt as you do now, and collect firewood, planks for your houses, and cedar for your canoes. The white man will give you work, and buy your fish and oil,"

"Ah, but we don't care to do as the white men wish."

"Whether or not," said I, "the white man will come . . . will teach your children to read printing, and to be like themselves."

"We do not want the white man. He steals what we have. We wish to live as we are." . . .

These were the first savages that I had ever seen, and they were probably at that time less known than any aboriginal people under British dominion.[6]

Banfield's report to Young, however, viewed the negotiations in a far more pragmatic light:

The following day [we] proceeded to make a treaty with the natives—Sheshat [Tseshaht] Tribe—and it is with much satisfaction I am enabled to state to you Sir that an arrangement amicable and satisfactory have been effected between the above named gentlemen [Stamp and Sproat] and the chiefs of the Sheshat tribe. The land selected for a mill site and buildings was quietly ceded to him after some slight hesitation on the part of the natives in immediately removing their lodges from the spot.

It was not their usual camping ground but since the first working party came down they erected temporary lodges. Captain Stamp made them a present of some 50 Bkts trinkets molasses and food. I explained to the chiefs the nature of Captain Stamp's settling among them which they thoroughly comprehend, and at present express entire satisfaction.

I likewise Sir told them it was by the express desire and sanction of his Excellency the Governor, that settlement of white people among them was allowed and that any injury or annoyance on their part to whites would be viewed with chastisement, also that whites would not be permitted to wantonly injure them. They put much confidence in Captain Stamp seeing the nature of his settlement is for a permanency.

I could not get them to remove to their old encampment consequently I put them on the place which I bought from them or made an exchange for a few blankets in February last . . .

Buildings Sir are progressing rapidly and the place assuming quite a civilized aspect.

BANFIELD EXPLORES THE NEARBY VALLEYS

Once the negotiations had been settled, Banfield took the opportunity to continue his exploration of the valleys inland from the head of the inlet (see Fig. 78, page 174):

I made a journey of two days through what I termed in a former communication the Yucultat valley. It proved to be a large lake some 30 miles [48 kilometres] in length running in a westerly direction [see Fig. 79, page 174] a continuation of the lake which Mr. Horn[e] first explored and which terminated in a small river and merely separated by a minor mountain from the Lake Okeaman in the Clayoquat district. A very rough tracing I have enclosed although inaccurate as regards distances, will convey the position and formation of the Clayoquat and Alberni waters the former Sir I am intimatly [sic] acquainted with long antecedent to this time. [See Fig. 80, page 174]

From his sketch map, it would seem that he referred to Sproat Lake as "Ah-nuk-lah Lake," connected by a trail to Great Central Lake, called Cla-coote Lake or Mah-howelth. He also noted a "Lake Nah-Mint flows into the Alberni 16 miles [26 kilometres] from Head"—clearly today's Nahmint Lake and River. He added a footnote "Many other lakes are in this neighbourhood." To the northeast, his "Chee-tan-o-ass" refers to the extensive flat lands beneath the southeastern end of the Beaufort escarpment.

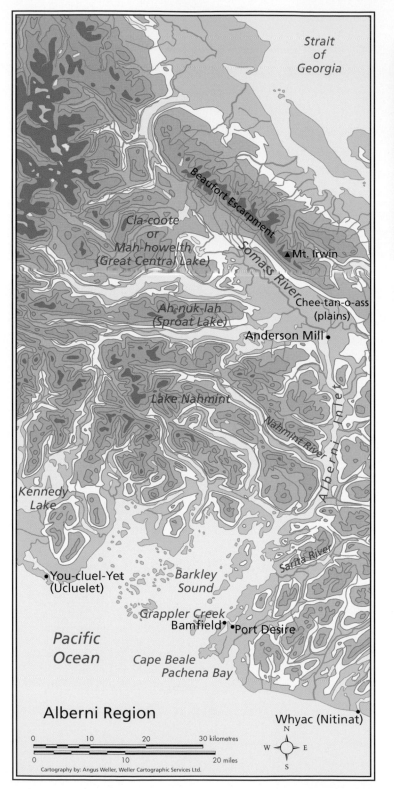

Alberni Region

Strait
of
Georgia

Beaufort Escarpment

Cla-coote
or
Mah-howelth
(Great Central Lake)

Somass River

▲ Mt. Irwin

Chee-tan-o-ass
(plains)

Ah-nuk-lah
(Sproat Lake)

Anderson Mill •

Lake Nahmint

Nahmint River

Alberni Inlet

Kennedy
Lake

Sarita River

• You-cluel-Yet
(Ucluelet)

Barkley
Sound

Grappler Creek
Bamfield •
• Port Desire

Pacific
Ocean

Cape Beale
Pachena Bay

Whyac (Nitinat)

0   10   20   30 kilometres
0   10   20 miles

N
W E
S

Cartography by: Angus Weller, Weller Cartographic Services Ltd.

(CLOCKWISE FROM LEFT) FIG 78   The region surrounding Alberni as explored by William Eddy Banfield between 1854 and 1862, while he served as Indian agent for the west coast of Vancouver Island. [Map by Angus Weller]

FIG 79   In 1913 Leonard Frank of Alberni took this photograph of Sproat Lake, the traditional territory of the Hupacasath (previously Opetchesaht) branch of the Nuu-chah-nulth people. [Author's collection]

FIG 80   William Banfield's report to the colonial secretary of September 6, 1860, included this sketch map of the region of the lakes near Alberni, based on his own explorations and hearsay from locals. [Courtesy of the Royal BC Museum and Archives, Victoria]

The sketch also showed the location of the mill and a dotted line heading east, marked "Nanimo track."

The lake he identifies as "Okeaman" is probably Kennedy Lake, considerably displaced. There is a Tia-o-qui-aht people's village, Okeamin, where the Kennedy River flows into the Tofino arm of Clayoquot Sound. The following year, Captain Richards of the survey ship HMS *Hecate* learned from local people of a large lake south and east of Tofino Inlet and connected to it by a fast-flowing stream, rich in salmon, but he was unable to explore it.

Banfield's report continued:

> But no agricultural land exists on the lake I have visited and marked on the sketch Ah-nuck-lah [*sic*]—there is another large lake adjoining this—which I also tried explore since Captain Stamp has been down in company with him but the river we found too rapid for canoes, but a trail connects both lakes some three fourths of a mile [1.2 kilometres] which I shall try at some future time—but the waters of this lake Mah-howelth must extend almost to the Gulf of Georgia if the Indians description is correct, but I am doubtful of any extent of agricultural land. Cranberry marshes exist to some extent.[7]

In April of the following year, Banfield returned to explore the two large lakes, and reported:

> I was at the lake, the larger of the two which feed the Somass River. I find no agricultural land exists on either side of this lake it is completely enclosed by mountains studded from base to apex with timber Sir, a species of Cypress [Yellow Cedar] exists on the mountain sides, admirably suited for boat building or fine finishing work, and white pine of good quality but not in large quantity.

The extreme length of the lake by computation about 35 miles [in fact, it is 20.5 miles, or 33 kilometres] running in a lateral direction with the island or about east and west nearly—about 3 miles at the head was frozen in, Sir.

> On the evening of the 20th April HMS *Hecate* arrived at Alberni. Mr. Mayne, the first Lieutenant proposes to open out if possible a new trail towards Nenimo [Nanaimo] and will start in a day or two. I have offered to accompany him, and he has kindly acceded to my request Sir I trust Mr Maynes efforts will be successful, and any little assistance on my part Sir will be cheerfully rendered.[8]

Banfield's last report concerned his discovery of some promising land for settlement close to his house on what had recently been named Grappler Creek, among the Ohiaht. For a short period, payments from Stamp had supplemented his stipend from Young, but he had recognized the conflict of interest and had decided to put distance between himself and the mill. Perhaps he had clashed with Stamp, who had a strong personality, or with Sproat, but he did not say so in his reports. After enthusing about the great richness of the fishing off Cape Beale, he described the immediate hinterland:

> At the point on Cape Beale where Captain Richards has marked a sandy beach, a village might be settled from twenty to fifty families. In the rear of this beach, probably not more than two hundred yards [183 metres], is a handsome lake running in an easterly direction and extending to within about a mile and a half [2.4 kilometres] of Banfield Creek. It is not environed by mountains or hills and the borders, as far as my observation has yet extended, are surrounded by willows and alders for a margin of a quarter of a mile or more and it has struck me as exceedingly rich lands and easily brought under cultivation and I should unhesitatingly pronounce it a most eligible and handsome locality.

Between this lake, Kichka, and Pachena Bay, is a tract of land some 2½ miles [4 kilometres] in length by about two thirds of a mile broad, the eastern end of which is a cranberry swamp and the southern part is higher and adapted for grazing and tillage.[9]

The rich land he described was, in the 1920s, part of the federal government's reserve for a national park of 232 square miles (600 square kilometres) between Port Renfrew and the Sarita River. This plan failed as a result of disagreements between the federal and provincial governments over mineral rights, but the province eventually established the Cape Beale headland as a provincial park. In 1971, it was incorporated into the Pacific Rim National Park, and is, today, the western end of the West Coast Trail.

BANFIELD'S MYSTERIOUS DEMISE

Within two months of Banfield's report on Cape Beale, he was dead.

DROWNED—Mr. Banfield, Indian Agent at Barclay Sound, and well known for many years in Victoria, was unfortunately drowned in the Sound last Monday afternoon. He had gone out in a canoe with an Indian to meet the schooner *Alberni*, which was expected in, and was never seen again.[10]

Banfield's associate, Peter Francis, nursed suspicions about this tragedy and went to investigate. In the spring he came to Victoria with his findings. Ohiaht men, including Kle-shin, the leader, had told him that it had been no accident. One of the band, Klatsmick, they said, had deliberately upset Banfield's canoe and prevented him from reboarding, with blows from his paddle. The body was never recovered. To bring the accused to Victoria for trial, Douglas dispatched the superintendent of police, Horace Smith, in a naval gunboat.

On November 3, 1864, Klatsmick was tried for the murder of William Banfield, the attorney general prosecuting. Klatsmick pleaded not guilty, but two key witnesses, Francis and Kle-shin, both testified that the accused had confessed to killing Banfield with two thrusts of his knife, and had even boasted of it. Francis added that the accused had offered him "a lot of skins" if he did not give testimony. After a heated debate about whether an unconverted Indian could understand the nature of testimony under oath, the court acquitted Klatsmick, who returned to his village, where he continued to boast openly of his deed (see Fig. 81, page 177).

An apparent motive later emerged. Previously, Banfield had been the unwitting accessory to the murder of one of Klatsmick's kinsmen, who had been his house guest. Under the traditional Ohiaht code of justice, Banfield, in failing to protect his guest, even though the man had left, had incurred a blood-debt. So, in local eyes, not only was Klatsmick entitled to exact retribution from Banfield, but family honour bound him to do so—and to proclaim the fact. This rationale was not raised at the trial in Victoria.

PROGRESS AND PROBLEMS AT THE MILL

In the meantime, the Anderson Mill came into production. By the end of 1860, several outbuildings, including stores and bunkhouses, had been erected, the heavy foundations for the sawmill were complete, and logging was under way. By mid-1861, *Meg Merrilies* carried the first cargo of 30,000 feet (9,144 metres) of lumber. Douglas declared Alberni a port of entry and appointed Stamp as collector of customs and magistrate of the going concern. An 87-foot (26-metre) schooner was under construction, and 250 acres (100 hectares) of farms were producing peas, barley, and oats.

Despite the severe winter of 1861–62, when ice in the inlet prevented ships from getting to within four miles (six kilometres) of the mill, 14 ships carried a total of over 8,000,000 linear feet (2,500,000 metres) of rough and dressed lumber, plus four cargoes of spars in 1862. Stamp donated one of those spars—159 feet (48 metres) long—to Kew Gardens in London, where it served as the flagstaff for the next 58 years (see Fig. 82, page 178).

In a disagreement early in 1864, Stamp parted company with the Andersons, and Sproat replaced him as manager and magistrate. But already the mill was facing difficulties. Once the trees in the immediate vicinity or close to the shore had been felled, the supply of logs to the voracious blades of the mill became a limiting factor. Huge trees could only be brought to the mill by long teams of oxen that skidded them along cordwood roads (see Fig. 83, page 178), or by floating them down shallow, rocky streams. Logging railroads overcame this problem, but they came along too late for the Anderson Mill. At the close of 1864, it was forced to cease operations, having by then produced a total of 35,000,000 board feet (83,000 cubic metres) of lumber, but without profit for the investors.

SPROAT'S LATER YEARS

Gilbert Sproat returned to England in 1865, whereupon he organized the London Committee for watching the affairs of British Columbia, to lobby the colonial administration. When BC joined the Canadian confederation in 1871, Sproat became the province's first agent-general in London. By this time, he had developed a strong interest in ethnology, in particular the culture and language of the people of the Nootka and Alberni region, whom he termed the Aht tribes and the 14 First Nations, are now called the Nuu-chah-nulth, meaning "all along the mountains and sea." [11] In 1868 he published a book, *Scenes and Studies of Savage Life*, still recognized as an outstanding description of First Nations life on Vancouver Island's west coast (see Fig. 84, page 179).

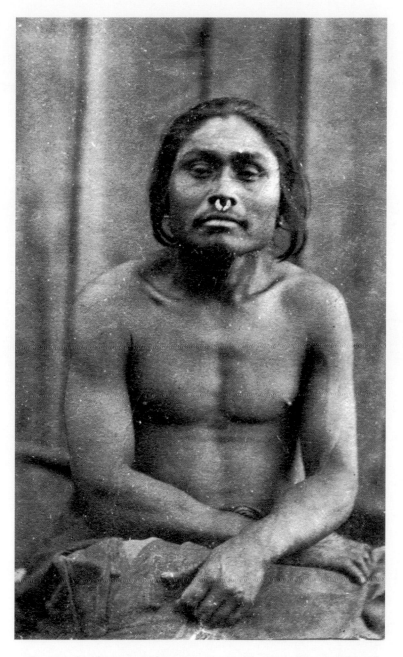

FIG 81 Carlo Gentile's portrait of an unnamed man of the Ohiaht (Huu-ay-aht) people. Before his murder, William Banfield would have known this man as a neighbour. [Courtesy of Greene Frogge Press]

FIG 82 (LEFT)   The 48-metre tall flagstaff at the Royal Botanic Gardens at Kew originated as a Douglas fir from Alberni. The Anderson company donated the spar, erected in 1861 as the world's tallest flagpole. Seen here in January 1909, the Union Flag flies at half mast to mourn the passing of Queen Victoria. [© Copyright the Board of Trustees of the Royal Botanic Gardens, Kew, London, UK]

FIG 83 (BELOW)   A 12-oxen team hauls logs from timber giants harvested in Alberni-area forests to the Anderson Mill. A cordwood road made from smaller spars provides a stable and smooth-riding track. [Courtesy of the Royal BC Museum and Archives, Victoria]

Sproat returned to BC in 1876, and was appointed to a new commission set up to reconcile differing views of Indian reserves between the dominion and the province. During the next three and a half years, he laboured strenuously to bring a measure of justice to the allocation of land for First Nations, but hardliners in the government of BC thwarted all his efforts.

He retired to Victoria in 1898, writing extensively to correct perceived misrepresentations in the early history of the two colonies. The journalist and former premier, Amor de Cosmos, is credited with remarking, "Sproat has forgotten more in one day than most of us could learn in a lifetime."

The island's toponymy commemorates all three men—Stamp, Sproat, and Banfield—by a river, a lake, and a small community on a creek. The unfortunate last of these suffered one final indignity: having his name misspelled as Bamfield for posterity.

FIG 84 Carlo Gentile described this couple as "Alberni Chief & his wife." Historian John Hayman identifies the man as Quatjenam, the second leader of the Opetchesaht tribe, Alberni. [Courtesy of Greene Frogge Press]

FIG 85 Captain and Mrs. Richards and officers of HMS *Plumper* in 1862. Richards is standing to his wife's left. Lieutenant Mayne is at far right; Pender is seated to Mrs. Richards's right, with Bedwell to his right. [Courtesy of the Royal BC Museum and Archives, Victoria]

CHAPTER THIRTEEN

GEORGE RICHARDS AND
THE MEN OF *PLUMPER*

IN DECEMBER 1856, THE HEAD of the Royal Navy's hydrographic surveying office, (known in the service as the Hydrographer), was Rear Admiral John Washington. He appointed Captain George Henry Richards, RN, to the command of HMS *Plumper* for a multi-purpose surveying voyage to the waters surrounding the colony of Vancouver Island. Requested for some years by the governor, James Douglas, this commission had at last been mobilized in response to several concerns: the increasing presence of American settlers and prospectors; the strong possibility of rich placer gold deposits along the Fraser River; and ambiguity in the Oregon Treaty of 1846 about the location of the water boundary between US and British territories on the Pacific coast.

Washington could not have selected a more experienced and capable officer than Richards. The son of a naval officer, at the age of 13 he followed his father into the service. While still a midshipman, he joined HMS *Sulphur*, initially under Captain Frederick Beechey, then Captain Sir Edward Belcher—both stern disciplinarians—on an extended surveying voyage to the Pacific.

In 1837 he called into Nootka Sound to verify Cook's astronomy. He also participated in surveys of the Falkland Islands and Patagonia, and, for four years, the rugged, complex coasts of New Zealand.

He saw military action during hostilities in the Opium War in China and in Argentina, earning commendations for bravery. As second in command to Belcher in HMS *Assistance*, he spent two years in the Arctic searching for the Franklin expedition. During this time, Richards gained further distinction for undertaking 2,000 miles of dog-sled journeys, including one of 93 days. After rising steadily through the ranks, he was promoted to captain in 1854, at age 34. *Plumper* was his first command.

Plumper, commissioned in 1848, was a barque-rigged, screw sloop of 484 tons (439 tonnes), 140 feet (42.6 metres) long; it carried 12 guns and up to 7 ship's boats of various sizes, to be used for survey operations. Modifications for charting meant that accommodation for officers and crew was cramped. Under steam, *Plumper* could just manage six-and-a-half knots. A major disadvantage came when the ship was changing between sail and steam. The propeller, eight-and-a-half feet (2.6 metres) in diameter, acted as a drogue under sail, so it had to be laboriously dismounted through the hull, then reinstalled when required.

During his initial inspection of his new command, Richards and his first officer, Lieutenant William Moriarty, discovered that *Plumper* needed repairs, which postponed their departure by a few months. Further troubles during their outbound voyage caused two more months' delay in Rio de Janeiro. These problems meant that they had to transit the Strait of Magellan in mid-winter, losing even more time. It was not until November 10, 1857, that *Plumper* entered Esquimalt and anchored.

On the face of it, this mission might not seem to have been a voyage of exploration. It was carried out initially in *Plumper*, later re-equipped with HMS *Hecate*, and eventually continued in HMS *Beaver*. It had come to retrace earlier work by the various Spaniards, Cook, and Vancouver—true explorers all. Richards's task might seem merely to bring greater detail and accuracy to an existing chart, rather than venturing into the unknown. However, the latest available cartography contained significant gaps and errors, as those reliant on such documents well knew.

As a result of the 13 years that the team devoted to charting the coast and adjacent waters of the island, and the mainland as far as the Alaskan boundary, 994 miles (1,600 kilometres) in all, it was among the most accurately and thoroughly surveyed of any of the world's coastlines, and their work most certainly did involve true exploration, both by sea and on land.

Richards faced a challenging technical task. Moreover, he had to serve, simultaneously, four masters: the Hydrographer, the admiral commanding the Pacific Station, the colonial governor, and Captain James Prevost, RN, of HMS *Satellite*, his senior officer on the International Boundary Commission.

Plumper's complement of officers included Moriarty and two more lieutenants qualified to take watch command, an engineer, a surgeon, a paymaster, and six specialist survey officers, called masters, of different grades and experience (see Fig. 85, page 180). The number of the crew is not on record, but since there were three masts, sails, and rigging to handle, as well as seven boats to man and the furnace to stoke, the complement would have been sizable, perhaps a hundred in all. In view of the risk of having seamen leave to join the gold rush, Douglas arranged that the entire crews of *Plumper* and *Satellite* (and later *Hecate* and *Beaver*) would have their pay doubled from the colony's funds for their time in local waters.

Richards's first duty on arrival was to report to Prevost, the senior British representative for maritime aspects on the Anglo-American Boundary Commission. They were to meet with their counterparts to agree on, and erect, a monument at the location where the 49th parallel—the negotiated border—crossed the coast (see Fig. 86, page 183). After that, Richards was to make "an accurate nautical survey of such portions of the channels and islands which lie between Vancouvers island and the Continent of America." This was needed to provide a chart on which to base the potentially heated discussion about the water boundary through the San Juan Archipelago.

By the time these two tasks had been accomplished, and *Plumper* could start on more general charting of the Gulf (soon to be termed the Strait) of Georgia, it was spring of 1860. Not that these two surveys alone had occupied the interim two years; other duties had interrupted and taken priority. Gold had been confirmed in the Thompson and Fraser rivers, bringing many prospectors through Victoria headed for the diggings. *Plumper*'s urgent mission was to survey the treacherous Fraser estuary and upstream as far as Fort Langley, and Burrard Inlet—major points of access to the goldfields.

Douglas also called on Richards to help quell the conflict instigated by the notorious Ned McGowan among the mostly American miners. He detached one of his officers, Lieutenant Charles Mayne, RN, to continue the Fraser survey aboard a shallow-draft sternwheeler as far as Yale. At Douglas's request, Mayne also surveyed the Lillooet region.

Between meeting these demands, Richards found time to resurvey the strategic harbours of Victoria, Esquimalt, and Nanaimo, where he was able to incorporate land details supplied by the colonial surveyor, Joseph Pemberton. In October 1858 he prepared, at the request of Douglas, a summary of the harbours of Vancouver Island. He was able to describe those within the Strait of Juan de Fuca and as far as Nanaimo, but acknowledged that:

> Of the several inlets and sounds which indent the Western Coast of the Island, but little is yet known; since the time of Vancouver, they have rarely been visited except by sealers and small vessels who trade with the natives for oil and fish . . . Many years since, I visited Nootka Sound which probably may be taken as a type of the others in their general characteristic, deep and narrow channels, studded with Islands and thickly timbered . . . It is more than probable that when the tide of emigration shall set in the direction of Vancouver Island these Inlets will become of great importance, particularly that of Nitinat or Barclay Sound on the S.W. Coast close to the entrance of Fuca Strait, and the head of whose waters have been reached in little more than [a few] days Journey on foot, from the Coast a few miles North of Nanaimo harbour on the East Coast. Mr. Horn[e] a gentleman of the Hudson Bay Company who made this journey informs me that he crossed a very extensive lake in the centre of the Island and that much good and open land exists in its neighbourhood entirely free from the dense forests which fringe the whole sea Coast of the Island.[1]

FIG 86 The obelisk marking the 49th parallel at Point Roberts, erected in 1862 by the Joint Boundary Commission for the Treaty of Washington, 1846. [Author's collection]

FIG 87 Late in October 1859, photographer Francis Claudet captured this daguerreotype image of a field gun, tents, and men of the US Third Artillery in position near the HBC's Belle View farm on San Juan Island. This was at the peak of the armed standoff later known as "The Pig War." [Courtesy of the Royal BC Museum and Archives, Victoria)

The next year, Richards accompanied Horne on his annual trading trip from Qualicum to Alberni. Noting the ridge of the Beaufort Range, over which they scrambled to get to Alberni, he felt that although it might answer as a trail for foot travellers, it was too steep to ever be considered for a roadway. Two years later, he would send one of his officers to try to find just such a route from the Alberni end, where the new settlement was under way.

Also during 1859, tension with American squatters on San Juan Island increased to the point of an armed standoff. *Plumper* was among the three naval ships ordered by Douglas to blockade the disputed island, confronting a substantial military force which included field artillery and an irascible American brigadier (see Fig. 87, page 184). *Plumper* conveyed a troop of red-coated Royal Engineers and marines with orders to oppose further landings. At the last minute, cooler heads arrived to defuse the so-called "Pig War," and the belligerents retired to separate camps to await a diplomatic settlement of the issue of jurisdiction.

The engineers were from the recently arrived Columbia Detachment, camped at New Westminster to reinforce Douglas's proclamation the previous year of the colony of British Columbia. They were to establish roads and townships, and map the goldfields region. Though Douglas was governor of both colonies, authorities in London appointed the commander of the detachment, Colonel Richard Moody, RE, as lieutenant-governor of the new colony. Moody had been aboard *Plumper* during the San Juan confrontation. Among other activities, the engineers set up a printing press, enabling Richards to have some of his early draft charts printed and available for local use.

During the winter seasons, the surveyors had been drafting their charts and assembling data for the associated *Sailing Directions*, working in one half of a hut at Hospital Point,

Esquimalt. Richards had taken a small cottage close by for his wife Mary—the daughter of a Royal Engineer officer—and their three young children.

Although *Plumper* had served reasonably well for local work, by the end of 1859, Richards had identified its limitations with regard to navigating the many narrow channels north of the Strait of Georgia, where tidal flows could reach eight knots. Moreover, he had crew problems. He had to operate *Plumper* short-handed by up to 14 men, and the contracts of many of the remainder were due to expire soon. It would be impossible to find local replacements. He requested that *Plumper* be replaced with, preferably, a more powerful paddlewheel sloop with greater space for a chartroom and accommodation.

In May 1858, *Plumper* had run aground near Waldron Island— an occupational hazard in surveying uncharted waters. A diver later inspected the damage, and recommended that the hull get attention in a dry dock. The nearest was at San Francisco, so the first few weeks of 1860 were lost in repairs. When *Plumper* returned after coaling in Nanaimo, the crew charted up the east coast of the island as far as Fort Rupert, today's Port McNeill.

LIEUTENANT MAYNE AND DR. WOOD EXPLORE THE COURTENAY VALLEY

As the survey parties in ship's boats worked their way past the northern end of Denman Island, Mayne went on a two-day exploration of the Courtenay River. The ship's surgeon-lieutenant, Charles Wood, accompanied him to collect botanical and other natural history specimens. Four local guides completed the party.

Mayne's report to Richards described the potential difficulties for vessels of any draft to navigate even a short distance into the river: a wide, low-lying tidal estuary flanked a narrow, shallow, winding stream. After barely two miles in their boat and only a few more by canoe, the party's progress was blocked by fallen trees. The men explored both banks on foot and discovered, beyond a thick fringe of willow and maple trees, that three good-sized prairies gave way to much denser forest, through which Mayne estimated they would manage to progress at only six to eight miles a day. He reported that:

> The three prairies we visited contained together about 5000 or 6000 acres [20 to 24 square kilometres] of perfectly clear land ready for the plough, the soil a rich vegetable mould, the whole well watered and on sufficient slope to make drainage very easy for the few swampy patches here and there which require it, and with abundant timber for building and fencing . . .
>
> In summer the whole plain is covered with berries, for which the Indians go there. They well know the value of the land, & informed me several times that it was very good: that all the Indians went there in summer to gather berries and would therefore require a great many blankets for it. They perfectly understand, as do the Indians where ever a white man shows himself that the time is drawing near when they will lose their land and asked me several times when we were coming to live there.
>
> They say bears, wolves, and deer are very plentiful. I saw three of the latter and abundant indications of the presence of the others. Grouse are numerous also. In the season, about 2 months hence, the river is full of salmon, and the sands at the mouth of the river are now covered in ducks & geese.
>
> Altogether I consider this a most desirable place for a settle-ment, though the land at present clear is not perhaps sufficient for a very large one.

From his guides Mayne learned the local name of the main river, "Tzõ-õ-õme" (Tsolum) and the one joining it two miles from the mouth, the "Pûnt-lûch" (Puntledge), which:

> comes down the large valley south of Mt Beecher and I think it takes its rise in the Central Lake. I remember Mr. Pemberton, the Colonial Surveyor, mentioning a river running, if I remember right, from the central lake through this valley, which he had seen from behind the Alphabetical [Beaufort] range.[2]

They rejoined *Plumper* at anchor in Henry Bay, Denman Island, and the survey of the coast continued northward. Theirs was a full hydrographic survey. The resultant chart would show the coastlines—as evidenced by the high-water mark—on both sides of the Strait of Georgia, and include all the many islands between. It would also show the depths of water throughout the area surveyed.

Another task for the surveyors was toponymy—the naming of the many features that they charted. Washington had instructed Richards to observe, where possible, place names already given by Vancouver and the Spanish expedition of 1792. He was also to note "the Native name with its meaning, if it have any." Where no toponym existed, Richards followed the customary practice of honouring naval superiors, fellow officers, members of the crew, other warships, or his personal circle. Inland from the Courtenay estuary, a prominent peak, Mount Washington, carries the name of Richards's superior. The two rivers noted by Mayne kept the local names he had collected. The nearby headland retained the Spanish Cape Lazo.

Plumper and the survey boats—often away from the ship for ten days at a time—made their way northward for the summer, coaling as necessary at Nanaimo (see Fig. 88, page 187). In July, Mayne left the ship to make another expe-dition into the mainland interior. This time, he started from the head of Jervis Inlet, seeking a route through the Coast Mountains to Bridge River and the upper Fraser. He was gone for two-and-a-half weeks, on an extremely arduous trek.

NANAIMO

FIG 88 Edward Bedwell of HMS *Plumper* painted this view of Nanaimo in 1860. His ship (for some reason, with the funnel omitted) lies in the centre, at anchor. He also shows the coaling pier, bastion, and, the pithead, a compound with chimney and heaps of extracted coal. [Courtesy of the Royal BC Museum and Archives, Victoria]

FIG 89 A studio portrait of sub-lieutenant Phillip Hankin, third mate on HMS *Plumper*, personal assistant and protégé to Captain Henry Richards, taken in 1858 or 1859. [Courtesy of the Royal BC Museum and Archives, Victoria]

Soon afterward, he made a boat survey of Howe Sound as far as Squamish.

Richards was also very active in boat operations, usually taking Philip Hankin, his third officer, who was new to surveying but keen to learn. Richards much appreciated Hankin's skill at cooking fish curry while they were away from the ship. During *Plumper*'s journey out, Hankin had prepared just such a dish for the Queen of the Sandwich Islands (later Hawaii).

Hankin had managed to arrange a berth on the mission after having talked with Daniel Pender, when they were both writing their exams for a mate's (sub-lieutenant) ticket. Pender, already appointed second master for the voyage, suggested that his friend apply. Hankin had earlier served on *Plumper* as a midshipman under a different skipper, and had not enjoyed the experience, but this new expedition sounded intriguing, and so it turned out. He proved to be a quick, assiduous learner, recognized by Richards, who also appointed him captain's personal assistant (see Fig. 89).

Two years into the mission, news arrived of Hankin's promotion to lieutenant; this meant that he was entitled to return to England for reassignment at his new rank. He left *Plumper*, his friends, and his much-respected captain regretfully, to make his own way home. Richards learned that his request for a larger and more powerful ship had been granted; HMS *Hecate* was being readied for survey work. Richards suggested that Hankin apply to join *Hecate*, and said that he would also request Hankin's assignment.

Plumper's final voyage of the 1860 season continued the survey north from Fort Rupert and around the northern tip of the island, where Richards noted, "The north end of Vancouver Id. at any rate near the coast is high, rising in very remarkable hummicky hills (like waves rounded on their summits) and densely wooded." After entering the open Pacific, they continued their reconnaissance down the west coast.

EXPLORATIONS INTO QUATSINO SOUND

Heading south, Richards sought a sheltered harbour where he could land and make astro observations for longitude. He found an inlet, marked but unnamed, on Kellett's 1847 version of Vancouver's chart (although later editions had called it Quatsinough). Guided by locals, they anchored in a cove on the north side (Koprino Harbour) opposite a large village (Koskimo) on the south, and met the locals:

> Very wild, savage looking chaps naked as the day they were born. Women ditto—except for a clout of cloth round the waist. They are very civil people but a long way behind all the tribes in civilization.[3]

He learned that the clan's name was closer to Koskimo than Quatsinough, but on the chart he retained the established name for the inlet, which he soon learned was larger and more complex than shown (see Fig. 99, page 206).

Accompanied by Dr. Wood and second master Daniel Pender, Richards reconnoitred the eastern extent of the inlet.

> Finding it a far more extensive place than I had anticipated and more than we shall be able to finish with all our force during the next week. We passed several native villages which prove that the inhabitants must have been more numerous than they are at present or else that they are very migratory. Many of the villages were deserted.

In fact, it was the height of the salmon run, and the villagers were most likely away fishing. Another boat party discovered, on the north side nearer the entrance, a sheltered side channel, which Richards called Winter Harbour.

Richards sent William Brown, the paymaster, and Francis Brockton, the ship's engineer, with local guides to check on reports that from a place at the far end of the inlet (Coal Harbour) there was a trading trail connecting with Fort Rupert. After a difficult hike of some 12 miles, Brown reached the fort and the HBC factor, Captain Billy Mitchell, gave him much-appreciated sacks of potatoes and fresh vegetables for *Plumper*'s larder. Brockton spent the time looking for, finding, and digging coal from local seams.

RICHARDS REVISITS NOOTKA

By now it was mid-September, and the weather almost constant fog and rain. It seemed that winter was about to set in, and Richards was keen to revisit Nootka Sound after an absence of 23 years.

After leaving Quatsino, *Plumper* passed the feature marked "Woody Pt." Richards felt that the name given by James Cook was ambiguous.

> This pt is a bold promontory with a remarkable double Islet [Solander Island] lying off it. It is very badly named altho by Capt Cook. First it ought to be a Cape and not a point, and next all the coast is densely wooded equally so with Woody Point. I shall call it Cape Cook.

He later named the promontory, of which the cape was an extremity, Brooks Peninsula, after a name already given to the adjacent inlet.

Richards employed an excellent Kwakwaka'wakw interpreter and guide known as Rupert Jim, who demonstrated his local knowledge as they passed various places along the coastline, providing local names such as Nesparti and Kai-o-quot—neither of which was shown on the Vancouver-Kellett chart of 1849—the size of villages, and even the number of sea otter pelts they currently had for sale.

Richards later noted:

> It is astonishing how soon every piece of intelligence is conveyed from one tribe to another—even tho they may be hostile towards each other.

A few miles north of Nootka, he recorded:

> We saw some very remarkable mountains today—but so many and such a sameness in appearance that they almost confused me—some I certainly recognized as old friends seen on the East coast but up to this time I have not been able to identify the real Conuma peak—for positive certainty.

Two hours after sunset, *Plumper* gingerly entered Friendly Cove, Richards relying on his memory of his previous visit, and anchored.

> The cove is extremely small and I was almost inclined to think I was mistaken it so very small did it appear by the almost darkness.

In the morning they discovered that they had managed to anchor in the best place. Richards wanted to make his observations at the same spot he had used during the earlier *Sulphur* visit. Most of the inhabitants—who, he learned, numbered 457—were away fishing, but the two who remained managed to pilfer his chronometer. In pursuit, he sent a boat with Jim, who captured the thieves and recovered the precious instrument. He clapped the two in irons to await the arrival of Maquinna, the current leader and grandson to the one he had met more than two decades earlier.

The following day Maquinna and a few close relatives arrived and, at Richards's request, berated the two prisoners, who fled, clearly terrified. Then Richards presented Maquinna and his family with gifts, and some trading took place. Richards remembered this leader's mother as a "pretty little, almost white girl" of noble demeanour; she was now an elderly woman. Richards, with Pender and Wood, visited the clan's winter village at Tahsis. They learned that:

> From Tasis to Nimpkish on the east side is a journey from 3 to 4 days. The great lake [presumably Woss] being only half a day from here. The weather was remarkably fine and we had an excellent view of all the peaks—also got latitude and time [a chronometer check].[4]

After a week of fine weather, *Plumper* left Nootka Sound, to anchor two days later in Esquimalt. For the remainder of the year, they surveyed the Fraser estuary and the nearby inlets of the mainland, and completed their charts. Mary Richards gave birth to a son, whom they named Vancouver. A few days later, *Plumper*'s replacement, HMS *Hecate*, arrived, and, on New Year's Day, 1861, Richards and his surveying officers transferred to their new vessel. Moriarty was to accompany *Plumper* home. Mayne received a well-deserved promotion to first officer leaving the opportunity for Hankin, who had arrived aboard *Hecate* as first officer, to take up the duty of second officer.

FIG 90 An *Illustrated London News* engraving, from a painting by sub-lieutenant Edward Bedwell, RN, shows HMS *Plumper* at anchor in Port Harvey, Johnstone Strait, with survey parties departing in the ship's boats. A signal beacon has been set up on shore as a reference point. The peak in the distance is Mount Berkeley. [*Illustrated London News*, March 1, 1862]

COASTAL SURVEYING IN THE MID-19TH CENTURY

In the era of Richards's survey, the line of the coast was determined in three stages. First, at a few locations, geographical coordinates would be found by astronomical measurements. Then, between such fixed points, traverses were run by measuring angles and estimating distances between intermediate, intervisible points also visible from boats offshore. Differences between the values of the closing point calculated from the traverse, and those obtained by astronomy, were adjusted systematically, giving corrected coordinates for each of the traverse stations. Third, the surveyor would draw the configuration of the coastline, interpolating between the stations, noting such elements as beaches, rocky areas, river estuaries, prominent shore features, mountains or villages, etc (see Fig. 90).

For the crucial task of recording soundings, or the depth of water at the lowest state of tide, the traverse stations were made clearly visible by erecting large tripod beacons. In ship's boats, teams of three surveyors, plus a recorder and a crew of rowers, traced lines of soundings whose positions were referenced to three of the stations. One man would heave a marked lead-line vertically beneath the boat, calling out the length of line between the bottom and the sea surface. Simultaneously, the other two observers, with sextants held horizontally, would each measure the angles between two different stations out of three. For each sounding, the recorder logged the depth, the two angles, and the time (see Fig. 91 a, b, c, page 193).

In the chartroom, surveyors drafted the configuration of the coastline, carefully recording the locations of the traverse stations. Using an instrument called a station pointer—three arms on a common axis that can be adjusted to show the pair of angles for each sounding—they aligned the arms with the observed stations on the chart to give the location of the boat at the time of sounding (see Fig. 108, page 218). The depth reading, corrected for the state of the tide, provided the figure to be recorded on the chart in its true position. In practice, there were usually more readings than necessary for navigation, so for clarity, redundant ones were removed in later drafts of the chart.

The tidal adjustment of soundings needs to be based on a thorough knowledge of the local tidal patterns. The Strait of Georgia, with tidal flows from around both ends of Vancouver Island, and many channels through two archipelagos, presents an extremely complex hydraulic system. Such data can only be gathered by regular observations of local tide gauges over extended periods of time. Richards and his hydrographers were experts in all of these techniques.

FIG 92 Paddlewheel sloop HMS *Hecate* at anchor in Esquimalt Harbour, a watercolour by Edward Bedwell, probably from 1862. Fisgard Lighthouse is seen at the far right. [Courtesy of the Royal BC Museum and Archives, Victoria]

CHAPTER FOURTEEN

HECATE IN THE WESTERN INLETS

Hms *Hecate* WAS A FAR more suitable craft for the work in prospect than *Plumper*: although older, it was larger, more powerful, spacious, and comfortable. At 816 tons (740 tonnes), it had nearly 70 per cent greater displacement. It was 165 feet (50.2 metres) long (18 per cent longer than *Plumper*). Critically, it was powered by a 240-nautical horsepower two-cylinder steam engine (a 300 per cent improvement) driving 23-foot-six-inch (7.2 metres) diameter paddlewheels on each side. Termed a paddlewheel sloop second class, *Hecate* had two masts, was rigged as a brig, and had been modified for surveying operations (see Fig. 92, page 194).

Aboard were 92 officers and men, and 13 boys. Two pivot guns, four smaller weapons, and four howitzers provided potent armament, while still leaving room for charting modifications. Launched in 1839, *Hecate* had seen four foreign-service commissions prior to Richards's command.

Shipwrights modified *Shark*, *Plumper*'s 32-foot pinnace, to operate under the conditions expected off the west coast, in order to serve as a much-needed tender to *Hecate*. They raised the gunwales, fitted a full deck, and rigged it as a schooner. Its major role would be to scout ahead of the main ship in uncharted waters, ensuring that submerged rocks, shoals, and similar hazards were identified and avoided. *Shark* could also carry larger survey parties, and for longer periods, away from the ship's anchorage. In addition, *Hecate* had its own pinnace, three smaller, sturdy whalers, and three slim and speedy gigs—a flotilla of boats to be called upon for surveying duties.

No sooner had Richards and his officers changed over to the new ship than there came a call to duty. A Peruvian merchant vessel, *Florencia*, was reported in trouble off Nootka. A gunboat, Hms *Forward*, had gone to assist, but was overdue. First *Hecate*, then *Plumper*, went in search, but made no contact. Richards recorded on his chart the location, just north of Ucluelet, where, in the final act of the drama, a gale blew the hapless vessel ashore, at Florencia Bay. *Plumper* departed for England at the end of January 1861

Lady Jane Franklin, widow of the Arctic explorer, arrived on tour with her niece Miss Sophia Cracroft as companion, and was

FIG 93 Phillip Hankin in 1862, by now second officer of HMS *Hecate* and appointed aide-de-camp to Lady Franklin during her visit to the colonies. [Courtesy of the Royal BC Museum and Archives, Victoria]

welcomed by Richards, who had helped search for her late husband and knew her well. He appointed Lieutenant Philip Hankin as her aide-de-camp for her stay (see Fig. 93), and Hankin also escorted the ladies as they travelled up the Fraser to the gold rush community of Yale. They were treated as distinguished guests throughout the two young colonies. Second master John Gowlland noted that she was "a fine cheerful, amiable old lady about 57—full of live and Energy—very observant of everything and always wanting to know the why & where for." Richards named a mountain feature on Broughton Strait the Franklin Range and a nearby island after Miss Cracroft.

Meanwhile, before the weather cleared sufficiently for the surveyors to return to their fieldwork, many charts and sailing directions needed to be brought to a condition suitable for dispatching to England. Other duties also interrupted their progress: with *Forward*, *Hecate* replaced buoys marking the treacherous entrance to the Fraser River, and, in company with two Royal Engineer officers, Richards inspected the western boundary marker at Point Roberts. Then the two ships—the largest up to that time—steamed up-river as far as the Royal Engineers camp and burgeoning community at New Westminster, to an excited welcome.

After coaling at Nanaimo, *Hecate* returned to Esquimalt in time to salute the new commander-in-chief, Rear Admiral Sir Thomas Maitland, in his flagship, HMS *Bacchante*, with four other warships of the Pacific Station. Further potential surveying time was sacrificed to the need for discussions of naval infrastructure with the admiral.

At long last, on the evening of April 16, *Hecate* cleared Esquimalt, bound for Alberni, joining up with *Shark* off Cape Beale. They anchored near Stamp's sawmill, which was just about to begin operating. All the surveyors in ship's boats set to work charting the canal, but they had little success:

During this 14 days not one without rain—almost constant & generally a heavy breeze. No sun, no sight of hills, very cold and perfect winter. Boats returned at end of fortnight all more or less damaged and having done little or no work.

While he was there, Richards noted the surrounding forest and farmland:

Splendid trees at Alberni for Spars. Many hundreds of acres of magnificent land—clear. Cap. Stamp has 100 acres [40.5 hectares] under cultivation. This is the most desirable agricultural district I have seen on the Id.

In a report to his superior, Admiral Washington, he elaborated:

I saw yesterday within a few hundred yards of the beach numbers of trees, which would make single lower masts for Line-of-Battle Ships or Frigates and of the finest quality . . . At this place they are decidedly superior to any I have seen on the Island. Certainly our government could save considerably by sending some of these spars to our establishments in China where no masts are to be obtained unless sent from England.[1]

MAYNE TRAVERSES THE ISLAND

During *Hecate*'s three-week stay at Alberni, Lieutenant Richard Mayne made another of his overland explorations. In Victoria, Richards had discussed with Governor James Douglas the desirability of finding a route for a road connection between Nanaimo and Alberni. Richards had seen for himself the Horne trail from Qualicum, which required crossing a steep ridge, and they hoped that a more direct, flatter route existed. He gave the problem to the now experienced and capable overlander, Mayne.

William Banfield, having just reconnoitred Great Central Lake, happened to be at the mill as *Hecate* arrived, and, as the local government agent, introduced himself. When he learned of the plan for Mayne to explore a route to Nanaimo, he offered his services as interpreter for the expedition, and was accepted.

The party consisted of Mayne, one sailor from *Hecate*'s crew, Banfield, and six packers, probably Tseshaht men, including their leader, an "old hunter." Richards, in a note briefing Douglas, observed:

The Indians know nothing whatever of the country, as their only mode of reaching Nanaimo hitherto has been by crossing the steep ridge-line of 1700 feet [518 metres] descending on Horne Lake—crossing it in canoe, thence across the land striking the East coast at Qualicum River—which is 32 miles [51.5 kilometres] from Nanaimo by sea. This route could scarcely be of much benefit and moreover the anchorage off Qualicum is exposed.[2]

He continued with the hope that Mayne could find a route between mounts Arrowsmith and Moriarty, adding reassurance that "He will do so unless he meets with insurmountable difficulties."

Mayne carried with him maps, a compass, and an aneroid barometer to measure approximate altitude. He described their route in detail in his final report to Richards, which was forwarded to Douglas, thence to the Colonial Office in London, which sent it to the Royal Geographical Society to publish in its *Journal*. After recounting their departure from Stamp's sawmill and the first two days' progress, more or less due east toward Nanaimo, he noted:

During the latter part of the day the old hunter . . . had been edging more northward than I liked; and I explained that we wanted to pass between Mounts Arrowsmith and Moriarty, and pointed it out on the chart to him. He insisted that if we went that way we should have to cross snow mountains, he having been there hunting; and he said he knew a way farther north by which we could get into the valley beyond the "steep ridge," though farther than that he did not know . . . I agreed to let him pilot . . . As it turned out, it was fortunate we did not try that way, for I afterwards found Arrowsmith and Moriarty are joined by a snow-covered ridge.

After crossing a ridge, which he noted at 1,200 feet [366 metres], he saw that they might have crossed further down at 700 to 800 feet [213 to 244 metres].

[W]e came to a good sized stream, 30 to 40 yards [27–37 metres] wide, running to the northward, which I called "Elk River" [now Cameron River] . . . we came to a small lake [Cameron Lake], about 3 miles [4.8 kilometres] long, and lying east and west, into which the Elk River empties itself. The soil from the mountain foot appeared very good and the elk are numerous; we saw upwards of a dozen, and shot one, without going out of our course.

Arrived at the lake, the Indians' knowledge of the country ceased; none of them had ever seen this lake before, and they gave up all charge. One old fellow expressed great disgust with my compass, because it could not tell me where the high mountain (Arrowsmith) was; but as I confidently asserted I knew the way to Nanaimo perfectly, they were content to go on.[3]

The guides proposed making a raft to save some arduous walking, and Mayne recorded that he agreed since, at that stage, he did not know how long the lake was. Later he realized that the raft had saved them some scrambling over steep rocks. As the lake terminated in a considerable river at its eastern end, they resumed on foot.

Banfield, too, kept notes that he summarized in a letter to Douglas on their arrival in Nanaimo. On the fifth and sixth days of their trip, after they had crossed a belt of thick woodland east of the lake, the landscape changed and they passed through:

Country very beautiful, open and ornamental. Complete park land—more resembling the best districts of Saanich than anything else I have seen—only Cedar and fir trees instead of oak—good agricultural land. I had no idea such land existed on the island to such an extent.[4]

He was referring to the gently rolling plains surrounding today's Coombs.

Under conditions of "incessant, or almost incessant, rain, and the mists over the gulf," Mayne had been unable to check his course from the peak of Texada Island or other known landmark, so, having misjudged the latitude of the lake, the party arrived at the head of Nanoose Harbour before continuing their woodland trek down the coast, southeast to Nanaimo. Mayne noted that they had crossed "two small gorges, through which the two streams marked westward of Nanoose, are 50 to 60 yards [46 to 55 metres] wide." These would have been the Englishman and the South Englishman rivers. He informed Douglas that "except for these and some other fallen timber, there would be no difficulty in riding a horse by the way we came."

At Nanaimo he was able to compare notes with Adam Horne, who had crossed the island several times on trading trips to Alberni, and together they devised an alternative return route that would skirt to the south of what are now the Nanoose Hills around Kidney Lake, then follow the original plan to locate a pass between the two mountains, and thence to Alberni.

Although Mayne had found the journey so far to be easy, compared with his previous expeditions, three of his packers were in bad shape, unable to make the return. Horne persuaded one, then three, of his local people to join the team and act as guides for the initial part. The weather had improved, so, after crossing the Nanoose (South Englishman) River and getting to higher ground on the western side:

> We came to a clear bare nob, from which I had a splendid view of both Moriarty and Arrowsmith; and, alas for the direct route! An equally clear view of a ridge about 2000 feet [600 metres] high joining the two. The Indians, of course, chuckled immensely when we saw this proof of their superior knowledge, and the old hunter said we should be up to our necks in snow if we tried to cross it. I had, however, not the slightest wish to try the experiment.

Instead, keeping to the foothills, they rejoined their outbound route at the eastern end of Elk (Cameron) Lake. They found the raft they had built and used previously, and again paddled the length of the lake. To their disappointment, this time they were unable to shoot an elk, and had to restrict rations. Mayne wanted a closer view of Arrowsmith, so, instead of looking for the lowest pass of the ridge, they made their way to the crest of the ridgeline to the south.

> Just when we were beginning to descend, and had almost given up the hope of seeing anything, we came to a clear spot, and saw Mount Arrowsmith, as it is seldom seen, perfectly clear to the very top.[5]

Mayne's final report included a map showing both his outward and return routes, with two suggestions for the line of the road (see Fig. 94, page 200). He pointed out that either of these would work, but that the final choice should depend on the route of the main east coastal road that would eventually connect Victoria and Nanaimo with the agricultural lands of the Courtenay Valley. Another consideration would be any intentions for making use of Nanoose, the "magnificent harbour for loading and unloading vessels." His report concluded by recognizing the help provided by Banfield's knowledge of the Nootkan language, but misspelling his name.

The Royal Geographical Society again published Mayne's report in its *Journal*—the third of such accounts. These, with his journal of the time aboard the two ships, formed his 1862 book, *Four Years in British Columbia and Vancouver Island*.

By the time the expedition returned to Alberni, *Hecate* had departed, headed for Uchucklesaht Inlet. Mayne hired a canoe to chase the ship and caught up with it by nightfall, to resume his shipboard duties. The surveyors were continuing to chart the multitude of islands and side channels of Barkley Sound, which Richards described in his private journal as "the most extensive and broken up place it is possible to imagine." Richards also noted that Mayne had "perfectly succeeded & made a good sketch of the country."

During a second visit to the mill at the head of the Alberni Inlet, carpenters made necessary repairs to the boats. *Hecate* then returned to Esquimalt, towing a gift from Captain Stamp for the recently arrived admiral: a spar for a new topmast for *Bacchante*. Stamp, of course, intended his gift to show off the quality and size of spars he could supply to the Royal Navy.

Two more weeks of prime survey time were lost to other duties: meetings about lighthouses and about the Rifle Volunteer Militia, and transporting a cargo of iron monuments for the RE Boundary Survey team. After coaling at Nanaimo, they steamed north along the coast, passing Capes Lazo and Mudge. Richards noted that here the two tidal streams from the ends of the

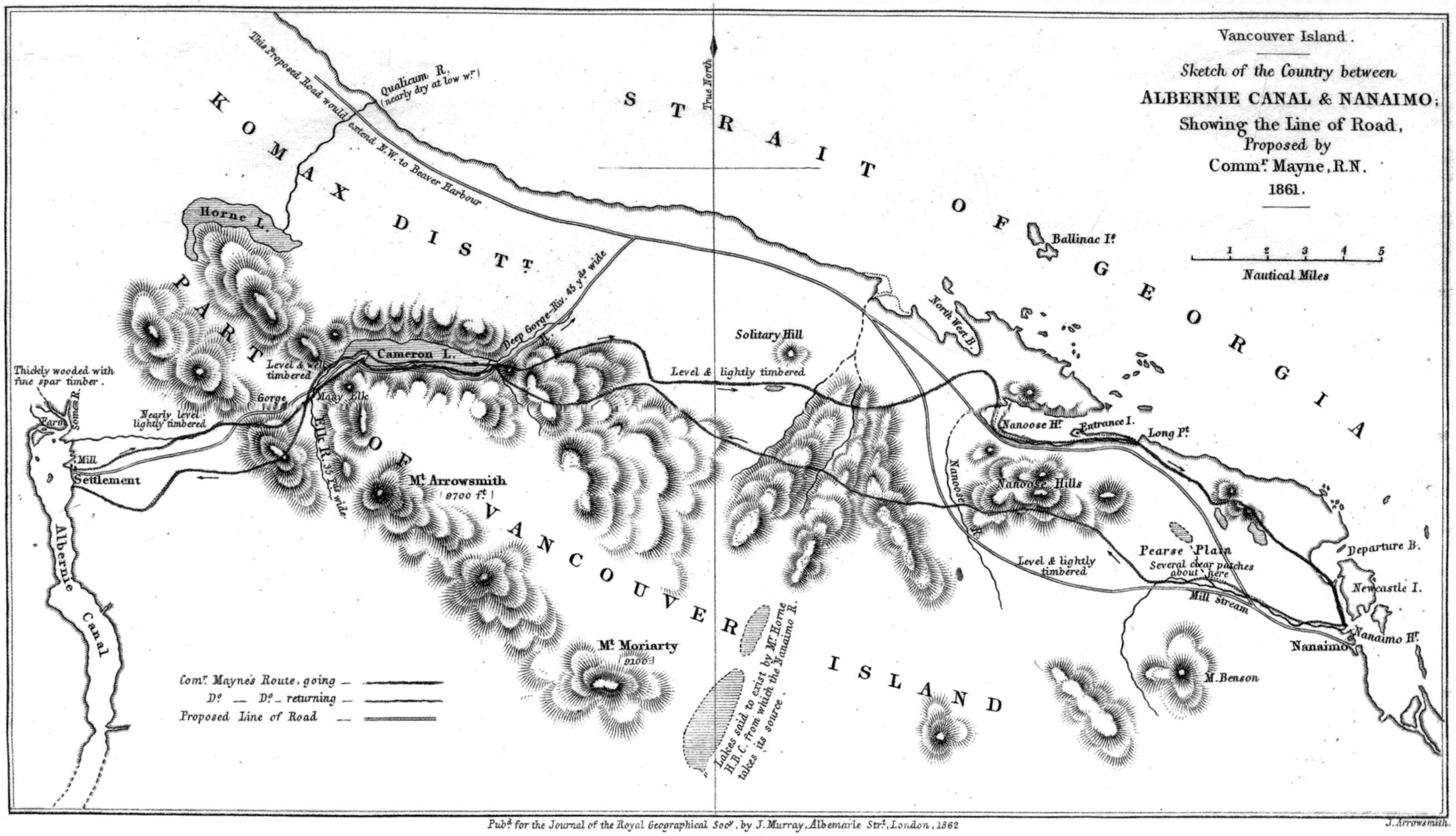
Vancouver Island.
Sketch of the Country between
ALBERNIE CANAL & NANAIMO;
Showing the Line of Road,
Proposed by
Commr. Mayne, R.N.
1861.
Nautical Miles
STRAIT OF GEORGIA
KOMAX DISTT.
PART OF VANCOUVER ISLAND
True North
This Proposed Road would extend N.W. to Beaver Harbour
Qualicum R. (nearly dry at low wr.)
Horne L.
Cameron L.
Deep Gorge Riv. 45 yds. wide
Solitary Hill
Level & lightly timbered
Ballinac Is.
North West B.
Nanoose Hr.
Entrance I.
Long Pt.
Nanoose Hills
Pearse Plain
Several clear patches about here
Level & lightly timbered
Mill Stream
Departure B.
Newcastle I.
Nanaimo Hr.
Nanaimo
M. Benson
Mt. Moriarty
Mt. Arrowsmith
Lakes said to exist by Mr. Horne H.B.C. from which the Nanaimo R. takes its source.
Thickly wooded with fine spar timber.
Farm
Somass R.
Mill
Settlement
Nearly level lightly timbered
Gorge
Level & well timbered
Elk R.
Albernie Canal
Commr. Mayne's Route, going
Do. Do. returning
Proposed Line of Road
Pubd. for the Journal of the Royal Geographical Socy. by J. Murray, Albemarle Str., London, 1862
J. Arrowsmith.

FIG 94 The map of lieutenant Richard Mayne's two-way traverse of the island in 1860, published in the *Journal of the Royal Geographical Society* in London in 1862. Mayne shows his outward and inward tracks, with his proposed alignment of a road between Alberni and Nanaimo. [Author's collection, Royal Geographical Society, London, 1862]

island met "at or near the moments of high and low water." At Seymour Narrows, with its as yet unsuspected, hidden hazard, he recorded:

> Passed thro Seymour Narrows, the tide of 3 knots (ebb) with us, and as usual, confused rips and swirls in the Narrows. Our steam was low and we found it difficult to steer in consequence. A ship should pass thro under good power—it is better to keep just eastd of the rips in the Narrows. [See Fig. 95]

Richards little realized that *Hecate* had been in serious danger from the swirling eddies around Ripple Rock. They anchored for the night "in Alert Bay, Cormorant Id, which is a very excellent stopping place abreast Nimpkish River in 7 fms [12.8 metres]."

At the nearby Fort Rupert, almost derelict and deserted, the carpenters took time to:

> [c]ut 5 logs of Yellow Cypress [Cedar] here—each log about 18 feet [5 metres] long by 15 to 18 inches [38 to 46 centimetres] in diameter. This wood is evidently not scarce . . . but it took us 2 whole days to get out these 5 logs . . . so we may be able to bring it into general use for boat building and repairing; it is the only wood in the Id available for such purposes and is very superior.

Continuing north, through Goletas Channel and around to Cape Scott, they found the sea significantly calmer than on their previous visit, but conditions soon deteriorated. Richards wanted to fix the positions of the notoriously dangerous Triangle Islands off Cape Scott, but could only "make such an examination of them as the unfavourable nature of the weather would permit" (see Fig. 96, page 203).

Hecate carried on steaming south for Woody Point (which Richards had renamed the previous year as Cape Cook, and later

FIG 95 Seymour Narrows photographed in 1958 looking west over Wilfred Point and Menzies Bay. It shows the turbulence caused by an ebbing tide over the infamous Ripple Rock during work preparatory to blowing up the hazard from below. [Courtesy of Museum at Campbell River]

became Brooks Peninsula.) Richards was correct in recognizing the special nature of this dramatic coastal feature: more recent studies have discovered that it was a refugium, an area free of glaciation during the most recent ice age.

"Thick squally" weather prevented any more survey work, so they continued as far as Clayoquot Sound. Richards had previously sent Second Master John Thomas Gowlland to reconnoitre the entrance and find a safe route to a good anchorage for *Hecate*. It was already dark, so they stood off, awaiting first light. At dawn, a two-gun signal summoned Gowlland to come and guide them in.

> After threading a passage good enough but with numerous reefs on either side, and passed thro one or two narrow passages and over some shoals of 4½ fathoms [*Hecate* drew about 2½ fathoms] we anchored in a very good berth 4 miles [6 kilometres] within the Sound under Mr. Gowlland's pilotage, and moored the ship.[6]

Some local guides were aboard, but, had Richards followed their advice to take a different entrance, *Hecate* would surely have foundered.

From the ship's sheltered anchorage near the village of Ahousaht, Richards sent out all the survey parties, provisioned for 12 days, to investigate another maze of islands and channels. As Mayne described it:

> We found sundry arms and passages hitherto unknown, and discovered that one previously marked on the charts as Brazo de Topino [*sic*] [Tofino] was inaccurately described—the extent proving to be not more than half that laid down by former explorers.[7]

While they were at the anchorage, the Ahousaht people told them more of the local region.

The natives give information of an extensive lake between this place [Clayoquot Sound] and Barclay Sound, which is entered by a rapid river only navigable for canoes. I am inclined to think from their sketch that it empties itself into or near Port Cox.[8]

That sketch was misleading: Port Cox, an early fur-trading site, was near the village of Opitsaht at the southern tip of Meares Island, in the middle of the sound. The "extensive lake" was most likely Kennedy Lake, emptying into Tofino Inlet at the extreme southeast.

After three weeks, they left for Alberni where they found that the sawmill was in production, at 20,000 board feet [47 cubic metres] a day. On leaving Barkley Sound, Richards turned north, hoping to find conditions at Cape Scott more favourable for charting the northwest tip of the island. Yet again, northwesterly winds signalled that this would not be possible, so he decided to turn south to obtain more soundings at the entrance to the Strait of Juan de Fuca.

HECATE RUNS AGROUND

Outside the entrance to the strait they ran into one of the all-too-common dense fogs, which required them to slowly feel their way by frequent soundings. Richards had just handed over the watch to Mayne to go below for his breakfast when alarms sounded:

> [The captain] had hardly reached his cabin when he heard the orders, "Hard a port!—"Stop her!"—"Reverse engines!"—shouted from the bridge, and rushed on deck just in time to find the ship landed on a nest of rocks, over which the surf was sullenly breaking . . . we discovered that we were two miles inside Cape Flattery . . . the ship swung broadside to the rocks and began to bump fearfully.[9]

FIG 96 Triangle Island photographed during an all-too-frequent storm by Jim Lamont. Captain Richards's struggle to survey this area can be appreciated.

FIG 97 Portrait dated about 1880 of Rear Admiral Richard Charles Mayne, RN, CB, FRGS. He later served as a member of parliament from 1886 to 1892. [Courtesy of the Royal BC Museum and Archives, Victoria]

With the assistance of an American schooner, which happened to be at anchor nearby, and after an hour thudding on the rocks, the crew managed to get *Hecate* off and limping toward Esquimalt. Following a thorough examination by fleet divers, and temporary patching, Admiral Maitland agreed that *Hecate* needed to be repaired in a dry dock. So, for the second time in this mission, Richards took his damaged ship to San Francisco, this time accompanied for security by the naval sloop *Mutiné* until they had cleared Cape Flattery.

While they had been at anchor in Clayoquot Sound, a canoe had delivered mail to them. One of the official dispatches for Richards brought the unexpected news that Mayne had been promoted to the rank of commander. Normally, this would mean that he return to Britain for reassignment, but since he was needed on *Hecate* for the rest of the season, his current assignment took priority. Commander Mayne remained with the ship until mid-October when repairs were complete, and then left for home. In his report, Richards praised Mayne:

> A rare instance of an officer, not brought up from youth in the surveying service having qualified himself by untiring applications for the highest positions he can be called on to fill.[10]

A few years later, Richards, by then the Hydrographer, gave Captain Mayne command of HMS *Nassau* and responsibility for a three-year voyage recharting the increasingly busy Strait of Magellan (preferred by steamships to rounding the Horn) and the southern coast of Chile. Mayne concluded his career as a rear admiral and a member of council of the Royal Geographical Society (see Fig. 97).

Before *Hecate* left San Francisco, Mayne's relief as first officer, Lieutenant Henry Hand, came aboard, and they sailed for Esquimalt, arriving at the beginning of November. Poor weather prevented further survey work that year, but considerable effort was required in constructing a stone pillar at the international boundary on the cliff at Point Roberts. The winter of 1861–62 was particularly severe: gales at sea, and temperatures on land as low as 9°F (-13°C) at night. Victoria Harbour froze over, locking in the anchored *Hecate* for a few days. The surveyors kept busy preparing charts and sailing instructions, while the crew repaired, painted, and refitted the ship's flotilla of boats.

"SUCH AN INFINITY OF ROCKS"—THE 1862 SEASON

Not until early April 1862 could Richards commence the new survey season. After coaling as usual at Nanaimo, they headed once more for Fort Rupert. In his private journal, he recorded in considerable detail the names, sizes, and locations of communities of the different peoples living in the region. He also noted their linguistic differences:

> The Rupert language is very extensively spoken, entirely so between Cape Mudge at the South to Cape Caution on the main, both on the Island and Continental shores and as far round as Port Brooks on the west side of the Id. There appear to be 4 principal dialects, or rather distinct languages—the Songhees between Sooke and Cowitchin; then the Nanaimo to C Mudge including Fraser River; the Rupert; and the Barclay Sound which latter is spoken from C Beale to Nootka with slight variations.

The weather remained too poor for extensive work on the outside coast. *Shark's* decking, having been made from unseasoned planks, had warped and now leaked badly (see Fig. 98, page 206); the schooner was unfit for the task ahead so, under Hankin, it returned to Esquimalt to be properly repaired. As *Hecate* rounded Cape Scott, they managed to get some soundings and headed for Quatsino Sound, to find two nights' respite. Then they tried

again to get boat parties to the north, but a freshening gale soon forced a return to Winter Harbour (see Fig. 99, page 206). Most of the villagers were away, fishing for halibut around the islands. Some Koskimo people whom they had befriended earlier returned, bringing their pretty young daughter, Yak-y-koss. The girl's head had been elongated into a cone as a baby by traditional methods (see Fig. 100, page 206); nevertheless, her innocent charm delighted the visitors.

Two days later, *Hecate* dropped off two survey parties at San Josef Bay in whalers, with orders to chart the Scott Islands and the coast as far as Quatsino. The ship returned to the previous safe anchorage. Wanting to find a vantage point on the nearby coast from which he could see along it and perhaps also view the islands, Richards took Hankin and his boat's crew on a hike:

> The trail to the sea was passable, but the water being rather high, we could not get along the shore to the NW, but had to strike inland where I have rarely found such walking in my life: on the tops of banks or along fallen logs, and the bush so thick as to entirely puzzle one. After an hour or two's scrambling, we gained a few hundred yards and again came out on the coast scratched and torn and done up—and did not get near the point.

Presumably, he was trying to reach today's Lippy Point, about three miles north of the entrance to the sound.

> Fortunately for our reputation, it came on to rain & blow from the SE so that it would have been useless proceeding. We returned by the rocks and I determined the next time I tried I would study the tide if possible. But this is difficult country, one moderately fine day in a week at the utmost. Got back at 5 PM, soaking wet and not sorry to be home.

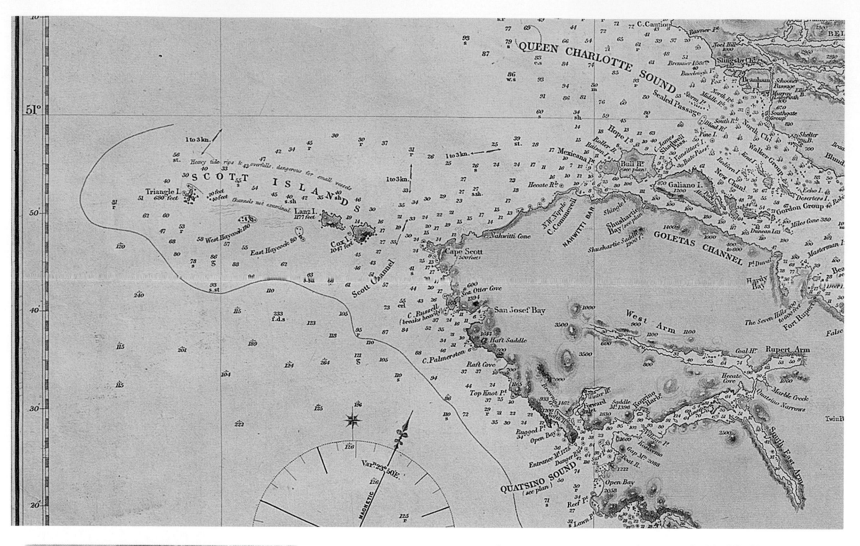

(CLOCKWISE FROM BOTTOM LEFT) FIG 98 *"Shark* in difficulties," an engraving in Mayne's book *Four Years in British Columbia and Vancouver Island,* shows the pinnace—iced-up and shipping water—off San Juan Island. Men try to attract notice and help from shore. [Courtesy of the Greater Victoria Public Library, Mayne]

FIG 99 The section of Admiralty chart #1917 covering the northwestern tip of Vancouver Island, showing the extensive and complex Quatsino Sound and Triangle and the other Scott islands, both areas are extremely difficult to survey. [Courtesy of Hydrographic Office, Taunton, UK]

FIG 100 Yak-y-koss the "cone-headed girl" of the Koskemo band, who became a favourite of Captain Richards. Koskemo and other Quatsino groups would bind the heads of girl babies between boards to elongate the skull. [Courtesy of the Greater Victoria Public Library, Mayne]

This from a man who had made a 90-day, solo journey by dogsled in the Arctic (see Fig. 101)!

They had experienced at first hand the conditions facing many shipwrecked mariners on the island's stormy west coast, who, even if they managed to get ashore, found themselves imprisoned there by an impenetrable barricade of salal and poisonous devil's club bushes. Two days later, he tried again:

> Walked across to the outside Coast again, and by dint of climbing precipices and Scrambling thro brush, we managed to reach the point from which Woody Cape is seen and one of the offlying Islets to the NWd to which I was able to get true bearings and fix my position . . . We reached the Ship at 6:30 PM after a most fatiguing day having taken four hours to walk a little over a mile, and three to return. It is very difficult to get along the coast by walking at any time—but unless at low water almost impossible.

After nearly two weeks, the whalers returned. Master Daniel Pender reported having experienced a "severe cruize."

> [S]trong SE gales had prevailed scarcely without interruption and [Pender] had met with some escapes. He had been at Cape Scott for 5 days, weather bound. The Indians had been very civil to his party . . . He had visited Scott and Lanz Ids, found no shelter there and landing very bad. The natives dread the SE gale on this coast . . . There are bad tide rips, near the Cape and Scott Ids both.

Four of the people from Cape Scott, in a canoe, kindly accompanied Pender's whaler back to Quatsino, down a coast

> on which the surf constantly breaks and off lying reefs extend frequently a mile from the shore. I was glad enough to get our boat back . . . [The locals] rarely fail in their prognostication of the

FIG 101 George Henry Richards, now wearing the insignia of post-captain (four rings) on his sleeve. The photograph is undated but was probably taken in 1861 or 1862. [Courtesy of the Royal BC Museum and Archives, Victoria]

weather and study the set of the Clouds and general appearance thoroughly before they start on this west coast from one place to another. The SE wind is their great enemy . . .

It is very remarkable the prevalence of SE winds at this season when nothing by NWds [northwestwards] were looked for. We have had 3 days of SE gales and rain regularly in a week. The natives look on upon these winds as their natural enemy. They call it Mitlass, and always speak of it as peshak, which means very bad. The NW wind they call Tsa-qua, it always brings fine weather.

They examined the many inlets between Quatsino and Nootka—Klaskino, Klaskish, Nasparti, Ououkinsh, Kyuquot, Esperanza, and Nuchatlitz. Richards, dismayed, commented:

Some of them [are] 20 to 30 miles [32 to 48 kilometres] in length—many sunken dangers lie off the islands and it will require great care and labour to survey this place . . . I have never seen a Coast so cut up as this—with such an infinity of rocks lying off it, most of them from 2 to 10 feet [0.6–3 metres] out of the water, many sunken.

Nor was the mid-May weather cooperative:

The NW winds have blown with great violence since they commenced [six days previously] so much so as to prevent our Sounding boats from Working frequently.

Richards was pleased by the treatment his team had received from the locals:

Our boats are constantly among them, far removed from the ship and quite in their power. They have always been foremost to help them, landing in a Surf a whole village has come down to haul the boat up or to launch her, and they have always shewn the most friendly feeling. I can safely say, having seen & had dealings with almost all the Native tribes in the world, I have never met a more friendly, harmless and well disposed set of people than those on Vancouver Island.[11]

On the evening of May 23, 1862, *Hecate* anchored in a "very snug cove" on the northern side of the entrance to Esperanza Inlet, near the place marked on the chart as Port Eliza, after one of the Spanish explorers of almost a century earlier. Since the next day was Her Majesty's birthday, Richards called it Queens Cove. A great many local people came to visit, and *Hecate*'s flotilla was dispersed on charting duties.

HANKIN AND WOOD TRAVERSE THE ISLAND

One of the missions leaving the cove was an overland exploration by a traditional trading route. Two years earlier, Richards had learned of an oolichan trail that led across the island, from Maquinna's winter village, Ehattesaht, at the northwestern extremity of Nootka Sound, to Cheslakees's village at the mouth of the Nimpkish River. In fact, this was the same trail that Hamilton Moffatt had followed in 1852, but Richards seems to have been unaware of that journey. Richards felt that his team should explore the trail, and proposed that Philip Hankin and Charles Wood undertake the expedition. When consulted, the visiting Mowachaht strongly advised against that idea—there had been a lot of snow, and the rivers were swollen, impossible to ford. From Kyuquot, they would find a far easier route.

Convinced, Richards modified the plan, and enlisted the services of four local Ehattesaht men to take the two officers to Kyuquot by canoe. There they would hire local guides and packers to accompany them across to Cheslakees's village, anticipating that this would take them three weeks. *Hecate* would await their arrival at Fort Rupert, near there.

Hankin was a good choice. He had a gift for languages, and had befriended a man from the Huu-ay-aht band, whom they called Friday, and who joined *Hecate*'s crew temporarily as a guide and seaman. Hankin had an excellent memory, and worked hard at learning Friday's dialect of the Wakashan, or Aht, languages, and he gained fluency as they surveyed the nearby inlets. Wood, in his report of their traverse, noted:

> I beg leave to offer my testimony to the great energy displayed by Lieut. Hankin who with his previous knowledge of Indian dialects & without an interpreter, within a few days made himself sufficiently master of the Cayuket language as to make our Indians perfectly understand his & my wishes in our progress across the Island.[12]

It seems that Hankin was too trusting in his negotiations with the Ehattesaht paddlers. He gave, as agreed, five blankets to the original paddlers to deliver them and their gear to Actiss, a village now called Kyuquot, on an island off the northern entrance to Kyuquot Sound. His mistake was to pay before the paddlers had met their side of the bargain. They stopped three miles short, set the expedition ashore, declaring that this was what they had undertaken, and left, laughing.

While neither Hankin nor Wood mentioned this initial difficulty in their reports, Richards learned from Gowlland what happened after they were abandoned. Hankin had managed to find two men with a tiny canoe and was attempting to continue on to Actiss, under worsening weather, when Gowlland happened to spot them and took them to the safety of the village. Gowlland, who had already spent a few weeks reconnoitring the sound, had established good relations with the resident people, the Kyuquot, and helped in negotiating for a canoe and seven packer-guides for the traverse of the oolichan trail.

Hankin found that he was able to converse with the locals using his command of the Huu-ay-aht dialect, but was less successful in persuading them of the need to get started. In addition to personal camp gear and food for the journey, Hankin carried his sextant and an artificial horizon for finding their latitudes along the route, and Wood carried equipment for collecting biological specimens. The packers brought baskets of dried halibut as their own rations. Their first objective lay 14 miles up Tahsish Inlet at the northeastern extremity of the sound, at the mouth of the Tahsish River. After six hours paddling they arrived, and camped for the night.

It began to rain heavily; the river was in spate, difficult and dangerous to either paddle up or wade against while burdened with gear. The packers grew increasingly reluctant to continue, and on the third day, Hankin reported "to my regret, told me they had made up their minds to return, so, shortly all our traps were in the Canoe, and we were on our way back to [Actiss]."

They camped again in their old spot. Hankin had understood that *Hecate* would be coming to Kyuquot in a few days, so he decided to wait for it. Not expecting to relaunch the expedition, he was generous with his food supplies. The villagers, whom Wood estimated to number 700, continued to be hospitable, and Hankin worked to expand his vocabulary. He had them draw in the sand the route that the surveying party would be taking, give the names of the various lakes and rivers they would pass, and estimate the distances between them, but these were not consistent. Wood began to assemble a collection of natural history specimens.

On his third day at Actiss, the weather having improved, Hankin calculated that they could still make the rendezvous with *Hecate* as planned. The local leader, Kâr-nê-nitt, pointed out

FIG 102   Martin Smith's recent photograph of Pinder Peak seen from Atluck Lake.

that because of the rains, this would be a difficult and dangerous journey. He negotiated an increase of two—to five—blankets, plus a shirt, per man, for the packers. Six men volunteered. Only two of them had been on the earlier attempt, and this was still too few to carry all the kit, provisions, and impedimenta of the expedition; they had to jettison something. It fell to Dr. Wood to give up his botanical collecting gear "greatly to [his] regret." Besides, since they were now behind schedule, they would have to forego any stops for scientific study.

As they started up the Tahsish River for the second time, Hankin realized that his food supply was now limited, but hoped to be able to shoot game for the pot; he also discovered that his packers were both unskilled at overland travel and reluctant. As they struggled through hilly, thickly wooded country, the noise of their passage frightened any animal worth shooting. The packers had told him that there would be plenty of elk, but they saw none. Heavy rain came on again, increasing the packers' anxiety, but Hankin urged them on. Following a trail, in some places they had to ford the ice-cold torrent. At one of those fordings, he recorded:

> The river was about 40 yards wide, nearly breast deep and fearfully rapid. We accomplished the crossing in safety, by all holding on to a long pole, and wading into the water at the same time; thus, by our united efforts resisting the force of the current.

Wood's report added that whereupon, "the Indians cheered we joining in at having got over our first difficulty."

Eventually they reached Atluck Lake, which Hankin described as:

> a beautiful sheet of water, running in a northwesterly direction, some 3½ miles in length, and 1½ wide [5.6 by 2.4 kilometres].

Lofty mountains rise on either side, where numbers of black bear find a safe and undisturbed retreat on its eastern side, towering high above the rest, lay a very peculiar pinnacle shaped mount, whose summit, some 1000 feet [300 metres] high, was covered with snow—to the northwestward of which were several almost needle pointed mountains of sharp, barren rock towering their blackened summits in fantastic forms above the waters of the lake. [See Fig. 102, page 210]

This pinnacle was probably Pinder Peak, now known to be 5,059 feet (1,542 metres) high, considerably higher than Hankin's estimate.

The packers felled a few small trees and lashed them together with strips of cedar bark into two rafts to take them all to the far end, with hard paddling. Hankin had brought a sounding line, but conditions prevented him getting the depth at the centre of the lake. They found the trail again, which led to a second lake, called Hoostan (now Huson, after an early prospector and surveyor). Wood noticed "a large patch of gentian in full and brilliant blossom," but considering the general paucity of interesting flora, he was relieved that he had not brought his plant press. While they built another raft, Hankin managed to shoot a grouse, his first fresh meat. He also obtained the latitude of their camp (see Fig. 103).

At the northern end of Hoostan, they found a good trail leading to a third small lake, Anutz. By this time, the officers were reduced to tea and dampers in the morning, and a shared can of beans and preserved meat in the evening, while the packers subsisted on "roots and ferns." Hankin planned to name the stream connecting the lakes Famine River, but this was not recorded on his map. After passing through a patch of land "like a neglected English park," which Hankin felt was "available for agriculture," the trail brought them to Lake Karmutzen (Nimpkish).

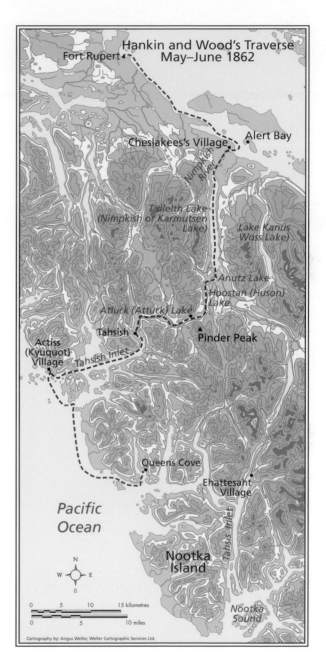

FIG 103 Map showing the trail followed by Lieutenant Hankin and Dr. Wood from Actiss (Kyuquot) across the island to Cheslakees's Village (Nimpkish) and Fort Rupert in June 1862. [Map by Angus Weller]

FIG 104 Phillip Hankin's manuscript sketch map of their traverse of Vancouver Island. [Courtesy of Land Title and Survey Authority, Victoria, BC]

A magnificent sheet of water sixteen or seventeen miles in length, with an average width of one mile and a half [25 to 27 by 2.4 kilometres]. It runs in a northwesterly direction into the Nimpkish River, thus completing an entire chain of lakes throughout the Island. I tried it for soundings with fifty fathoms.

They searched unsuccessfully for a canoe, but did find on the beach a log, 60 feet (18 metres) long, flattened on one side. After launching this and attempting to paddle it, Hankin fitted an outrigger to stop it from rolling, rigged a mast, and hoisted a blanket for a sail. They managed to make a few miles before headwinds prevented progress. They rested for a few hours before continuing to the head of the Nimpkish River, which was far too rapid to venture down aboard the log. They would need a good canoe. They found none, but a trail led them to Cheslakees, the main village of the Nimpkish ('Namgis) people.

> There are fifteen houses, and many Nimpkish Indians reside here during the salmon season . . . We found but one canoe here which we immediately hired, and arrived the same evening at Fort Rupert, where we were most hospitably entertained by Mr. Moffatt until the arrival of the ship.[13]

Hamilton Moffatt, having explored across the island by oolichan trail a decade earlier, would have known well what the two men had just experienced. From leaving Actiss for the second time, the traverse had taken them nine days (see Fig. 104). Hankin rewarded the packers with an extra blanket each, purchased from Moffatt's company store, plus a bag of ships biscuit. After a few days' rest, the packers returned to Actiss by canoe, around the north end of the island.

Two days later *Hecate* arrived, and the two overlanders climbed aboard. Richards recorded in his journal: "The Dr was much knocked up. The season for travelling was too early"—just as the locals had repeatedly warned them.

Apart from his temporary duty as ADC to Lady Franklin and his traverse, Hankin remained with *Hecate* throughout the voyage, including the return home. His later career makes a fascinating story, but it did not include further exploration of the island.

RICHARDS ATTEMPTS ONCE MORE TO CHART SCOTT ISLANDS

In early June, having seen Hankin and Wood leave for their overland adventure, Richards departed Queens Cove for Kyuquot, where he left three boat parties provisioned for two months to continue the survey, and steered north again for the Scott Islands. They found the place enveloped in thick fog. Thwarted, Richards noted:

> This is the third time I have been baulked in the examination of these Ids in consequence of fogs . . . On a Coast like this Strewed with dangers and subject to strong currents and furious gales with thick weather, it is certain that many serious and fatal disasters must be looked for—should sailing vessels or even steamers engage in a line to the Bentink Arm or any part of the Coast Westd of Vancouver Id.

Forced to abandon the attempt, he headed once more for Fort Rupert, where Hankin and Wood rejoined the ship. There they witnessed the ravages of a smallpox epidemic. The nearby village itself had been abandoned out of fear of contagion. Although Dr. Wood vaccinated all the local people who showed up, several died each day, and there was little Richards or Wood could do to alleviate the suffering. They carried on to Nanaimo, also deserted by locals in terror of the disease; nonetheless, *Hecate* did manage to take on coal before proceeding to Esquimalt.

In Nanaimo, Hankin and Wood each prepared a detailed report of their traverse. Richards forwarded both to Douglas, who, later that year, arranged for the *British Colonist* to publish Hankin's. Draftsmen incorporated his map of their route into the published charts.

After two frustrating weeks while naval duties fully occupied his time, Richards was able to resume the survey of the entrance to the Strait of Juan de Fuca. As a thrown horseman gets back in the saddle quickly, *Hecate* returned to the rocky site of its mishap off Neah Bay, Cape Flattery; two days were spent adding to the collection of soundings around the nearby bank or shoal (now known as Swiftsure), first recorded by the French count La Pérouse in 1786. Richards then returned to Nootka, Kyuquot, and Quatsino, completing any gaps that remained on their charts of the inlets' interior channels.

While they lay at anchor in Quatsino, Yak-y-koss, the cone-headed girl, and her parents came to visit and, as before, received gifts from Richards.

> Her parents evidently look upon her head as a source of great wealth for them . . . As I was interested in the poor child and civil to her at first, I think it right to carry it out, so I always make her presents . . . I gave her a cotton dress, 5 reels of cotton. A bar of soap and a comb . . . They value soap and I think they come onbd dirty to get it.

Three weeks later, having explored and charted the narrows and the two most distant channels, they completed the survey of "this very extensive inlet—the distance from the sea to the head of the west arm more than 40 miles [64 kilometres]."

At the end of July, *Hecate* left Quatsino to try, yet again, to survey close to the Scott Islands group. Finally, this time, the weather let up as they approached.

FIG 105   Daniel Pender, Master, RN, captain of HMS *Beaver*. Photographed by Carlo Gentile in 1864. [Courtesy of the Royal BC Museum and Archives, Victoria]

[W]e passed along the South side of the Islands, fixing the positions of the Haycocks and the western [Triangle] island very satisfactorily after a 4th attempt. Carried a line of soundings along the North side and passed thro the Scott Passage between Cox Island and North Cape . . . There were tide rips also in the other passages and I did not feel justified in attempting to pass thro in the ship where so much was at stake. They could not have been examined in boats any time. I have been there but I hope I may be able to accomplish it yet.

At anchor again in Queens Cove in Esperanza Inlet, Richards sent a message to Gowlland that all boat parties should return to the ship. The crews spent the next ten days completing the surveys of the Esperanza area. Then *Hecate* navigated the channels on the northern and eastern sides of Nootka Island, dropping Maquinna and his youngest wife off at Friendly Cove before taking a line of soundings around Estevan Point and into neighbouring Hesquiat Harbour. They returned to Esquimalt for, they hoped, some respite.

To Richards's frustration, yet again official duties took precedence. First, they had to chase some deserters from the flagship across the Strait of Juan de Fuca, then Douglas called for *Hecate*'s services. They were to tow the schooner *Explorer*, with 80 settlers accompanied by the governor and his entourage, to Cowichan as a planned community of agricultural pre-emptors. Richards was not impressed with the supposed farmers: "the would be settlers shew the greatest apathy and won't even accompany the gentlemen [Pemberton's surveyors] to see the district."

After returning to Victoria, they steamed through Haro Strait and into Saanich Inlet. Having spent two days ashore near Mount Newton with the local clergyman, Richards noted:

I am much pleased with what I saw of the Saanich district. The country is beautiful, soil very good—in many parts entirely clear, in most loosely wooded with fine Oaks & Maple . . . Mr. Lowe had a congregation of 29 on the Sunday of my visit.[14]

He recorded that the local settlers had lost most of their livestock in the recent severe winter. Crossing to Point Roberts, Richards inspected the stone obelisk, now completed, that marked the international boundary.

By this time, it was mid-September, but the survey season was not yet done. They headed to Shushartie, bound for more work in Queen Charlotte Sound, where they needed to locate and sound the shoal noted by George Vancouver, nearly 70 years earlier. Although the weather for the remainder of the year was not conducive to productive charting, Richards continued to work, reconnoitring the Queen Charlotte Islands (now Haida Gwaii) and the outer coast as far as Fort Simpson and Metlakatla on the lower Skeena River, the homeland of the Tsimshian Nation. He was using Vancouver's charts, which he found of only limited help.

HECATE RETURNS TO BRITAIN

After making farewell visits to the mill at Alberni and to New Westminster, and after coaling in Nanaimo, *Hecate* returned once more to Esquimalt, anchoring on December 6, 1862. There, Richards received confirmation that he, the ship, and most of the crew, were to return home. Master Daniel Pender (see Fig. 105, page 214), soon to be promoted to staff commander, would be in charge of the veteran HBC paddlewheeler *Beaver*, on charter and carrying the designation HMS, for a seven-year extension of the survey (see Fig. 106). Funded partly by the colonial governments, Pender and his crew were to navigate and chart the intricate waters north of Vancouver Island as far as the Alaskan border.

In his covering letter to Hankin's report, Richards informed Douglas that:

FIG 106   HMS *Beaver*, converted for hydrographic survey operations, at anchor in Victoria Harbour. For seven years after Richards and *Hecate* returned to England, Daniel Pender employed *Beaver* to chart the coasts north of Vancouver Island. [Courtesy of the Royal BC Museum and Archives, Victoria]

The survey of the greater part of the Western Coast has been completed and several new harbours and anchorages discovered, which, when published for general information, will, I think, prevent a recurrence or lessen the frequency of disasters which have annually befallen vessels navigating this boisterous neighbourhood.[15]

The *British Colonist*, reporting the imminent departure of the ship, trumpeted:

> Every nook and cranny of our coast has been explored and mapped. Every current has been marked; an excellent compendium of sailing directions published by Captain Richards making the navigation of our waters easy. In fact, it is due to Captain Richards and officers, to state that the first thorough survey of our Island has been made by them. Harbors or inlets have been marked on our Island that never existed, and large sheets of water that did not exist were unknown. All this *Hecate*'s Surveying Corps have settled definitely and correctly.[16]

Before the ship departed, the Vancouver Island House of Assembly passed a unanimous resolution:

> This House desires to express their appreciation of the eminently able and practical manner in which the duties of [the coast survey] have been performed; and that the thanks of this House are due to [Captain Richards and the officers of HMS *Hecate*] for the valuable services thereby conferred upon the colony.[17]

Hecate spent the whole of 1863 on the voyage back to Britain. Collecting survey data all the way, they sailed via San Francisco, Acapulco, Honolulu, various small islands in the South Pacific,

Port Jackson (Sydney) Australia, inside the Great Barrier Reef, Timor, Java, Simon's Bay (Cape Town), Madeira, and, to complete the circumnavigation, Woolwich, on the Thames estuary, where the crew were paid off. Their captain and most of the officers had been away nearly seven years, during which time they had surveyed 5,000 miles (8,000 kilometres) of coastline, and 5,000 square miles (13,000 square kilometres) of sea.

At Sydney, Richards received the news that Admiral Washington had died, and that he, Richards, would be appointed the Hydrographer upon his return. He gave his next ten years to that office, vigorously advancing the productivity and status of the Hydrographic Department in support of the worldwide operations of the Royal Navy. He was promoted to rear admiral, knighted into the Order of the Bath, and elected a fellow of the Royal Society (see Fig. 107, page 217).

The authoritative *Memoirs of Hydrography* of 1883 stated that:

> At the close of 1872, the chief event of Sir George Richards' official career as hydrographer took place, in the sailing of the *Challenger* on a scientific voyage of three years duration. There is but no doubt that he was the prime mover in that undertaking from start to finish, not only in a scientific sense, owing to his position as one of the council of the Royal Society, but . . . in successfully overcoming any monetary objection raised against its advancement.
>
> It is hardly necessary to add that the *Challenger*'s voyage proved a complete success in every way.[18]

This was the voyage that effectively gave birth to the science of oceanography. George Richards retired from the navy as a vice admiral in 1877, but was later promoted to admiral. He died in November 1896.

FIG 107 Admiral Sir George Henry Richards, KCB, FRS, FRGS. Portrait by Stephen Pearce, 1865, National Portrait Gallery, London. [© National Portrait Gallery, London]

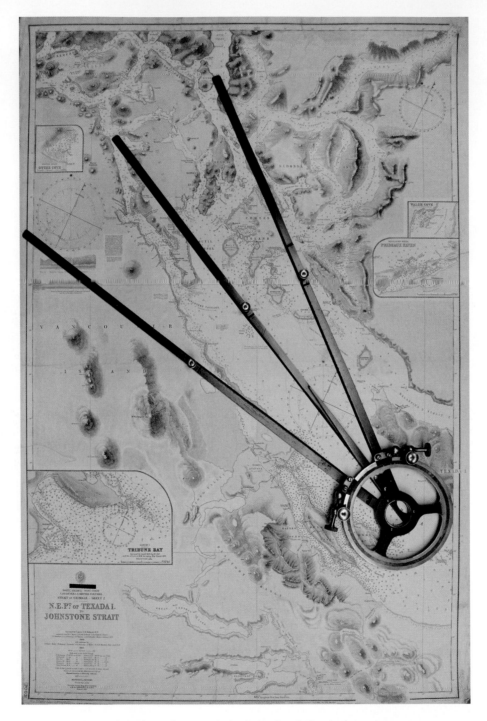

FIG 108 A station pointer, made by H. Hughes & Son in the early 1900s, positioned on Admiralty chart 580, surveyed by Captain Richards, and published in 1867. [Courtesy of Vancouver Maritime Museum]

AFTERWORD

THIS BOOK CONCLUDES IN 1862, with the departure of Captain Richards and HMS *Hecate*, but leaving HMS *Beaver* under the command of Daniel Pender to continue the hydrographic charting north. That same year, Victoria was incorporated as a city, so Joseph Pemberton, Benjamin Pearse, and other members of the survey department focused their efforts on real estate registration and similar tasks.

The following year saw the conclusion of the era of James Douglas as governor of both colonies—Vancouver Island and British Columbia. He was honoured for his contribution to British interests in the region with a knighthood. Two men replaced him: governors Arthur Edward Kennedy for the island, and Frederick Seymour for the mainland.

At the time of that change, knowledge about Vancouver Island was incomplete. Captain Richards had charted the coastline with excellent detail and accuracy; the southern and eastern coastal areas had been reconnoitred, and agricultural settlement started. A few traverses across the island, following oolichan trails, had revealed something of the mountainous interior. Some coal deposits had been found and exploitation was under way, but the economy of the island colony was far from being self sustaining.

The authorities in London knew this, and both new governors arrived with instructions to bring about the union of the two colonies. Within a few years this was done, and soon afterward, in 1871, the legislature of the united colony of British Columbia decided to join the Canadian confederation.

A number of exploring expeditions set out to complete the map of the island's interior, some with economic objectives, others out of curiosity and adventure. The colonial and then provincial survey departments also began a systematic reconnaissance of the unknown sectors of their territory. All such exploratory endeavours suffered from loss of manpower as a flood of volunteers departed for the tragic fields of Flanders.

GLOSSARY

Board-foot Unit of measurement used in the lumber industry for volume of cut lumber: the volume of one-foot length of a board one foot wide by one inch thick. 1,000 board-feet converts to 1.66 cubic metres.

Braza Spanish unit of measurement equivalent to a fathom, or about 1.67 metres.

Cadastre The system of documenting and registering real property boundaries. Also called "legal" or "tax" mapping.

Careen (naut.) To turn a ship on its side for cleaning, caulking, or repairing the hull.

Chinook Jargon or chinuk wawa The trading language used throughout the Pacific Northwest during the fur-trade and colonial eras. Based on the language of the Chinook people of the Columbia estuary, but modified to include French, English, Spanish, and even Polynesian terms, and a simplified grammar. McLoughlin, Douglas, McNeill, and other company men were all fluent speakers.

Chronometer An exceptionally precise clock, watch, or other timepiece.

Datum (chart) The level below which depths are indicated on a marine chart and above which heights of the tide are expressed. It usually indicates the mean level of low water at ordinary spring tide.

Dead reckoning A system of navigation or estimating the position of a ship without the use of any astronomical observation, but allowing for tides, currents, ship's speed, windage, and course steered.

Gazetteer A geographical dictionary or index of place names.

Geodesy (n.) Geodetic (adj.) The mathematical science of calculating or measuring the shape of the Earth or large areas of land. High-precision observation and spherical geometry are normally involved.

Gyre A large-scale circular motion of the ocean caused by the rotation of the Earth and friction of the wind.

Hydrography Specialized mapping or charting of oceans, lakes, rivers, and other surface waters, emphasizing depths of water.

Hydrographer A surveyor specializing in hydrography. The Hydrographer is also the title of the chief of the British Hydrographic Service

Kuroshio Current The North Pacific equivalent to the Gulf Stream, part of the North Pacific gyre, conveying warm water from Taiwan, northeast past Japan, and toward the coast of North America.

Latitude The angle at the centre of the Earth between a point on the Earth's surface and the equator, north or south. Since Vancouver Island and its vicinity lie within the northern hemisphere, either the qualifier, or the term latitude, have been omitted in this work as redundant.

League A league is a measurement of distance formerly used throughout Western Europe and Latin America, although its length varied depending on the place and the era. A nautical league was calculated by measuring about one minute ($\frac{1}{60}$ th of a degree) of arc along a meridian. The length varied depending on the degree of flattening of the meridians at the poles, but for practical purposes, it was usually taken as three nautical miles. In modern times, the nautical mile has been set by international agreement at 1.852 kilometres, so that a league at sea is 5.556 kilometres. This has been used throughout *A Perfect Eden*.

Lee shore (naut.) The situation of a ship positioned or manouevring close to shore when the wind is blowing toward that shore. Perilous for vessels reliant on sails.

Lunar distance A method for finding longitude at sea by observation of the moon against the background of fixed stars and calculated comparison with tables in the *Nautical Almanac*, to determine the Greenwich time of the observation.

Oolichan or grease trail Traditional overland trade route in the Pacific Northwest used to bring grease from oolichan ("candle fish"), harvested by coastal people, into the interior.

Pinnace (naut.) A ship's boat fitted with a mast and sails or rowed by up to sixteen oars. Used for inshore charting work prior to advent of inboard engines.

RE The [Corps of the] Royal Engineers, a technical service of the British army. Members of the corps are known, collectively and individually, as "sappers."

RGS (**The Royal Geographical Society**) The London-based learned society founded in 1830, dedicated to worldwide geographical exploration, research, and education.

RN (**naut.**) Pertaining to the British Royal Navy. Added to the rank of officers and men, e.g.: Henry Richards, Captain, RN.

Running survey (naut.) A method of charting a coastline while remaining aboard ship and under way. Angles between identified points along the coastline are measured and recorded as well as the vessel's course and estimated distance run.

Station pointer (naut.) A three-armed protractor used to chart a vessel's position from two simultaneous, horizontal, sextant angles taken between three fixed points ("stations") on shore.

Toponymy The geographical place names of a region.

Voltigeurs A lightly armed militia formed by the HBC, mainly from mixed-race and French Canadian employees who were skilled backwoodsmen.

ENDNOTES

EPIGRAPH

1 Glazebrook, *Hargrave Correspondence*, pp. 420–421.

CHAPTER ONE: THREE PUZZLING VOYAGES

1 Vining, *An Inglorious Columbus; Or, Evidence That Hwui Shan and a Party of Buddhist Monks from Afghanistan Discovered America in the Fifth Century, A.D.*, pp. 263–299.

2 Drake, *The World Encompassed by Francis Drake*, p. 115.

3 Purchas, *Hakluytus Posthumus or Purchas his Pilgrimes*, Vol XIV, p. 415 ff. Also: Williams, *Voyages*, p. 413.

CHAPTER TWO: FIRST CONFIRMED ENCOUNTERS

1 Beals, *Juan Pérez on the Northwest Coast*, Bucareli to Pérez, December 24, 1773, p. 25.

2 Ibid., p. 75.

3 Ibid., Pérez to Bucareli, August 31, 1774, pp. 53–54.

4 Ibid., Mourelle's "Narrative of Pérez's Voyage in 1774," from Martinez's diary, pp. 112–117.

5 Ibid., Pérez to Bucareli, November 3, 1774, pp. 56–57.

6 Bancroft, *History of the Northwest Coast,* Vol 27, p. 168.

7 Barnett and Nicandri, *Arctic Ambitions*, p. 213.

8 Rickman, *Captain Cook's Last Voyage*, p. 240.

9 Cook, *A Voyage to the Pacific Ocean*, Vol 2, p. 343.

10 Walbran, "The Cruise of the Imperial Eagle," *Victoria Daily Colonist*, March 2, 1901.

11 Ibid.

12 Layland, *The Land of Heart's Delight*, Fig. 23, p. 37.

CHAPTER THREE: SPANIARDS TAKE POSSESSION OF NUCA

1 Wagner, *Spanish Explorations*, p. 85.

2 Ibid., p. 138.

3 Ibid., p. 152.

4 Ibid., p. 148.

5 Ibid., p. 171.

6 Ibid., p. 176.

7 Ibid., p. 152.

CHAPTER FOUR: MALASPINA'S EXPEDITION ARRIVES AND EXPLORES

1 Vaughan, *Voyages of Enlightenment*, p. 3.

2 Jane, *Spanish Voyage to Vancouver*, p. 33.

3 Ibid., p. 36.

4 Ibid., p. 41.

5 Ibid., p. 46.

6 Wagner, *Spanish Explorations*, p. 254.

7 Ibid., p. 258.

8 Jane, *Spanish Voyage to Vancouver*, p. 54.

9 Ibid., p. 57.

10 Ibid., p. 61.

11 Ibid., p. 68.

12 Ibid., p. 138.

CHAPTER FIVE: THE ISLAND OF QUADRA AND VANCOUVER

1 Lamb, *Voyage of George Vancouver*, p. 283.

2 Ibid., p. 569.

3 Ibid., p. 620.

4 Ibid., p. 625.

5 Ibid., p. 672.

6 Ibid., p. 1390.

CHAPTER SIX: "A CONVENIENT SITUATION FOR AN ESTABLISHMENT"

1 Glazebrook, *Hargrave Correspondence*, Finlayson to Hargrave, February 21, 1833.

2 HBC Archives B 223/b/15 fo. 62.

3 Rich, *The Letters of Dr. John McLoughlin*, pp. 286–287.

4 McLoughlin to Simpson, March 1840, HBC Archives B223/b/26.

5 Simpson to McLoughlin, March 1, 1842.

6 Simpson, *Narrative of a Journey*, p. 182.

7 *Simpson's London Correspondence*, November 25, 1841.

8 Simpson, *Narrative*, p. 239.

9 Douglas to McLoughlin, October 1, 1840. HBC Archives B 223/b/28.

10 Simpson to Governor and Committee, March 1, 1842, HBC Archives.

11 Williams, HB *Miscellany*, vol. 30.

12 Douglas to McLoughlin July 12, 1842. "The Founding of Fort Victoria," *The Beaver*, March 1943, p. 7.

13 Glazebrook, *Hargrave Correspondence*, pp. 420–421.

CHAPTER SEVEN: FORT VICTORIA

1 "Letters of Charles Ross," *BC Historical Quarterly*, vol. 7, 1943.

2 Report by Warre and Vavasour, October 26, 1845, BC Archives.

3 Vavasour's report to Holloway, March 1, 1846, BC Archives.

4 Finlayson's memoirs, BC Archives.

5 Seemann, *Narrative of the Voyage*, p. 100.

6 Ibid., p. 170.

7 Seemann, *Narrative*, p. 110.

8 Ibid., p. 112.

[9] Gordon to Duntz, October 7, 1846. Colonial Office Records 305/1.

[10] *Illustrated London News*, February 27, 1847.

[11] Seymour to Admiralty, February 8, 1847. Colonial Records 114A/416/2.

[12] Kane, *Paul Kane's Frontier*, p. 100 ff.

CHAPTER EIGHT: THE NEW COLONY IS PROCLAIMED

[1] Simpson to Governor and Committee, June 30, 1849, HBC Archives A/12/4 fo. 532.

[2] Bowsfield, *Fort Victoria Letters*, Douglas to Barclay September 3, 1849.

[3] McKay, "Recollections of a Chief Trader," p. 11.

[4] Bowsfield, *Fort Victoria Letters*, Douglas to Barclay, June 23, 1852.

[5] Ibid., September 3, 1849.

[6] Ibid., May 7, 1851.

[7] Pemberton, *Facts & Figures*, Appendix, p. 143.

CHAPTER NINE: EXPLORATIONS NORTH TO COMOX AND ACROSS TO ALBERNI

[1] *Colonial Despatches*, Douglas to Barclay, August 18, 1852.

[2] Douglas to Pakington, August 27, 1852.

[3] *Colonial Despatches*, addenda to Douglas's report.

[4] McKay to Douglas, October 22, 1852.

[5] McKay's "Nanaimo Daybook," October 13, 1852.

[6] McKay to Douglas, October 22, 1852.

[7] Douglas to McKay, October 27, 1852.

[8] Pemberton to Barclay, September 24, 1852. HBC Archives A.6/120.

[9] Ibid., March 26, 1853.

[10] Douglas's diary, August 24, 1853.

[11] Douglas to Newcastle, October 24, 1853, *Colonial Despatches*.

[12] *HBC Nanaimo Memoranda 1855–57*, http://www.nanaimoarchives.ca/index.php?p=1_182_HBC-Memoranda-1855–57.

[13] *Diary of A.G. Horne*, transcript, Nanaimo Community Archives.

[14] Douglas to Colonial Secretary, August 20, 1856, *Colonial Despatches*.

[15] Governor and Committee to Pemberton, October 8, 1853.

[16] Pemberton to Douglas, December 15, 1856.

CHAPTER TEN: MESACHIE, THE HAUNTED FOREST

[1] Pemberton to Douglas, November 12, 1857.

[2] Gooch, "Across Vancouver's Island," *Colburn's United Service Magazine*, 1886 Pt II.

CHAPTER ELEVEN: THE NEW DISTRICTS

[1] Pemberton to Barclay, February 1854.

[2] Surveys of Districts Nanaimo and Cowichan Valley, June 1859.

[3] Colonial Office Minutes re: Douglas Despatch to London, July 25, 1859.

CHAPTER TWELVE: "A MOST ELIGIBLE AND HANDSOME LOCALITY"

[1] Dr. Lorne Hammond of the Royal BC Museum has uncovered what little is known of Banfield's early years and his demise. He kindly loaned his yet-unpublished essay to the author.

[2] Colonial Correspondence, BCArch GR-1372, F-107, Francis and Banfield to Douglas, July 1, 1885.

[3] Ibid., Banfield to Young, October 24, 1859.

[4] Ibid., February 23, 1860.

[5] Ibid., July 3, 1860.

[6] Sproat, *Scenes and Studies of Savage Life*, p. 1.

[7] *Op cit* Banfield to Young, Report #8, September 6, 1860.

[8] Ibid., April 18, 1861.

[9] Ibid., August 22, 1862.

[10] *The Daily Colonist*, October 24, 1862.

[11] Nuu-chah-nulth Tribal Council website

CHAPTER THIRTEEN: GEORGE RICHARDS AND THE MEN OF *PLUMPER*

[1] Richards, memo to Douglas, October 23, 1858.

[2] Colonial Correspondence, BCArch GR-1373, F-1126 Mayne to Richards, April 19, 1860.

[3] Richards's journal, p. 76.

[4] Richards's journal, pp. 84–92.

CHAPTER FOURTEEN: *HECATE* IN THE WESTERN INLETS

[1] Richards's journal, p. 110 and *Note 93*.

[2] Richards to Douglas, April 25, 1861.

[3] Mayne's report to Richards, May, 1861.

[4] Colonial Correspondence, BCArch GR-1372, F-107 Banfield to Young, May 6, 1861.

[5] Mayne's Report. BCArch Library NWp 971M M472r.

[6] Richards's journal, p. 122.

[7] Mayne, *Four Years*, p. 235.

[8] Richards's journal, p. 124.

[9] Mayne, *Four years*, p. 237.

[10] Richards's journal, p. 17.

[11] Ibid., p. 179.

[12] BCArch GR-1372 F-1215. Woods report to Richards, June 14, 1862.

[13] Ibid., Hankin's report to Richards, June 17, 1862. Also *British Colonist*, December 13, 1862.

[14] Richards's journal, pp. 189–208.

[15] Richards to Douglas, June 20, 1862.

[16] *British Colonist*, November 17, 1862.

[17] Ibid., December 9, 1862.

[18] Dawson, *Memoirs of Hydrography*, p. 138.

SELECT BIBLIOGRAPHY

Bancroft, George, "Memorial on the Canal de Haro . . . ," in *Papers related to the Treaty of Washington*, Washington, DC: [US] Government printing office, 1872.

Bancroft, Hubert How and Henry Lebbeus Oak, *History of the Northwest Coast: 1543–1800*, San Francisco, CA: The History Company, 1890.

Banfield, William Eddy, "Letters to James Douglas and William Young," *Colonial Correspondence*, GR 1372, BC Archives, f 107 and f 588.

Barnett, James K. and David L. Nicandri, *Arctic Ambitions, Captain Cook and the Northwest Passage*, Victoria, BC: Heritage House (for the Anchorage Museum, AK), 2015.

Beaglehole, John, ed., *The Journals of Captain Cook on his Voyages of Discovery. Volume 3, The Voyage of the "Revolution" and "Discovery," 1776–1780*, Cambridge, UK: The Hakluyt Society, 1967.

Beals, Herbert K., *Juan Pérez on the Northwest Coast*, Portland, OR: Oregon Historical Society, 1989.

Beals, Herbert K., "The Juan Pérez-Josef De Cañizarez Map of the Northwest Coast," *Terrae Incognitae (Journal of the Society for the History of Discoveries)*, Volume XXVII, 1995.

Bishop, Raymond, "Drake's Course in the Pacific," *BC Historical Quarterly*, VIII #8, 1939.

Bowsfield, H., ed., *Fort Victoria Letters 1846–1851*, Winnipeg, MB: Hudson's Bay Record Society, 1979.

Clayton, Daniel W., *Islands of Truth, the Imperial Fashioning of Vancouver Island*, Vancouver, BC: University of Vancouver Press, 2000.

Colonial Despatches, *The Colonial Despatches of Vancouver Island and British Columbia 1846–1871*, (online) bcgenesis.uvic.ca.

Conner, Daniel and Lorraine Miller, *Master Mariner, Capt. James Cook and the Peoples of the Pacific*, Vancouver, BC: Douglas & McIntyre, 1978 and 1999.

Cook, Warren L. *Flood Tide of Empire: Spain and the Pacific Northwest 1543–1819*, New Haven, CT, and London, UK: Yale University Press, 1973.

Cutter, Donald C., *Malaspina and Galiano: Spanish Voyages to the Northwest Coast 1791 & 1792*, Vancouver, BC: Douglas & McIntyre, 1991.

Dawson, L.S., *Memoirs of Hydrography*, Eastbourne, UK: Henry W. Keay, 1883.

Doe, Nick, "A Russian map of Gabriola–1849," *Shale*, No. 3, January 2002, Gabriola, BC: Gabriola Historical & Museum Society, 2002.

Drake, Francis and Francis Fletcher, William Sandys Wright Vaux (ed.), *The World Encompassed by Sir Francis Drake*, Cambridge UK: Cambridge Library Collection–Hakluyt First Series No. 16 (reprint), 2010.

Dorricott, Linda and Deidre Cullon, eds., *The Private Journal of Captain G.H. Richards: The Vancouver Island Survey (1860–1862)*, Vancouver, BC: Ronsdale Press, 2012.

Douglas, James, "Report of a Canoe Expedition along the East Coast of Vancouver Island," communicated by the Colonial Office to the Royal Geographical Society and read at the meeting 28 February, 1853.

Duff, Wilson, *The Indian History of British Columbia*, Vol 1 "The Impact of the White Man," Victoria, BC: Anthropology in British Columbia, Memoire #5, Provincial Museum of BC, 1964.

Duff, Wilson, "The Fort Victoria Treaties," *BC Studies* #3, Autumn 1969.

Elms, Lindsay, *Beyond Nootka, A Historical Perspective of Vancouver Island Mountains*, Courtenay, BC: Misthorn Press, 1996. See also his website: http://members.shaw.ca/beyondnootka/articles/island6000.html.

Fisher, Robin, *Contact and Conflict, Indian-European Relations in British Columbia, 1774–1890*, Vancouver, BC: University of British Columbia Press, 1977.

Glazebrook, G.P. de T., ed., *The Hargrave Correspondence 1821–1843*, Toronto, ON: The Champlain Society, 1938.

Gooch, Captain T. Sherlock, "Across Vancouver's Island," Colburn's *United Service Magazine and Journal of the Army, Navy and Auxiliary Forces*, Pt II, London, UK: Simpkin, Marshall & Co, 1886.

Gough, Barry, *The Royal Navy and the Northwest Coast of North America, 1810–1914*, Vancouver, BC: University of British Columbia Press, 1971.

Gough, Barry, *Distant Dominion: Britain and the Northwest Coast of North America, 1579–1809*, Vancouver, BC: University of British Columbia Press, 1980.

Gough, Barry, *Fortune's a River: The Collision of Empires in Northwest America*, Madeira Park, BC: Harbour Publishing, 2007.

Greene, Ronald A., *Carlo Gentile, Gold Rush Photographer, 1863–1866*, Victoria, BC: Greene Frogge Press, 2015.

Haycox, Stephen, James Barnett, and Caedmon Liburd, eds., *Enlightenment and Exploration in the North Pacific 1741–1805*, Seattle, WA: University of Washington Press, 1997.

Hayes, Derek, *British Columbia: A New Historical Atlas*, Vancouver, BC: Douglas & McIntyre, 2012.

Hill, Beth with Cathy Converse, *The Remarkable World of Frances Barkley 1769–1845*, Victoria, BC: TouchWood Editions, 2003.

Horton, John (*see* Vassilopoulos).

Hudson's Bay Company Archives, for letters and orders, (online) gov.mb.ca/chc/archives/hbca.

Hudson's Bay Company, *Nanaimo Memoranda 1855–57*, (online) www.nanaimo-archives.ca/transcripts-recordings/hbc-nanaimo-memoranda-1855–1857.

Inglis, Robin, ed. *Spain and the North Pacific Coast, Essays in Recognition of the Bicentennial of the Malaspina Expedition, 1791–1792*, Vancouver, BC: Vancouver Maritime Museum Society, 1992.

Inglis, Robin, *Historical Dictionary of the Discovery and Exploration of the Northwest Coast of America*, Lanham, MD: Scarecrow Press, 2008.

Ireland, Willard, "First Impressions," *BC Historical Quarterly*, Volume XV, 1951.

Jane, Cecil, translator, *A Spanish Voyage to Vancouver and the North-West Coast of America*, London, UK: The Argonaut Press, 1930.

Kane, Paul, *Paul Kane's Frontier: Including Wanderings of an Artist Among the Indians of North America*, Austin, TX: University of Texas Press, 1971.

Keddie, Grant, *Songhees Pictorial, A History of the Songhees People as Seen by Outsiders, 1790–1912*, Victoria, BC: Royal BC Museum, 2003.

Kemp, Peter, *The Oxford Companion to Ships and the Sea*, London, UK: Oxford University Press, 1976.

Kendrick, John, ed., (intro), *The Voyage of Sutil and Mexiana 1792, The Last Spanish Exploration of the Northwest Coast of America*, Spokane, WA: Arthur H. Clark Co., 1991.

Lamb, W. Kaye, "The Founding of Fort Victoria," *British Columbia Historical Quarterly*, Vol. VII No 2, 1943.

Lamb, W. Kaye, ed., *The Voyage of George Vancouver 1791–1795*, London, UK: The Hakluyt Society, 1964.

Layland, Michael, *The Land of Heart's Delight: Early Maps and Charts of Vancouver Island*, Victoria, BC: TouchWood Editions, 2013.

Leland, Charles G., *Fusang or The Discovery of America*, New York, NY: J.W. Bouton, 1875.

Lok, Michael, See Purchas Vol XIV p. 415 ff.

Mackie, Richard, "J.D. Pemberton," *Dictionary of Canadian Biography Online*, www.biographi.ca, Ottawa, ON: National Archives of Canada, 1990.

Mayne, Richard C., *Four Years in British Columbia and Vancouver Island*, London, UK: John Murray, 1862.

McCabe, James O., *The San Juan Water Boundary Question*, Toronto, ON: University of Toronto Press, 1965.

McDowell, Jim, *José Narváez: The Forgotten Explorer*, Spokane, WA: Arthur Clark, 1998.

McDowell, Jim, *Uncharted Waters, The Explorations of José Narváez (1768–1840)*, Vancouver, BC: Ronsdale Press, 2015.

McKay, Joseph William, *Recollections of a Chief Trader in the Hudson's Bay Company*. (Transcript in Nanaimo Centennial Museum.)

Meares, John, *Voyages Made in the Years 1788 and 1789 from China to the North West Coast of America*, London, UK: Logographic Press, 1790.

Miller, Gordon, *Voyages to the New World and Beyond*, Vancouver, BC: Douglas & McIntyre, 2011.

Olshin, Benjamin B., *The Mystery of the Marco Polo Maps*, Chicago, IL: University of Chicago Press, 2014.

Palau, Mercedes *et al*, *NUTKA 1792, Viaje a la Costa Noroeste de la América Septentrional por Juan Francisco de la Bodega y Quadra . . . 1792*, Madrid, ES: Ministerio de Asuntos Exteiores de España, 1998.

Palau, Mercedes, *et al*, *Nootka Regreso a una Historia Olvidada*, Madrid, ES: Ministrio de Asuntos Exteriores de Espanã, 2000.

Pemberton, J. Despard, *Facts and Figures Relating to Vancouver Island and British Columbia Showing What to Expect and How to Get There*, London, UK: Longman, Green, Longman, and Roberts, 1860.

Pemberton's reports and correspondence are in the Archives of Manitoba, *J.D.P.'s Correspondence, 1851–1855*, location code A.6/120 also A11/74, microfilm #47.

Pritchard, Allan, *Vancouver Island Letters of Edmund Hope Verney 1862–65*. Vancouver, BC: University of British Columbia Press, 1996.

Purchas, Samuel, *Hakluytus posthumus or Purchas his Pilgrimes*, London, UK: Hakluyt Society Extra Series no. 14–33, 1905 (reprint of 1625 edition.)

Rich, E.E., ed., *The Letters of John McLoughlin from Fort Vancouver to the Governor and Committee*, Vol. II, Second Series, 2013, The Champlain Society, (online) www.champlainsociety.utpjournals.press.

Richards, Captain George Henry, RN; for his journal, see Dorricott and Coulon.

Rickman, John, *Journal of Captain Cook's Last Voyage to the Pacific Ocean on Discovery performed in the Years 1776, 1777, 1778, 1779*, London, UK: E. Newberry, 1781. Reprinted Amsterdam, NL: N. Israel 1967, p. 240.

Roberts, John E., *A Discovery Journal: George Vancouver's First Survey Season–1792*, Victoria, BC: Trafford Publishing, 2005.

Ruggles, Richard I., *A Country So Interesting; The Hudson's Bay Company and Two Centuries of Mapping 1670–1870*, Montreal, QC, and Kingston, ON: McGill–Queen's University Press, 1991.

Saavedra, Santiago (dir) *et al*, *To The Totem Shore, The Spanish Presence on the Northwest Coast,* Madrid, ES: Ediciones El Viso (for the Pavilion of Spain, World Exposition, Vancouver, BC, 1986.)

Sampson, Harriet Susan, "My Father, J.D. Pemberton: 1821–93," *BC Historical Quarterly,* Volume VIII, No. 2, 1944.

Sandilands, R.W., "The History of Hydrographic Surveying in British Columbia," unpublished transcript of a paper presented in Victoria, BC, January 28, 1965. [A bound copy is in the library, University of Victoria, VK 597 C32 S2.]

Scott, Andrew, *The Encyclopedia of Raincoast Place Names, A Complete Reference to Coastal British Columbia*, Vancouver, BC: Harbour Publishing, 2009.

Seeman, Berthold, *Narrative of the Voyage of HMS Herald During the Years 1845–51*, London, UK: Reeve & Co., Volume 1, 1853.

Simpson, George, *Narrative of a Journey Round the World: During the Years 1841 and 1842*, London, UK: Henry Colburn, 1847.

Sobel, Dava and William J.H. Andrewes, *The Illustrated Longitude; The True Story of a Lone Genius Who Solved the Greatest Scientific Problem of His Time*, London, UK, New York, NY and Toronto, ON: The Penguin Group, 1998.

Sproat, Gilbert Malcolm, *Scenes and Studies of Savage Life*, London, UK: Smith, Elder and Co., 1868.

Suttles, Wayne, ed., *Handbook of North American Indians*, Vol. 7, *Northwest Coast*, Washington, DC: Smithsonian Institution, 1990.

Tovell, Freeman M., *At the Far Reaches of EMPIRE; the Life of Juan Francisco de la Bodega y Quadra*, Vancouver, BC: University of British Columbia Press, 2008.

Twigg, Alan, "Finding Juan de Fuca in Kefalonia" in *British Columbia History*, Vol. 6 No. 4, Victoria, BC: British Columbia Historical Federation, Winter 2013.

Vassilopoulos, Peter, *John Horton: Mariner Artist*, Surrey, BC: Heritage House Pub. Co., 2007.

Vaughan, Thomas, E.A.P. Crownhart-Vaughan, and Mercedes Palau Baquero, *Malaspina on the Northwest Coast: Voyages of Enlightenment*, Portland, OR: Oregon Historical Society, 1977.

Vining, Edward Payson, *An Inglorious Columbus; Or, Evidence that Hwui Shan and a Party of Buddhist Monks from Afghanistan Discovered America in the Fifth Century, A.D.*, New York, NY: D. Appleton and Company, 1885.

Vouri, Michael, *The Pig War; Standoff at Griffen Bay*, Friday Harbor, WA: Griffen Bay Bookstore, 1999.

Wagner, Henry R., "Confidential Instructions . . . Mourelle," *Spanish Explorations in the Strait of Juan de Fuca*, Santa Ana, CA: Fine Arts Press, 1933.

Wagner, Henry R., *Cartography of the Northwest Coast of America to the Year 1800*, Berkeley, CA: University of California Press, 1937. Reprinted, Amsterdam, NL: N. Israel, 1968.

Walbran, Capt. John T., *British Columbia Coast Names Their Origin and History*, Vancouver, BC: Douglas & McIntyre, 1971 (reprint of 1909 first edition).

Washington, John, *Hydrographic Instructions for Capt. George Richards About to Proceed to Vancouver's Island*, Taunton, UK: British Hydrographic Office, Misc. file #2, folder 3, item 2. March 1857, British Columbia Archives call number GR 284.

LIST OF ILLUSTRATIONS

WEBSITES OF CONTRIBUTING ARTISTS AND PHOTOGRAPHERS

Michael Felber, michaeljfelber.com
Mark (and Harry) Heine, markheine.com
John Horton, johnhorton.ca
Jim Lamont, facebook.com/jim.lamont.330
Mark Meyers, rsma-web.co.uk
Gordon Miller, gordonmiller.ca
Chris Sheppard, 500px.com/fundyrocks
Martin Smith, summitpost.org/users/vancouver-islander/26998
Alan Twigg, alantwigg.com
Angus Weller, mapmatrix.com

ACKNOWLEDGEMENTS

I have many people and organizations to acknowledge for their contributions in bringing this book to publication. I offer my sincere thanks to them all — their cooperation, in so many different ways, has been indispensable.

The British Columbia Arts Council, for another grant under its program of Project Assistance for Creative Writers.

The several friends, colleagues, and advisors who provided guidance in developing the text: Graham Brazier, Lorne Hammond, Peter Johnson, Grant Keddie, Sharon Keen, Kevin Neary, and Ross Tweedale.

The wonderful artists, painters, and photographers who most generously granted permission to include their work: Michael Felber, Mark Heine (for work by his father, Harry) John Horton, Jim Lamont, Gordon Miller, Mark Myers, Chris Sheppard, and Martin Smith. Their websites are listed on page 232.

The Nanaimo cartographer, Angus Weller, generated the series of location maps, and that of the island on pages ii–iii, based on his original digital files, but modified to meet this book's requirements. Angus devoted effort and expertise far beyond what I had imagined, and achieved a result far superior to what might have been expected. His website is also listed.

Other individuals who kindly provided images from their own collections for me to share with my readers: Ron Greene, Derek Hayes, Alan Twigg, Eric and Alisa Waschke; and those who guided me toward images I needed: Lindsay Elms, Mark Hipfner, and Robin Inglis.

I thank Robin Inglis, also, for most graciously agreeing to provide a foreword for this book, and for his encouragement.

I am grateful as well to the staff at various repositories of maps and images from whom I have obtained permission to use material in their care: the Royal BC Museum and Archives; the Land Title and Survey Authority; the Greater Victoria Public Library; the BC Legislature Library; Christ Church Cathedral, Victoria; the Hudson's Bay Company Archives; the Museo Naval and the Museo de América, both in Madrid; the Royal Ontario Museum; the Campbell River Museum and Archives; the Canadian Coast Guard, the Vancouver Maritime Museum; the National Portrait Gallery, London; the Royal Geographical Society Map Room; the Royal Botanic Gardens, Kew; and the Library of Congress; The National Library of Australia, the State Library of NSW.

My editor, the experienced and eagle-eyed Marlyn Horsdal. It has, again, been a most rewarding experience to work with her, and with my publishing team at TouchWood Editions: Pat and Rodger Touchie, Taryn Boyd, Pete Kohut, Renée Layberry, Tori Elliott, and John Walls.

Once more, and above all, my thanks go to my wife, Jean, for her support, encouragement, editorial skills, and so much more.

INDEX